Banking and Social Cohesion

Banking and Social Cohesion

Alternative Responses to a Global Market

Edited by
Christophe Guene and
Edward Mayo

JON CARPENTER

Contact details:

INAISE – International Association of
Investors in the Social Economy
Rue d'Arlon 40
B-1000 Brussels, Belgium
Tel 32-(0)2.234.57.97
Fax 32-(0)2.234.57.98
E-mail inaise@inaise.org
Web http://www.inaise.org

NEF – New Economics Foundation
Cinnamon House
6-8 Cole Street
London SE1 4YH
United Kingdom
Tel 44-(0)171-407.7447
Fax 44-(0)171-407.6473
E-mail info@neweconomics.org
Web http://neweconomics.org

This book is also published in French with the title
Banques et Cohésion Sociale – Réponses à un Marché Globalisé
and can be ordered from
Editions Charles Léopold Mayer (FPH)
38, rue Saint-Sabin
F-75011 Paris
France
Tel 33-(0)1 43 14 75 75
Fax 33-(0)1 43 14 75 99
E-mail paris@fph.fr

Books published by Jon Carpenter may be ordered from bookshops or (post free)
from
Jon Carpenter Publishing, Alder House, Market Street, Charlbury, OX7 3PH
Please send for our free catalogue
Credit card orders should be phoned or faxed to 01689 870437
or 01608 811969

First published in 2001 by
Jon Carpenter Publishing
Alder House, Market Street, Charlbury, Oxfordshire OX7 3PH
Tel / fax 01608 811969

ISBN 1 897766 69 6
Printed in England by Antony Rowe Ltd., Chippenham

Contents

Innovating for social cohesion

The Portuguese Presidency of the European Union gave a strong impulse to the implementation of the European Employment Pact. At the Lisbon Summit of 24 and 25 March 2000, efforts were dedicated to the objective of growth for Europe, based on innovation and knowledge, energetic pursuit of job creation, and research into greater social cohesion.

But while overall economic development reaches a high level in the European Union as a whole, exclusion also continues to grow; it is affecting vulnerable social groups and bringing serious repercussions for integration, especially among young people. The fight against social exclusion is a top priority, and initiatives which aim to promote job creation at a local level are to be encouraged.

The new financial organisations which have emerged over the last ten years, such as credit co-operatives servicing the local economy or fair trading; micro-finance organisations; and banking organisations with an environmental, community or ethical bias, have all made remarkable achievements in terms of funding and support. For example, the micro-credit movement, well developed in Third World countries, is now making its presence increasingly felt in the industrialised world; and, through community credit programmes which enable the unemployed to create their own jobs, it demonstrates the vast potential for initiative that exists amongst socially excluded people.

This social and community finance movement deserves to be developed further, especially by those committed to the European social model which seeks to reinforce social cohesion and reject all forms of exclusion. The revision of European banking directives provides an opportunity to explore the possibilities of creating a legal and regulatory framework. We should find ways to make sure people without either jobs or the financial tools which enable job creation have access to credit.

INAISE, and its new book 'Banking and social cohesion', is providing essential work on some of the central issues of social and community finance. I welcome this initiative as a significant factor in the building of stronger social cohesion in the European Union.

Michel Rocard, MEP
President of the Employment and Social Affairs Committee

Making sense with money

Ever since money has existed people have tried to make sense of it and with it. Examples of social investment go back to 14th century Italy and beyond. The development of universal welfare and full employment strategies in a post war world distracted us. In 1971 the decision to take the United States off the Gold Standard, and so remove the last fixed link between paper money and real goods, effectively redefined money. In the three decades since the divergence of the money economy from the world of manufacture and trade have become marked. At the same time we have witnessed a growing gap in wealth distribution. We are in a period of substantial wealth creation, both through earned income and the transfer of wealth from one generation to the next. Yet, persistent poverty and inequality exists – especially among women, children, refugees and minority communities. Today, more than ever, we need to make sense with money.

New wealth creators and their ideas about balancing market and public responsibility are providing new resources to assist social, environmental and economic change. Their rejection of the thesis that nothing can be done has spawned new financial intermediaries – social banks; guarantee funds; alternative finance networks; reinvestment trusts; social venture capital funds.

For the first two decades, many of these worked quietly and mostly successfully at the margin, innovating, recreating the connections between money and its uses. Yet 'suddenly' Governments and think tanks have discovered social finance and see in it, perhaps, part of the answers to the issues that have so far evaded them.

It is like the lily pond. Several days before the pond is completely covered by lily pads, the water is only half covered. A week before that it is only a quarter covered. A month before that there are just one or two. So, while the lily pads have been there for a while and grow imperceptibly all summer long, only in the last parts of the cycle do we notice their 'sudden' appearance and comment on their beauty and simplicity.

The social finance pond is not yet half covered and needs nourishment to grow – particularly capital. The first plants took root from the ideas of people. Given a chance to become sustainable, they will continue to flourish and bloom long after governments have gone in search of still newer solutions to society's intractable social and economic problems. Let us not lose sight of the words of Margaret Mead:

'Never doubt that a small group of thoughtful, committed citizens can change the world; indeed it's the only thing that ever does.'

Malcolm Hayday
President, INAISE

Acknowledgements

The editors are extremely grateful to the numerous people and organisations without whose support, advice and opinion this book would not have been possible as it is. We would like to thank the European Commission Third System and Employment pilot action programme for having co-financed this book. We would like to thank all the authors who have most positively responded to the challenge of this project. None of this would however have been possible without the INAISE members, Malcolm Hayday (president) and the secretariat team and its co-ordinator Viviane Vandemeulebroucke and especially Danyal Sattar for his unique ideas and human skills.

Finally, we all are especially indebted to all those past and present social pioneers, who at one point have decided to change the course of fatality, with intelligence and dedication to the common good.

E. M., C. G.

Introduction
A problem here to stay

Ed Mayo (NEF) & Christophe Guene (INAISE)

Banks are not charities. But in some countries, charities are becoming banks. In other countries, the state is engaging banks in addressing poverty and social cohesion. Banks, long used to public criticism, have had to think afresh when faced with the challenge of being wanted for their services in sectors that were previously neglected.

If these appear to be confusing times for banks, and for the state and third sector alike, there is at least an underlying logic being played out. Alongside an era of visible and accelerating market change in financial services, the seeds of a new mixed economy of welfare are emerging, that promise to elevate financial services to a prominent new social role in twenty-first century European societies. No blueprint for this is yet fully formed, although opportunities and the warning signs are perhaps furthest advanced in Anglo-American nations. But experimentation in these new markets is already underway, reflected in the experience of the pioneers documented in this book.

These experiments should be seen as testing the ground for what may come. They embrace a wide variety of markets and financial services and cover providers dedicated to specialist markets, and mainstream banks, often operating in the reflected space of the public sector, at local, regional or national level. Such a complex ecology of emerging practice will make it hard to yet generalize about strategies for success. By presenting contributions from the leading practitioners and observers in Europe, but also beyond, the aim of this book is to do justice to the diversity of experience at a formative stage.

This field of work, is not the reinvention of banking, but the application, and in some cases rediscovery, of banking techniques and in particular, credit for the purpose of social gain. Social banking we define as where suppliers of financial services take a positive interest in the social outcomes and effects of their activities. In its basic form, this merely requires that a bank be conscious of its social impact, for example through a social audit, as the Co-operative Bank in the UK and SBN Bank in Denmark have done. In a more advanced form, it enables banks to re-engineer products, processes or services in order to improve social impact. A prime example would be to enable disadvantaged people and communities to access financial services and to use them to good purpose.

Social banking is therefore a distinct approach to banking. It is also challenging. Intuitively, it feels like taking small-scale, more costly and risky products and selling them to people who may not be able to afford average cost. But as a number of contributors to this book have demonstrated, there are tricks up the sleeve of the social banker, which address cost, risk and return. It also has commercial benefits. Banks have done much, and certainly can do more, to embrace diversity and root out race discrimination in lending. That has to be a good move when ethnic minorities in Europe have a disposable income of many billions of euros.

Trends in banking

The energetic innovation in social banking catalogued by authors in this book comes at a time of unprecedented change in the wider structure of the banking industry. Advances in information technology allow banks to carry out far greater market segmentation, based on data analysis and, increasingly, credit scoring. This means more intense competition for profitable business and creates a fundamental change in the traditional economics of banking. It exposes and reduces traditional cross-subsidies across the industry, but also provides opportunities for cross-selling other financial products.

Mergers and acquisitions in the sector more than tripled in the year up to mid 1998, as domestic markets opened up to competition. The desire to create a level playing field in EU banking markets, coupled with the arrival to a common currency, have been important drivers. And there is a long way for rationalisation to go. Europe is far from having a consolidated financial services sector. Mergers are predominantly national, rather than EU-wide, in focus. The UK remains unusual for having offloaded its state and mutual banking sectors into the private sector. The share of retail banking in EU countries held by non-domestic banks is low in every case. While EMU offers a single currency and European Central Bank, it retains eleven different national authorities for the regulation of banking. Whereas in the USA a diverse regional banking industry was the result of targeted legislation dating back to 1933, in Europe it has been the result of language and culture.

Yet a number of changes that have worked their way through the US banking system over the last decade are sure to make their mark on the European banking industry. Not least of these is the shift in the way states finance social security and pensions from pay-as-you-go to funded systems. If European householders follow the US, UK trend and shift their savings from bank deposits to towards securities, then the landscape of European financial markets and with it, in particular, the financing of companies, will change dramatically.

Technological advances also change the way services are delivered. In the UK, since 1987 the number of bank branches of the five main high-street banks has declined by a third. In turn, this has a series of social impacts. Within Europe the UK has moved furthest away from the local provision of financial services, concentrating business banking services in particular on a smaller number of larger banks with fewer branches. In countries such as France and Germany a similar process of rationalisation, including mergers, is under way and is expected to continue as European monetary and financial integration progresses. The traditional delivery system through locally and regionally orientated banks is therefore under threat.

Closure of the last branch in town is still a rare occurrence in Europe. But where it has happened, it compromises retail businesses handling cash, and contributes to the decline of high-streets. Customers go elsewhere for their banking, taking their retail spending with them. One scenario is that, without an active approach to social banking, the new landscape of financial services across Europe in ten years time will contain tens of thousands of towns and villages turned into economic ghost towns by financial withdrawal.

On the other hand, there remains a long tradition of mutual and co-operative bank ownership. This ownership structure has often involved local and regional authorities, in turn engendering local community responsibility among smaller banks. A number of countries retain a tradition of mutual/co-operative bank lending in the agricultural and small (urban) business sectors, based on long-standing traditions of lending to small farmers and artisans.

There also exist a number of state-backed, specialist banks lending directly to the small business sector (for example, KfW and Deutsche Ausgleichsbank in Germany) or for refinancing such loans (Caisse des Depots in France). The German 'development' banks advance implicitly subsidised loans, as well as disbursing explicit loan subsidies, and have established benchmark margins and loan standards. As a consequence they make fixed and variable interest-rate medium and long-term loans more readily accessible. The implicit subsidy derives both from the ability of the state underwritten institutions to raise low cost finance and from their non-profit tax status. However, the German financial system has essentially become geared towards supporting established medium-sized enterprises, the 'Mittelstand' is less good at meeting the needs of the micro and small business end.

Who is involved in social banking?

There are three main groups of actors in relation to social banking in Europe. The first is mainstream private sector banks, engaged in social lending as a minority part of their activities. The second is the state, including state-owned banks, operating with social objectives. The third we could loosely call specialist lenders to the third system. These are financial institutions dedicated in all their activities to social objectives, either operating on a for-profit basis as a bank (typically a small one) or on a non-profit basis, often operating as an intermediary in partnership with banks or the state.

A diverse European tradition exists of each of these, going back to the establishment of the Monte-di-Pieta in Italy in the fifteenth century. Investors in the social economy such as the Co-operative Bank of Lamia in Greece, date back to the beginning of the twentieth century, while most have emerged over the last ten years. In Europe, such groups finance up to 15,000 third system projects a year and have invested over $1 billion over the last decade.

Differences between countries relate to differences in regulatory and policy framework. In France, for example, specific legislation allowed the establishment of flexible local investment clubs (Cigales), which invest equity in local enterprises and wind up after a set period. Over ten years they have invested over £1.25 million of equity into micro-enterprises with sums as low as £3,000. In Belgium, Hefboom attracts state support for its enterprise finance and development work for marginalised groups. Credit unions were pioneered in nineteenth century rural Germany at a time of famine and have developed in Ireland, the UK and Poland. Ironically, strict regulation of deposit-taking and lending in Germany means that, despite their success elsewhere, credit unions are not now permitted.

Table 1: Social Banking Target Markets

Market	Examples of need
Low-income consumers consumer credit.	Savings mechanism, payment service,
Small business finance	Development finance
Micro-enterprise for individuals and families	Start-up / working capital, business skills
Third system social enterprise	Project finance, working capital, facility finance
Ecological enterprise	Development finance

But this is also a world-wide industry. Micro-finance reaches more than 13 million people in developing countries. Progressive legislation around community reinvestment in the USA has aided efforts to establish 310 community finance initiatives which control capital of over $6.5 billion for community economic ventures. Many of these emerged from a process of local community protests at the activities of mainstream banks, on issues such as the withdrawal of financial services from localities and racial discrimination in lending. Such initiatives now look to catalyse community economic development, particularly in the fields of affordable housing and small businesses.

In post-war Europe, organising social housing for those in need has been seen as the function of the state. Instead, many pioneers of specialist social banking initiatives emerge from an interest in the unconventional enterprises of the third system. This concept includes not just the traditional core bodies of the social economy, mutuals, co-operatives and associations, but also new organisational models which fit neither the classical public or private sector forms. They:

- try to find solutions rather than to place themselves in a new market sector;
- often refer to factors such as social solidarity, democratic organisations or the primacy of the individual over capital;
- are often the result of public/private partnerships and have a close relationship with their local communities;
- do not have the market as their sole source of income instead securing public subsidies, donations or loans – they often have very mixed income;
- often give specific attention to disadvantaged people;
- have small-scale structures with larger numbers of non-active associates of unpaid volunteers.

The third system is therefore an important market for a number of social banks. The European Commission too in its report 'The Third System and Employment' sees it as a new dynamic force.

'The social economy and the activities oriented to meet the needs unsatisfied by the market can lead to the development of a new sense of entrepreneurship particularly valuable for economic and social development at local level. This sense of entrepreneurship is closer to the aspirations and values of people that do not seek profit making but rather the development of socially useful activities or jobs. These forms of entrepreneurship have a useful role in promoting social cohesion and economic local (sic) performance'.

Social banking, however, also relates to personal financial services, from bank accounts to mortgages, and to micro- and small business lending, which is a fast growing area of concern. Banks are key providers of external debt finance for such businesses. There are no stock markets for small and medium enterprises (as opposed to companies). Venture capital funds have increasingly refused to provide seed-corn capital for business start-ups, because of high fixed costs, lack of information and the lack of a track record. However, because of the relatively fixed transaction costs of making a loan, they tend to prefer larger to smaller loans, unless small borrowers are likely to take up other financial products as well.

How does it work?

The common feature of social banking is that it is about social as well as financial matters. Social banking attempts to target certain socially beneficial activities for positive investment. However, social banking is not just an issue of outcomes, although this is the ultimate test of effectiveness. It is also an issue of method. The social dimension allows the financing institutions to innovate around method to reduce risk and improve returns. Without this, social banking would simply duplicate mainstream banking by looking for bankable projects with social return that could have received finance anyway. Instead, social banking methods widen the frame of those able to access finance.

In some cases, this is possible to do this simply through operating with institutions able to develop specialist knowledge of the relevant market, be it financing co-operatives or ecological enterprises. Even in a competitive financial services market, enterprises with bankable propositions may not win finance. A major reason for these finance gaps is because banks do not know enough about borrowers. Such 'information asymmetries', in the vocabulary of banking literature, are often greater for smaller firms and unconventional enterprises, especially those without a track record.

Other methods set out in the course of this book, address the cost structure of lending, including transaction costs, risk and return. By reducing costs, again, social banking can widen access to capital. These range from partnerships with state bodies and partial subsidies through to mutual approaches capable of reducing risk, lowering transaction costs or offloading costs onto borrowers, and innovative models of risk assessment.

In economic terms, therefore, social banking is able to release for the benefit of society the positive externalities associated with social cohesion, including increased economic participation and improved social capital. As the 1998 UK report *Small is Bankable* sets out:

> 'In terms of simple economic theory, three factors affect the provision of private finance for each circle: the *demand* for finance, the *supply* of finance and *market imperfections* which may mean that finance is under- or over-supplied to certain groups.
>
> There are, in addition, two types of market imperfection. *Market inefficiencies* occur when those who supply finance do not allocate it on the basis of the expected rate of return, after an adjustment for risk, even though they could earn a competitive return. *Market failures* occur when those who supply finance are deemed not to be acting in the collective best interest of the wider community.'

The common feature of all social banking is therefore that it widens access to capital and improves overall social and economic cohesion.

There are, of course, a variety of forms of financial services. Most people for example need key 'lifeline' financial services to get by. These include paying bills, cashing cheques, home insurance, a place to save and a way of getting credit, for example in a crisis. The impact on people of not having these services, so-called 'financial exclusion', is an issue of increasing concern. It is not simply a question of cost or inconvenience. It is a denial of citizenship.

These services are passive financial services, in the sense that they can help to protect people from risk, allowing them to control their finances and smooth over financial shocks from paying for school uniforms to facing the cost of funerals. The majority of contributions in this book, however, focus on active financial services, in particular credit, which can be used to promote livelihoods.

One way of understanding society's needs for credit, and the extent to which they are met, is provided in Figure 1, in the form of four nested circles. This could be understood as relating to a geographical area or a section of the population.

Circle 1 is the circle of current investment. This includes the total loan activity of all lenders.

Circle 2 is the circle of bankable potential loans. These loans meet existing underwriting criteria but are more labour intensive, for example because they are smaller or non-traditional loans, or are time-consuming to the lender because the borrowers need more assistance in applying for them.

Circle 3 is the circle of potential deals, which can be made bankable with third party support. These are loans, which could be made if outside participants are brought into the project to provide the guarantees, subsidy, equity or technical assistance necessary to make marginally bankable deals feasible.

Circle 4 is the circle of total economic needs. Credit will not be appropriate to meet unmet economic needs at this point. Public services, expenditure or grants are required.

An agenda of widening access to private capital will look for creative ways to increase current investment (circle 1) by enabling bankable and partially bankable proposals (circles 2 and 3) to win appropriate finance. Examples of actions by mainstream banks to do this include: loan targets for disadvantaged groups, flexibility on loan conditions, consideration of underwriting standards, for example in relation to credit history, support for specialist non-profit initiatives, proactive marketing, support for money advice, technical assistance, improvement of banking facilities, review of branch closures and bank staff training. An alternative is to increase public investment (circle 4) or improve the extent to which public investment is compatible with incentives for private investment.

Does it work?

The range of social banking therefore extends from grant dependent organisations, state backed agencies right through to profitable banks. There are two key factors, which influence financial sustainability. The first is an attitude towards repayments and write-offs. An excellent example is community loan funds in the USA, which have a long history and have experienced cumulative loan loss records of 1.1 per cent. The second factor is whether an institution operates at an appropriate scale. Triodos Bank, for example, has pursued a strategy of devel-

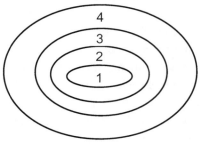

Figure 1: Social Cohesion and Credit Needs

Circle 1: Current investment
Circle 2: Bankable potential loans
Circle 3: Bankable with third party support
Circle 4: Total community economic needs

oping substantial banking assets in Holland, Belgium and the UK.

There may, however, remain arguments for subsidies. One initiative with an apparently low level of financial sustainability is the Prince's Youth Business Trust (PYBT), which operates in the UK, India and a range of other countries around the world. In the UK, total expenditure (*after* write-offs and provisioning of around 40 per cent) amounts to no more than £3,700 per young unemployed person supported to start an enterprise. Moreover, two-thirds of the businesses they support survive, and half of those whose businesses fail do not return to the dole queue. This compares favourably to the £8,500 a year the government would have to pay them if they remained unemployed.

A study by INAISE reports that half of the initiatives studied in the field of investors in the social economy required less than ECU 8,000 to create a job. These figures demonstrate true value for money and the benefit of applying a new economic framework, which can encompass social and financial returns.

These trends are examined by a number of authors in the book. Chapter one, 'The banking system and market failure', takes a first look at the funding gap and its background. Elaine Kempson analyses bank exclusion in the UK, and the political opportunities for tackling it; Daniel Immergluck describes the way that deregulation and segmented banking services have excluded poor communities and small enterprises in the US; Paul Gosling looks to the future, and the impact of new technology – which can act as an inclusive as well as exclusive force; Masaru Kataoka takes this further, in his description of the finance gap against the background of Japan's major banking crisis; and Paul Dembinski broadens the issue to ask how economic institutions could have permitted this gap to arise in the first place, and current theoretical shortcomings in understanding and interpreting it.

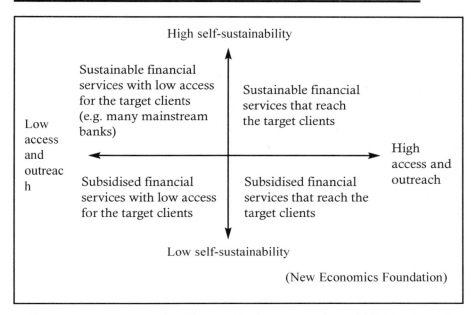

High self-sustainability

Sustainable financial
services with low access
for the target clients   Sustainable financial
(e.g. many mainstream   services that reach
banks)   the target clients

Low
access
and   High
outreac   access and
h   Subsidised financial   Subsidised financial   outreach
            services with low access   services that reach the
            for the target clients   target clients

Low self-sustainability

(New Economics Foundation)

Chapter two, 'New banking pioneers' looks at enterprises which are attempting to bridge the funding gap. M. Pilar Ramirez demonstrates workable examples in countries across the South, and Rosalind Copisarow extends this to show how institutions in Northern Europe can adopt similar practices. Lynn Pikholz and Ronald Grzywinski describe a US community bank which, according to orthodox economic arguments, should not even function but in reality is doing very well; Bettina Schmoll a German environmental bank which now covers the full range of social problems; Laura Foschi and Francesco Bicciato the first ethical bank in Italy; and Christophe Perritaz the wider arguments about the use of money within the community at large.

In chapter three, 'Learning from past (mutual) banking pioneers' Joseph Stampfer writes about the co-operative banking movement in Germany, and Thierry Groussin and David Vallat about the popular credit movement in France; MHA Jeucken and BJ Krouwel look at the Netherlands' only co-operative banking group, with its origins in agricultural communities and its future as a large successful commercial enterprise; Paul Jones takes a more recent example, a credit union set up in the north-west of England in the 1980s, and sets this in its historical context to ask where the UK credit union movement is heading; and Heidi Muthers-Haas and Helmut Mathers draw lessons from the history of the co-operative banking movement which should direct the movement's future.

Chapter four, 'The mainstream banks' social responsibility and action' starts looking at how the funding gap could be closed. Jacques Zeegers turns the question round, to ask how banks should see their role in a social market economy, from employment to social inclusion; Leo Schuster analyses the role of indirect stakeholders, and banks' capacity for 'corporate citizenship'; Peter Hughes and Andrew Robinson describe one UK bank's development of a social responsibility portfolio; James Giuseppi looks more widely at performance across Europe, concluding with comparative ratings; Patrick Ochs looks at 'added social wealth' and the conditions by which banks can create financial services with social added value; Udo Reifner takes the specific example of 'social banking', to ask how profit and social responsibility can work together, as well as the products this partnership can offer; and writers working for the US Treasury describe the impact of the Community Reinvestment Act, which has levered large sums back into low-income communities across the US.

Chapter five, 'Re-socialising banks: between re-regulation and welfare banking' asks how, ultimately, the funding gap could be abolished. Andy Mullineux goes back to the UK 'social exclusion' agenda, to ask what legislative framework could facilitate this; Koert Jansen describes the Dutch 'green investment scheme', which has had major success attracting ethical investment in the Netherlands; Maria Nowak analyses the problems with introducing micro-credit schemes into the French social and welfare system; Pat Conaty explores the potential for increasing the entire volume of social finance across Europe; Malcolm Lynch writes about the, and the complexities of regulation, particularly in the context of the work of the Basel Committee on Banking Supervision; and Jan Evers looks at the US CRA, and the implications for European legislation.

ENDNOTES
1   Adapted from a model in the Woodstock Institute (1991), *Making CRA work for you,* Chicago.

Chapter one

The banking system and market failure

Bank exclusion in the United Kingdom

Elaine Kempson
(Personal Finance Research Centre, University of Bristol, UK)

Deregulation of financial services has widened access to banking services for most people in the UK, but a minority have needs that are largely unmet by a competitive market. These needs include both personal and micro-enterprise banking and in, both cases, similar groups of people are affected for broadly similar reasons. The underlying explanation is that financial service providers view meeting the basic banking needs of people on low incomes as an uneconomic proposition. However, pressure from a government that is committed to financial and social inclusion has created a climate within which banks and other providers are investigating the potential for new product development at this end of the market.

Who is affected by bank exclusion?

Although only a minority of people is affected by bank exclusion, they are particularly concentrated among specific groups: people living on low incomes, tenants and those living in run-down and disadvantaged areas. Even among these groups it affects people in some circumstances more than it does others. People with an unstable work history, young people, women and people from African Caribbean, Pakistani or Bangladeshi communities are especially likely to be excluded.

Personal banking

Recent research has found that between 6 and 9 per cent of people in the UK do not have either a savings account or a current account with bank or building society.[1] About twice that number specifically lack a current account. In addition to these people there is another 3 per cent of people who have an account but stopped using it (Kempson and Whyley, 1998a).

In general the youngest and oldest age groups have the highest likelihood of being unbanked. And women are more likely to have no bank account than men at all ages, but especially so if they are over 70. In terms of family circumstances, lone parents and single pensioners are the least likely to have an account – especially if they are women.

Financial circumstances clearly play a big part. People who are unemployed or not working through sickness or disability are especially likely to be unbanked and are consequently, greatly over-represented relative to their proportions in the population as a whole. The longer people have been out of work, the less likely they are to have an account. So that half of people who have been out of work for more than ten years lack an account, compared with just over a quarter of those who last worked one year ago.

The lower a person's income and the more money they get in the form of benefits, the greater the likelihood of them not having a current account. Consequently, more than half (54 per cent) of people who receive income-related benefits because they are unable to work or have children and a low wage do not have an account.

Although only 8 per cent of people with an account are from one of the ethnic minority communities, the small numbers of ethnic minorities in the population hide the extent to which they are over-represented among non-account holders. Two groups stand out as having a very high likelihood of being unbanked: the Pakistanis, where 55 per cent of individuals do not have an account; and Bangladeshis, where the figure is 64 per cent. As might possibly be expected, these proportions are even higher for women than they are for men with 67 per cent of Pakistani women and 74 per cent of Bangladeshi women not having a current account of their own.

Of course many of these factors are inter-related and it is useful to be able to disentangle their effects. For example, are pensioners less likely to have a bank account because of their age, because they are no longer in work and needing an account for their wages or because they have a low income? Multivariate analysis techniques allow these interrelationships to be explored and to assess the extent to which individual characteristics (like age, being in work and income) have an independent effect net of all other characteristics (Kempson and Whyley, 1998a).

The factors that had the largest influence were ethnicity and economic circumstances. Being Pakistani, for example makes you four times as likely to be unbanked as a white person in similar personal and economic circumstances; while being Bangladeshi triples the odds. There seem to be a number of related reasons for this. These include a suspicion of British banks caused by language and cultural barriers, coupled with alleged racism by a minority of bank staff. In addition, the limited availability of Islamic banking products acts as a further barrier to use. Interestingly though, while African Caribbeans are very likely to be unbanked, this is largely explained by their family and financial circumstances rather than factors related to ethnicity.

Income per se does not have a large effect, although being out of work does. People who are not in paid employment are up to three times more likely to be unbanked than people who have a full-time work, but are identical in all other respects. Moreover, all other things being equal, a person who is in receipt of income-related benefit is twice as likely to have no account as someone not claiming any form of social security benefit. There are a number explanations for this finding. Some people who are not in paid work have never had an account. Some are refused bank accounts outright, some are offered one with such limited facilities that they choose to do without, while others do not even bother applying because they think their application will be turned down. A second group have had an account in the past. They either close it down when they cease to have a wage coming, in order to keep tighter control over their money, or they get into financial difficulties and the bank closes their account because they are over-drawn.

Surprisingly, gender does not have a significant independent effect, even though women are less likely to have an account than men. In other words, women are over-represented among the unbanked not because they are female, but because they are less likely to have an earned income from full-time work. Some of these women became mothers at an early age before they had opened an account; others have given up an account in their own name when they stop work to care for children. Following relationship breakdown, some women who are left on a very low income and without access to a bank account prefer a cash budget to keep control over their money. Others are refused an account when they apply or do not apply at all because they believe they will be refused.

In other words, there is a complex set of reasons why a minority of people do not have a bank account. For some it is because they have been refused one – or believe they would be. While for others, especially the very elderly, there is a clear preference for maintaining a cash budget, because that is how they have always managed their affairs. For most, however, it is because there are barriers that deter them from using a bank account, ranging from a fear of using an account which allows you to overdraw, to feeling alienated from banks.

Micro-entrepreneurs

There are around 3.3 million micro-enterprises in the UK, with fewer than five employees – the great majority of which are sole traders. Among these, particular groups of people are both less likely to run businesses and, if they do so, more commonly encounter difficulties gaining access to bank funding. The evidence, however, is much less comprehensive than it is for personal banking.

Women and young people, aged under 25 are greatly under-represented among micro-entrepreneurs relative to their numbers in the workforce. And this is despite the fact that, if they are in business at all, women and young people are especially likely to have a micro-business. Similarly, African Caribbean people are under-represented among micro-entrepreneurs, although Asians (including people from Indian, Pakistani and Bangladeshi communities) are all much more likely to have their own business than people of white British origin (Kempson and Whyley, 1998b).

The available evidence suggests that between 15 and 20 per cent of micro-entrepreneurs approaching the banks for finance are unsuccessful in their attempt to raise credit. Qualitative research with women entrepreneurs found that half of them had faced difficulties raising finance (Carter and Cannon, 1988). While a number of studies have found that particular ethnic minority groups have dispro-portionate levels of difficulty raising money for micro-enterprises (Cosh and Hughes, 1997; Jones et al, 1997; Metcalf et al, 1997). For example, while 21 per cent of white entrepreneurs who had applied for a bank loan had encountered difficulties, 29 per cent of Asians and 39 per cent of African Caribbeans had done so. And among Asians, Pakistanis were twice as likely to have encountered diffi-culties as Indians.

There are clearly a number of factors that act to restrict access to bank finance by micro-entrepreneurs generally, but tend to impact disproportionately on the groups identified above. These include:
* bank lending criteria
* terms and costs of loans and current accounts
* fear and feelings of alienation
* alleged discrimination

Bank lending criteria frequently include appropriate business experience, investment of personal capital and collateral. Yet all three present a huge stum-bling block for young people with little work experience of any kind; women returning to the labour force after caring for a family; and people 'pushed' into self-employment as a result of long-term unemployment. These people find it difficult to open business accounts, just as they do for their personal banking.

At the same time, there is some evidence that the terms and higher than average costs of bank finance deter some micro-entrepreneurs from applying, as does the cost of a current business account.

Young people, women, the long-term unemployed and some ethnic minorities are, as we have seen, under-represented among those using personal bank accounts. As a consequence many of them are unused to dealing with banks and are at a distinct disadvantage when it comes to making a business case for finance.

Added to which, women and ethnic minorities frequently report discrimina-tion. African Caribbeans feel particularly disadvantaged in this respect and report that their loan applications are viewed more negatively than those from either white or Asian applicants (Jones et al, 1997). Likewise, women accuse banks of being sexist and patronising (Carter and Cannon, 1988); while Pakistani and Bangladeshi entrepreneurs believe that the high street banks often fail to under-stand the nature of the business they wish to run (Herbert and Kempson, 1996). Indeed, it has been found that funding of Asian businesses is both highly selective and stereotypical, so that those who are not running businesses that are considered typically Asian (such as take-away restaurants or corner shops) tend to be turned down for loans (Jones at al, 1997).

What are the unmet needs?

Among both personal customers and micro-entrepreneurs who are excluded from banks, there is a clear need for simple, transparent products, that reduce both the risk of financial difficulties and, as a consequence, the barriers to access.

Bank accounts

For personal customers, the prime need is for a basic account to handle money on a day-to-day basis. Such an account would include facilities for:
- paying cash and cheques in
- holding money until it is needed and
- spreading the cost of bills

What they do not want is revolving credit facilities, such as overdrafts or credit cards.

Savings accounts would not meet the needs of most of the unbanked as they do not offer facilities for spreading the cost of bills. And current accounts are considered unsuitable, and therefore avoided, for two main reasons. First, there is the fact that they carry the possibility of unauthorised overdrawing. Secondly, the lack of transparency of such accounts is also problematic as it is difficult to identify, at any one time, which transactions have cleared the account. Together, these two shortcomings mean that people on very low incomes, which are stretched to the limit, often incur bank charges that are equivalent to at least a third of their weekly income.

In addition, the fact that bank accounts carry the possibility of overdrawing, means that anyone applying for an account is subject to credit scoring – which acts as a barrier for those not considered creditworthy.

What is needed is a basic account that falls some way between a savings account and a current account, offering both transparency and a range of facilities, including bill-payment. It would not permit overdraft, although it would offer a 'buffer zone' protecting those who inadvertently overdraw by a small amount for a few days. Such an account would not need to be credit scored and so could be offered to everyone, including those who are currently excluded (Kempson and Whyley 1999)

Credit and business finance

There are remarkable similarities in the needs for personal and business loans among those who are currently excluded by the banks. They require relatively small amounts of money, and non-bank lenders in this end of the market have found that risks of default are greatly reduced by offering a series of short-term small loans rather than a single larger one for a longer period. Moreover, it becomes possible to increase the amounts lent, depending on the repayment history of previous loans (Loeff, 1999, forthcoming; Rowlingson, 1994).

Borrowers also welcome the repayment systems offered by the non-bank lenders; while the lenders themselves find that they reduce levels of default. Typically, these place a personal obligation on the borrower to make the payment to a known individual at a set place and time. So, companies specialising in credit for the unbanked normally have agents who collect the repayments door-to-door on a fixed routine. Micro-lenders often employ group lending techniques where members of a group meet to pool their repayments for forwarding to the lender.

The third key element of credit in this market is the need for some flexibility over the timing of repayments at times of genuine pressure on household or business finances. Borrowers welcome being able to reschedule from time-to-time without incurring penalties for missed payments and almost all commercial and social lenders who provide credit at this end of the market adopt this practice.

Providers

A common complaint by both individuals and micro-entrepreneurs who are excluded from banks is that the banks are too remote and do not understand what it is like to live on a very low-income or to run a micro-business with a very small turnover. They, therefore, express a desire to deal with organisations that do have that understanding, although they would also like them to be reputable, large organisations that are secure financially. At the same time, there is a strong desire to be able to move on to mainstream banking if this becomes appropriate (Whyley and Kempson 1999). This suggests that the most appropriate method of delivery for both basic banking and credit is a bank working in co-operation with a not-for-profit organisation such as the Post Office, a credit union or a microlender.

Why have the banks not met these needs?

On the whole, the banks have not met the needs outlined above, because they consider them uneconomic. There is little profit to be made from a basic bank account or small loans with a higher than average risk of default. The need for a more personal service also adds to the cost. Moreover, such customers offer very limited opportunities for cross selling. In a competitive market, banks inevitable expend far more effort in creating new products and delivery systems for higher income users with more sophisticated banking requirements than they do for those on low incomes whose needs are modest. This need not remain so.

And how might they do so?

A number of banks in the UK have recognised that many of the people they do not serve may, with time, become mainstream customers. Research has shown that only a third of people in the lowest income quintile were still on such low incomes three years later (Jarvis and Jenkins 1997). Likewise, the experience of microlenders suggests that a high proportion of the micro-entrepreneurs they lend to not only remain trading but actually expand their businesses. In other words, many of those who seem unbankable now will almost certainly be considered bankable at some time in the future.

In addition, developments in technology mean that new products could be designed that would meet the needs of the unbanked. Indeed, some of the basic bank accounts developed for young people could well be adapted to meet the needs of people on low incomes. A number of banks are exploring this possibility and a small number have already launched new products.

Thirdly, there are growing opportunities for banks to be working with intermediaries such as the Post Office, credit unions and microlenders. Indeed, many of the banks are now developing links with these organisations.

The current UK government has given impetus to these developments with its emphasis on combating financial exclusion. The UK government is committed to delivering all social security payments by automatic cash transfer into bank accounts by the year 2003, so that all benefit claimants will need an account by that date. In addition, self-employment is one of the options suggested to unemployed people who must sign up to the New Deal – a scheme designed to help the unemployed find work. Access to start-up finance is an important component of assisting people to become self-employed. Two government action teams, working within the remit of the Social Exclusion unit, have looked at access to personal financial services and business start-up finance. Both are expected to produce far-reaching reports.

While financial exclusion remains a serious issue of concern, the political and commercial climate in the UK (if not continental Europe) has never been more favourably disposed to tackling it; only time will tell how far those who are excluded from banking can have their needs met.

REFERENCES
Carter and Cannon (1988) 'Women in business' *Employment Gazette* Oct pp 565-571
Cosh and Hughes (1997) 'Size, financial structure and profitability: Uk companies in the 19980s' in Hughes A and Storey D *Finance and the small firm*. Routledge (1997)
Loeff, A et al (1999, forthcoming) *Reducing cost and managing risk in lending to micro-enterprises. Handbook for micro-lending in Europe*. FACET
Herbert A and Kempson E (1996) *Credit and ethnic minorities* Policy Studies Institute
Jones T, McEvoy D and Barrett G (1997) 'Raising capital for the ethnic minority small firms' in Hughes A and Storey D *Finance and the small firm*. Routledge (1997)
Kempson E and Whyley C (1998a) *Access to current accounts*. British Bankers Association
Kempson E and Whyley C (1998b) *Benchmarking in micro-lending: country report for the United Kingdom*. Personal Finance Research Cenre, University of Bristol
Kempson E and Whyley C (1999) *Kept out or opted out: understanding and combating financial exclusion*. Policy Press
Metcalf H, Modood T and Virdee S (1997) *Asian self-employment*. Policy Studies Institute
Rowlingson K (1994) *Moneylenders and their customers*. Policy Studies Institute.
FOOTNOTE
1   Building societies are mutual organisations that were, originally, set up as organisa-

tions that offered facilities for savings and house purchase loans. Since they were de-regulated, many have converted to banks and those that remain now offer a full range of banking facilities.

New technology and banking exclusion

Paul Gosling

New technology has been a major factor in the withdrawal of bank branches from low income areas, but as the townships of South Africa have proved they can also be the means by which banking facilities are extended to a previously marginalised community.

The financial services industry has gone through a commercial revolution in the last decade. Call centres and the internet have given corporations the opportunity to enter the banking market at a lower cost than existing branch-based banks. This approach has been led in the UK by Direct Line – backed by the Royal Bank of Scotland – in the insurance sector, and by First Direct – a subsidiary of the Midland Bank and part of the giant global business the Hongkong and Shanghai Banking Corporation – in banking.

Other financial services companies are also moving into new technology banking. Prudential has launched its high interest bearing Egg accounts, which will be mainly serviced through what the company hopes will quickly become Britain's largest internet banking operation.

But the biggest threat to the traditional banks comes from outside the sector. An amazing array of new competitors has entered the banking industry. These corporations are focusing on low cost operations using call centres, the internet, outsourcing and high quality computer databases built up from other activities. They hope that they can use strong non-banking brands to quickly build large customer numbers to benefit from economies of scale and low core costs, to compete by undercutting established banks.

Companies adopting this approach include Virgin Direct, the airline to music global brand, which entered financial services through insurance and savings products, and which aims to launch its own banking operation without a branch network. GE Capital is a major credit card issuer and lender, based in the UK from a call centre in Leeds, which is part of the United States' General Electric corporation. British Gas has its own credit card, built up by a strong customer database. AT&T, the largest telecoms operator in the US, is also one of the world's largest credit card issuers. Other market entrants include the Ford Motor Company.

It is the supermarkets that are causing the most damage to the banks, apart from the Prudential whose Egg account has captured £3bn of savings – half of the total gained by the new banks at the expense of the traditional ones. Tesco and Sainsbury have launched attractive new bank accounts, combined with other financial products, wrapped into their loyalty cards which offer discounts and bonuses to valued customers.

These supermarket banks are an extension to the established principle of own-branded products. The difference is that instead of own-brand baked beans, production of which is outsourced, this time it is a banking service. The product again is outsourced. Responsibility for the mechanics of the accounts lies with smaller banks trying to improve their own economies of scale – the Royal Bank of Scotland and the Bank of Scotland.

In the longer term, these supermarket banks are likely to present an even greater threat to the traditional banks. Loyalty cards may become general purpose 'smart cards', containing computer chips making them effectively minia-ture computers but in the size and style of a credit card. These smart loyalty cards will be capable of storing reward points, personal bank account details and be a credit and debit card. They could hold several currencies for frequent travellers. But they could also be electronic purses.

Electronic purses cause bankers to lose sleep. They store a monetary value on a multi-purpose smart card, which can be topped-up from a cash machine; money can be down-loaded electronically on a personal computer with a smart card reader (these will soon be standard); or even over a mobile phone (mobiles containing smart card readers are already in low volume production). Not just the branch network, but the cash machine network could soon be made redundant.

Once smart cards become generally adopted, the governments will be fully involved. The British Government is in discussion with the banks about incor-porating public access codes onto the smart cards that they issue. Functions are likely to include passports, driving licences, public transport concessions, public building access and even library membership. However, it could be the super-markets rather than the banks that cream off the largest share of this potentially lucrative market using the strength of their existing loyalty cards.

Lower cost base

The driving factor behind these strong new competitors to the banks is their lower cost base. It is the expensive branch networks that particularly penalise the old banks. Figures quoted by the Department of Trade and Industry (part of the UK Government) show that a financial transaction conducted through a bank branch typically costs $1.07; over a telephone call centre the cost is 52 cents; using a cash machine it falls to 27 cents; but over the internet it is just one cent.[1]

It is easy to see, then, that First Direct which has no bank branches but a strong call centre base is able to very strongly cost-cut compared with a bank like NatWest's which has a massive network of 1,730 branches despite having already closed 220. However, this is as nothing compared with the advantage that Prudential's Egg will have once it is firmly established as an internet bank. Not only is Egg able to avoid the investment in fixed assets and staffing associated with branches, it is also using a method by which customers are directly 'self-servicing' – they are inputting their own details and issuing their own instructions to the computers directly.

While branch networks have largely survived (although badly damaged, to the detriment of poorer communities) many of the remaining branches are barely viable. Even a small loss of customers will make many more branches redundant. The emphasis now is on branches turning 'tellers into sellers', as the expression goes, to make branches more like non-banking retail outlets, staffed by experts in pensions, insurance policies and savings products. This requires a heavy investment by the banks in re-training and recruitment. It also explains why our high streets are being transformed as old, large branches are being converted into cafes and bars, while new branches appear between shoe shops and pharmacies.

Many fewer tellers are needed now, with the reliance on cheques reduced, and the introduction of automatic cheque reading facilities. These 'back office' functions are now fulfilled, typically, on industrial estates in low wages regions. Call centres are usually located in similar environments. The loss of traditional branch banking is not only damaging to low income customers, but also helps to drive down skills and wages within much of the banking industry.

There is a further factor assisted by new technology which is to the detriment of poorer customers. Direct Line's shockwaves through the insurance industry were created by its significant reducation in premiums compared with its established competitors. This was only partly reflecting its lower operating costs. It also was the result of a radical difference in pricing policy.

Insurance has traditionally been about pooling risk. Direct Line was much more pro-active in correctly assessing risk. Potential high risk customers were not sought or encouraged. Instead, lower risk customers were given extremely attractive premium quotes. Insurance became less about sharing risk across a large group of people, and more about allocating it to those people most likely to crash their cars or be a victim of crime.

An equivalent process is more slowly happening in the banking industry. Even those banks which persist with large branch networks are keen to charge those customers who use branch banking, compared with those who use the internet, call centres or cash machines. Established banks will be better situated to compete with new entrants to the market if they can offer their lowest charges to their most lucrative customers. An example of this new approach has been adopted by Germany's BHW Bank, which offers a 50% discount on bank charges to customers moving to phone or PC banking. Some US banks have even offered $50 to each customer who signed up for internet banking. Citigroup in the US, which claims to have invented home banking, found that PC banking only took off when it was made free of bank charges.

These approaches, when they become more common, will mark the most significant push yet away from branch banking towards home banking, especially for the more lucrative customer with access to a home PC. After all, banks are just as interested in how much profit a customer can earn them as they are in how much it costs the bank to service them. So customers who take out other financial products – such as insurance or pensions – through their bank, or who persistently have high levels of deposits in their accounts, will find their bank charges fall. This directly mirrors the approach taken to grocery shopping by the major supermarket chains. Conversely, poorer customers can expect to gradually pay more for their banking. Asking all customers to accept a pooling of costs is being phased out in banking, in the same way that the pooling of risks is disappearing in insurance.

In both cases, the power of computer databases to analyse the value and cost of customers is the key factor in enabling financial services providers to assess whether customers earn them profits or losses. In the past banks analysed products sold, but knew little about profiles of individual customers. A bank typically would have no idea about whether a particular person was a customer for just one product, or for a whole of products. Consequently, it had little idea how loyal a customer was, or how much they generated in profits.

All that is changing. Banks have had to invest massively in new computer systems, which are helping to further revolutionise the banking industry. A typical financial services call centre today will have a fully integrated customer database as well as caller line identification. When a call is received, the phone number called from will be displayed on a screen. This number will be compared with the database, and the customer calling can normally be identified. Instantly, the customer's details will be displayed on screen, showing which products they have bought, the balance in all accounts, and details of any recent complaints or disputes.

It will be much easier to make detailed customer profiles, illustrating the level of profit a customer generates, or, alternatively, that the customer actually loses the bank money. This type of sophisticated analysis has already been conducted by one computer company, which is now retailing products from a competitor especially to sell to troublesome customers to reduce the workload on its call centres.

Not all the banks have yet converted their computer systems to operate at this level. When they do, poorer customers can expect to notice their bank charges rise further.

Internet service providers

It is unlikely that we have yet seen the extent to which new technology will damage the traditional banking industry. It may not simply be internet banking that drives a new wave of cost cutting and therefore branch closures by the banks, it could also be the developing role to be played by internet service providers (ISPs).

ISPs are controlling the virtual retail environment of the internet, and helping to re-define the role of banks for the 21st Century. Banks, after all, are essentially facilitators for commerce. If much of the commerce in the future is to be conducted over the internet, it is the corporations that control the contact between business and consumer – or between business buyer and business seller – which can become the banks of the future.

Major corporations are now recognising the potentially enormous significance of becoming ISPs – those benefits can include commissions on sales of advertised products, advertising revenue, promotion of own brand products and of the corporate brand. Media companies ranging from News Corporation to Disney, IT corporations like Microsoft and supermarkets including Tesco have all moved into this market.

Banks, too, recognise these opportunities. The Prudential, Barclays and the giant Citigroup of the United States have all become free membership ISPs. Their services will not only be aimed at customers who use home or work PCs to do their banking. They will be equally important as more people use mobile phones as integrated electronic communication devices. In South Africa, the Nedcar bank even gives its more wealthy customers a free mobile phone, enabling them to build up stronger customer profiles.

Clearly, the growing significance of the internet and the mobile phone will be further damaging to poorer customers without access to either. It is another aspect of the growing trend towards valuing wealthy clients, devaluing others.

Does it have to be like this?

Clearly not. When the African National Congress replaced South Africa's Nationalist Party in government, its commitment to opening up society to blacks was at the heart of its policy objectives. Businesses were told in no uncertain terms, if they wanted to be successful in modern South Africa they had to ensure that they were working with blacks – promoting black staff, recruiting more blacks, and servicing more blacks as their customers. The businesses took notice.

Banks, in effect, had to sign up more black customers. But if they took on more customers by opening more branches they would lose money. They decided to find cheaper ways to service the extra customers. At the same time, the ANC government was looking for partnerships with banks to pay welfare payments to pensioners and the unemployed.

Cash machines have been installed by the Absa bank in the middle of the bush, where even phones are a rarity, using satellite communication systems. These automated telling machines (ATMs) not only dispense cash, they also take deposits and sell cinema tickets. South African banks are keen to extend their functions to provide a wider range of products. Similar machines in Japan, placed in workplaces, are used to order groceries for home deliveries.

Another major South African bank, First National, has created a network of advanced cash machines in Kwazulu Natal to make welfare payments to pensioners. Half a million pensioners are paid using this system, with payments authorised by smart cards and biometric testing to authenticate the card holder as the rightful beneficiary.

Creating networks of advanced cash machines installed in poorer areas may not be regarded by many as an adequate substitute for closed bank branches. However, the experience of South Africa does illustrate that banks can at low cost create an infrastructure which does service lower income customers (including benefit claimants) and reduce their economic marginalisation.

ENDNOTE
1   'The Knowledge Driven Economy' white paper, published by the Department of Trade and Industry, 1999.

Deregulation, segmentation and exclusion in the financial services sector: effects on the low-income side of the economy (lessons from the USA)

Daniel Immergluck
(Woodstock Institute, USA)

The last twenty years has been a period of major structural change for the financial services sector in the United States. Some of this restructuring has been prompted by technological change, but public policy has also helped to facilitate the increased mobility of capital to places where it brings the highest short-term private return but not necessarily the greatest long-term social return. While deregulation and technology have combined to provide a wider choice of services and increased price pressure in the lucrative segments of different financial markets, the pursuit of affluent customers has left lower-income consumers and very small firms at a disadvantage. The supply of capital to lower-income populations and communities has been volatile and susceptible to changes in international and national investment opportunities.

Financial services in the U.S. and in Europe are undergoing a simultaneous process of concentration and convergence. Since 1985, the number of commercial banks has declined precipitously in the U.S. from more than 14,000 to about 9,000 in 1997. The top 50 banking organizations in the U.S. now comprise over two-thirds of added value of all U.S. banks, up from less than half in 1985, and the assets of the top ten banks has increased by 70% in real dollars. After decades of European and Japanese dominance, two U.S. banking organizations, Citigroup and BankAmerica, rank among the top six banks in the world as of March of this year. In Europe, the largest bank is expected to have exceeded $1 trillion in assets by the time of this publication.

Consolidation is also occurring in securities and insurance industries, though at a somewhat slower pace than in banking. At the same time, the former independence of financial service industries has been eroded, with cross-industry mergers and acquisitions becoming commonplace. Beginning in the Great Depression of the 1930s, the U.S. had maintained a financial structure that separated lending (banks), investing (securities firms), and insurance activities. But in the last decade, these boundaries have begun to break down, with government deregulation accommodating the desire of financial service giants to build their economies of scale and scope.

Believing that the country is 'overbanked,' regulators, led by the Federal Reserve System, have encouraged mergers of banks in the U.S. Federal Reserve researchers have begun to argue for new techniques for analyzing the competitiveness of local banking markets, arguing that traditional techniques overstate levels of concentration.[1] Since controversy about very large mergers increased following the 'megamergers' of 1998, members of the Board of Governors of the Federal Reserve have spoken repeatedly of the advantages of banking consolidation.[2] In fact, only minimal scrutiny of bank mergers occurs in the U.S., despite regulations – such as the Community Reinvestment Act (CRA) — that call for evaluation of impacts on markets and communities.[3] No bank merger has been blocked due to CRA concerns since 1995, and even that merger was later approved. Of almost 60,000 CRA-covered applications to regulators from 1989 to 1996, only 24 were denied.[4] Even when mergers began resulting in institutions of a size rivaling the largest European banks, little change in the regulatory process occurred. Public hearings were held on the 1998 megamergers only after elected officials from areas being threatened with job losses called for them. In the end these mergers were approved without significant conditions.

In the case of cross-industry mergers and affiliations among banks, securities firms, and insurance companies, regulatory accommodation has occurred somewhat incrementally, with federal banking regulators allowing banks to operate further and further from their traditional core mission of taking deposits and making loans, primarily through affiliates owned by bank holding companies. Full-fledged convergence or integration, which would be facilitated by legislative changes, has been slowed primarily by the different industry players competing to influence the ground rules under which industry combinations would occur, with each industry preferring rules which gives its largest firms a competitive advantage.[5] This intrasectoral infighting has worked to the advantage of those wishing to slow the amalgamation and concentration of financial resources, although no end to such trends seems in sight.

One result of financial sector restructuring has been a concentration of financial power in a much smaller number of firms, without any real safety net or universality provisions to ensure that lower-income communities have access to the same types (and prices) of financial products that more affluent customers are routinely offered. True, the United States does have the CRA and fair lending laws, which in recent years have improved access to home purchase loans in underserved markets.[6] But financial capital has migrated out of the commercial bank sector into affiliated and unaffiliated firms, neither of which are covered by the CRA. The law has been more vigorously applied, but to a smaller segment of overall financial capital. In 1998, bank deposits accounted for 25% of household assets in the U.S., down from 55% in 1975. Similarly, banks and thrifts made just over 40% of mortgage loans in the U.S. in 1996, with relatively unregulated mortgage companies making the remaining portion. In 1977, banks and thrifts accounted for 80% of mortgage activity. Many of these mortgage lenders are in fact owned by bank holding companies (another result of convergence), but this portion of the parents' activity is not subject to CRA. Similarly, many of the deposits that were lost by banks during the 1980s' rise of money market mutual funds are now held by firms that are affiliated with large banks.

Market segmentation and exclusion

The convergence across industries, and not merely the consolidation of banks themselves, has fed the concentration of financial resources. Now, as financial service firms concentrate and converge, a third trend is occurring in the provision of financial services: escalating market segmentation. The financial powerhouses, which have begun to rival the largest European banks in size, actually contain a number of discrete business units which serve customer segments differentiated in ways that are highly correlated with class, race and neighborhood. The size of these corporations allows them to invest in and construct highly sophisticated data warehouses which provide them with a wealth of information to segment the market among their various product lines and units. Higher-income customers are targeted by large regional and increasingly national banks for a full range of services, including money management and investment services, low-cost home-equity lines of credit, and other products. Meanwhile, these banks shun lower-income customers by avoiding physical presences in low-income areas and by offering lower-priced services to higher-income customers. Moreover, internet banking, which some analysts expect to capture 10 % of the mortgage market by the year 2000, serves disproportionately affluent borrowers. Large institutions utilize computerization to score and segment the population into profitability sectors. This intensifies competition for the most lucrative customers, those with large cash management and investment needs, and reduces it for lower-income consumers and smaller firms, especially those not owned by affluent individuals.

Until the late 1980s, banking in the U.S. was essentially a local or statewide activity, with restrictions on interstate banking. Some states had maintained what were called unit banking laws, which prohibited even in-state branching. In 1994, with the Riegle-Neal Interstate Banking and Branching Efficiency Act, the last of the major mobility restrictions — the prohibition on interstate branching of single banking enterprises — fell. These mobility regulations maintained a banking system in which financial institutions were somewhat dependent on local economic conditions for their own success. As interstate banking restrictions fell, banks were no longer locally dependent and could provide financing throughout the country. This may have improved the competitive environment for borrowers where few local banks existed, but it also meant that banks could search nationally for more lucrative transactions. Thus, interstate mobility increased competition and reduced price for lucrative customers, but may have actually aggravated poorer service in less attractive market segments. Of course, some very large banks had already developed extensive international businesses, which were not subject to interstate restrictions, and so it was natural for them to replicate their capital mobility schemes within the U.S. once permitted to do so.

The continuing push by banks to focus more and more on middle- and higher-income market segments has left lower-income segments with relatively few providers offering a weaker selection of less attractive financial products. The growth of secondary markets in the 1980s provided an instant source of financing for nonbank mortgage companies, which often operate through independent mortgage brokers and do not rely on relatively costly physical branch presences.[7] These brokers tend to segment markets based on race and class, and tend to deliver products tailored to their segment of the market. Higher-income borrowers are courted by brokers offering access to a wide variety of conventional bank and mortgage company financing. Lower-income and especially minority communities are targeted by smaller numbers of brokers and mortgage companies. Many such lenders specialize in loans guaranteed by the Federal Housing Administration (FHA), which provides 100% guarantees that can lead to excessively risky lending. Some of these lenders concentrate their activity in lower-income and, especially, minority communities and experience relatively high foreclosure rates. This, combined with the program's poor performance at putting foreclosed properties back on the market, has contributed to pockets of property abandonment and blight in many lower-income urban neighborhoods.[8]

In addition to the mortgage lenders specializing in FHA loans, a set of providers has emerged in recent years that focus on 'subprime' loan products, designed to serve those not meeting conventional 'A' credit standards. Subprime lenders may specialize in 'B,' 'C' or some lower grade of loan, signifying higher risk. But market segmentation and the lack of competition in certain markets by prime lenders, especially large banks, allows some subprime firms to exploit less sophisticated loan applicants by offering them products that are priced higher than what they could qualify for from another lender. Frequently loans are 'packed' with extraneous fees and charges that are not based on cost and are not subject to well functioning competitive markets.[9] Repeated refinancing of debt and the rolling in of charges into the loans can put homeowners into very heavy debt situations.

Because prime lenders, especially banks, have recently been encouraged by CRA regulation to make home purchase loans to lower-income and minority borrowers, subprime lenders have had less success in the home purchase loan arena. But subprime lenders are often the dominant refinance and home improvement lenders in low-income markets.[10]

While lending units targeting lower-income segments of the market are often clearly differentiated firms from prime-lending depository institutions, the current trend of convergence and concentration has meant that, more and more, parent corporations own institutions serving these different markets. For example, First Union, the sixth largest commercial bank in the U.S. recently purchased The Money Store, one of the largest subprime lenders in the country. Conversely, Conseco, the parent company of GreenTree Financial, a major subprime lender, has recently applied to regulators to open a thrift, or savings bank. Many of the largest subprime lenders in the U.S. are affiliated with a major commercial bank (including Bank America, First Union, and Bank One) through a bank holding company structure. But again, the subprime units tend to be organized as mortgage companies, which are less scrutinized than CRA-regulated banks and thrifts.

In addition to the segmentation of residential credit, low-income communities are also the object of segmentation and exclusion in the market for basic financial services, including deposit accounts. Recent estimates are that one in eight U.S. families do not have a banking account. Low-income consumers tend to rely more heavily than others on storefront check-cashing outlets, which charge relatively high per-transaction fees for cashing checks and other services. Typical monthly costs for using these providers can be more than four times that of using a conventional depository institution. Banks and thrifts have generally avoided seeking out low-income retail account customers. This is evidenced by a decline in branches in low-income areas. Federal Reserve researchers found that, from 1985 to 1995, low- and moderate-income neighborhoods accounted for almost two thirds of the total decline in branches over this period, despite only accounting for only one-fifth of all branches in 1985. Over roughly the same period, the number of check-cashing outlets has tripled according to industry estimates.[11]

Segmentation and exclusion in financing small enterprises

In the small business arena, the lack of substantial secondary markets has meant that the role of nonbank lenders has been constrained. Banks continue to dominate small business lending, although larger firms have become less reliant on banks through issuing their own corporate debt. Finance companies are significant providers of small business loans, especially for retail firms, and may be increasing their role in specialty niches, but still comprise a significant minority of the market for small business loans. Segmentation, then, has occurred primarily within the banking industry itself. Large banks, until recently, were relatively inactive small business lenders, especially for very small firms needing relatively small loans (especially under $100,000). Smaller banks, especially those with assets of less than $5 billion made the bulk of small business loans. Their reliance on physical branches located in commercial areas, their willingness to invest in relationships with small firms, and their inability to compete with larger banks and mortgage companies on high-volume transaction businesses like mortgages and deposit services (especially automated tellers) all resulted in small banks doing a disproportionate share of small business loans.

In recent years, however, the advent of automated underwriting and data warehouse-based marketing has enabled large banks to penetrate small loan markets. Large banks have utilized computerization to identify likely loan candidates based on databases of firm information, including credit report data. They have also utilized automated underwriting to reduce the average transaction costs of small loans. After adjusting for mergers, small business loans of less than $100,000 at large banks (those with more than $5 billion in assets) grew by 19% from 1996 to 1997, compared to just 9% for all banks.

While the small business loan market had been segmented by loan size, with large banks making the larger loans and smaller banks making smaller loans, the segmentation is now shifting toward risk, geography, and race. Large banks, whose comparative advantage is in high-volume, low-cost automated processes and mass marketing, will increasingly target small firms with impeccable credit, especially those firms owned by individuals with high net worth. Meanwhile, smaller banks are seeing many of their 'best' customers flee to lower-cost commoditized credit from the large banks and are left making more traditional, relationship-based loans to firms that exhibit higher average credit risks. This segmentation will work to raise the price of credit for the small firm whose owner lacks high net worth or impeccable credit.

Another manifestation of segmentation of small business lending is geographical. Despite the growth of some mass marketed small business loans, small business lending remains highly correlated with branch location. Banks with branch networks tend to lend to firms quite near their branches. My analysis of Federal Reserve data for small business loans shows that, of the four very large bank holding companies in the Chicago metropolitan area (each with assets of $15 billion or more), only the one with a significant branch presence in lower-income neighborhoods made more than 12% of its small business loans in such areas. (The industry as a whole made 15% of all loans in such neighborhoods). The other three large bank holding companies have built up branch networks in relatively affluent, predominantly suburban areas. Together, less than 10% of their loans are made to firms in lower-income areas. Meanwhile the 5 small banks making the highest percentage (between 32% and 52%) of their loans to lower-income neighborhoods all had substantial branch presences in such areas.[12]

The segmentation of small business loan markets contributes to poor credit access by firms in those market segments not prized by mainstream, larger banks. Lower-income and minority neighborhoods receive fewer small business loans after controlling for the number and types of firms in the area.[13]

Moreover, black-owned businesses are rejected for bank loans at two and one-half times the rate as white-owned firms. This differential only drops to 2-to-1 when business characteristics are controlled for.[14] Minority-owned firms are forced to rely more on trade credit or personal resources to initiate and expand their operations.

Segmentation and CDFIs: opportunities and threats

The direct avoidance of lower-income market segments by banks can provide market opportunities for socially responsible community development financial institutions (CDFIs). CDFIs include community development banks (like South Shore Bank in Chicago), community development loan funds, community development credit unions, microenterprise loan funds, and community development venture capital funds. These alternative financial institutions utilize private, public and philanthropic capital to develop financial markets in communities that conventional banks and lenders have shunned. While estimates of the total size of the CDFI sector vary, true CDFIs control a very small portion of financial assets in the U.S., certainly only a fraction of a percent. Many are very small and will require a good deal of time and capital to grow to an appreciable scale.

Since CDFIs obtain much of their capital from private-sector financial institutions, particularly through the encouragement of CRA, their ability to expand will ultimately depend on an expansion of CRA requirements for nonbank financial institutions, including mortgage and finance companies, as well as securities and insurance firms.

While segmentation can provide opportunities for CDFIs to serve markets exploited by high-priced providers, it can also threaten their growth. In some cases, subprime lenders can dampen potential markets by leaving behind households whose finances are beyond the aid of a CDFI. When excessive fees and charges are built into financing packages or when loans are repeatedly refinanced with increased costs rolled in, borrowers can find themselves with such high levels of debt that even CDFIs, which generally can take greater risks than banks, cannot provide them with assistance. Thus, CDFIs may find it in their interest for such segmentation to be limited, and for 'predatory' practices to be curtailed.

NOTES
1   Anthony W. Cyrnak, 'Merger Policy and the New CRA Data,' Board of Governors of the Federal Reserve System, *Federal Reserve Bulletin*, September, 1998, 703-715.
2   See, for example, 'Remarks by Chairman Alan Greenspan: Changes in Small Business Finance,' at the Federal Reserve System Research Conference on Business Access to Capital and Credit, Arlington, VA, March 9, 1999.
3   The federal Community Reinvestment Act, which has been in place since 1977, requires banks and thrifts in the U.S. to serve the credit needs of their communities. Banks are examined every two years for compliance with the law and are given a 'CRA rating.' A bank's CRA performance is considered when it applies to regulators for permission for a variety of activities, including merging with another depository. The law is implemented through a set of regulations which were significantly modified in 1995 after several years of preparation.

4   These include all CRA-covered applications, not just for mergers and acquisitions. See Ken Thomas, The CRA Handbook, McGraw Hill, 1998.

5   The federal legislation which seeks to reduce barriers between banking and nonbanking financial activities has been called 'financial services modernization.' Most proposals to reduce barriers between banking and nonbank financial activities would allow for increased shifting of activities and assets from Community Reinvestment Act-regulated banks into unregulated entities. Amendments to expand the CRA to such nonbank affiliates have generally not been successful.

6   Increased enforcement of CRA and fair lending laws began in the early 1990s. From 1992 to 1995, home purchase loans to African-American borrowers in the U.S. increased by more than 125%, with loans to lower-income borrowers growing by 75%. Both of these groups saw lending increase faster than the overall rise of 54%.

7   In the U.S., the growth of large secondary markets, in which loans are purchased and sold after being originated, has increased the liquidity of lenders without direct access to deposits for funding loans. The two dominant players in mortgage secondary markets in the U.S. are the government-sponsored enterprises, Fannie Mae and Freddie Mac.

8   Calvin Bradford, *The Two Faces of FHA*, Chicago Fair Housing Alliance, 1998.

9   Norma Paz Garcia, *The Hard Sell: Combating Home Equity Lending Fraud in California*, Consumers Union, San Francisco, CA, 1998. Also see U.S. Senate Special Committee on Aging Hearings: 'Equity Predators: Stripping, Flipping, and Packing Their Way to Profits,' March 16, 1998.

10   Randall Scheesele, '1997 HMDA Highlights,' U.S. Department of Housing and Urban Development, November 1998. This analysis shows that subprime lending for refinancing in the U.S. grew from 45,000 transactions in 1993 to 461,000 in 1997, and increase of over 930%, while conventional refinancings declined by 52% over the same period. Subprime lenders accounted for at least 30 % of refinances of low-income homes but only 9 % of high-income ones. Researchers at the Kansas City Star found that fifteen of the top 20 lenders in Kansas City's minority neighborhoods are subprime lenders. See Ted Sickinger, 'Paying the Price for a Loan,' *Kansas City Star*, March 1, 1999.

11   The branch analysis is in Robert Avery, Raphael Bostic, Paul Calem, and Glenn Canner, 'Changes in the Distribution of Banking Offices,' *Federal Reserve Bulletin*, September, 1997. The check cashing outlet estimate is from Richard Oppel, Jr., 'The Stepchildren of Banking: Efforts to Serve Low-Income Areas Appear to Sputter,' *New York Times*, March 26, 1999.

12   Daniel Immergluck and Erin Mullen, *Getting Down to Business: Assessing Chicago Banks' Small Business Lending in Lower-Income Neighborhoods*, Woodstock Institute, 1998.

13   Daniel Immergluck 'Intrametropolitan Patterns of Small Business Lending: What Do the New CRA Data Reveal?' *Urban Affairs Review*, July, 1999. Also see Gregory Squires and Sally O'Connor, 'Access to Capital: Milwaukee's Small Business Lending Gaps,' presented at the Federal Reserve System Access to Business Capital and Credit Conference, May 9, 1999.

14   David Blanchflower, Phillip Levine, and David Zimmerman, 'Discrimination in the Small Business Credit Market,' National Bureau of Economic Research, November 1998.

The salaried-men mentality: bringing change to financing in Japan

Masaru Kataoka
(President of the Citizen's Bank, Japan)

Do banks with salaried-men mentality have a future?

Japan is in uproar about the financial industry's inability to tackle the problem of bad debts. A more serious problem, however, is the loss of the spirit to challenge and financial purpose.

The Japanese people were united in their efforts to escape from poverty after the war fifty years ago. Industry grew rapidly and there was always a strong demand for capital. It was a seller's market; financial institutions required land as collateral, earned good interest, and expanded their size. Additionally, governmental protective measures gave rise to the myth that 'banks don't go bankrupt.' The result was that bankers, whose job is supposed to be risk management, lost the necessary know-how and mindset. The unique Japanese-style 'ringi' system, reaching a decision by using a circular letter, blurred individual responsibility and removed the word 'responsibility' from their dictionaries.

When the bubble economy burst in the late eighties, the worth of Japan's total liabilities and net worth was halved. Since the Japanese economy recovered from nothing fifty years ago, this is not particularly daunting. Conversely, the problem is that the Japanese people became affluent, lost their spirit to challenge, lost their sense of purpose and direction, and lost their creativity – cannot take the next step. Employee-mentality, i.e. 'self-protection internally, arrogance externally,' became pervasive. Management urgently needs to overcome this situation. But if also management are hirelings, no hope is left.

Japan's social system gave priority to industrial production, and Japan's infrastructure *vis-à-vis* everyday life is not commensurate with the country's wealth. As people start to become wealthier themselves, their use of capital to eliminate poverty from the face of the earth is their historical destiny. Here a new purpose has to be found, and the spirit to challenge must be recovered.

Japanese financial institutions must be reformed from three perspectives. These are the market perspective, the community perspective, and the next-generation perspective. The market perspective means competing fairly with the rest of the world. The community perspective means going back to the basics, namely addressing community requirements through financing. This is because becoming engrossed in the money game — played with collateral as cards — cannot be a true foundation for a business enterprise.

Lending in order to nurture 'communal enterprises'

For sixteen years, I was an employee of a major bank. In 1989, the notion that 'engaging in enterprise is not for merely making money, but for learning to be part of society' prompted me to quit my job and set up the 'Citizen's Bank,' in collaboration with Eitai Credit Union of Tokyo. Since then we have, in collaboration with regional community banks and local governments, been lending without taking any collateral whatsoever, from the conviction that if an enterprise serves the community and is considered necessary by the community, it will necessarily survive as a business. What we check is that the enterprise is not being carried out with a primary objective of making money – that it stems from the will to 'tackle social issues.' Loans are up to a maximum of 10 million yen, at the long-term prime rate, and are paid back over a period of five years.

The number of loans made by the Citizen's Bank so far is around seventy, for a total of around 500 million yen. Not a single one has gone bad. Why? It is because we don't just lend money, but instead emphasise on 'nurturing' our clients. In other words, we make concerned organisations get involved, and aim to give the entrepreneur a hand in the creation of the business, through a system that runs from business school to counselling to financing to follow-ups after inauguration.

The borrowers thus far have all been enterprises that tackle problems which affect the day-to-day life, such as restaurants that serve only natural foods, home care services, catering for the elderly, transport for the disabled, manufacturing soap from waste oil, and so forth. I call such businesses 'communal enterprises.' Of these communal enterprises, there are around 27 categories that are in universal demand, in all regions of the nation. If these are properly supported in urban centres with populations of around 100,000, not only will there be a significant contribution to welfare of the elderly and the disabled, but also the 500,000 jobs created nationwide will serve to reinvigorate provincial areas. Entrepreneurial expertise garnered from regional successes can be exchanged with community banks world-wide; this should contribute to solving the largest problem developing nations face today, namely unemployment. This is my future plan. This is why I run the Citizen's Bank.

Citizens' hands will remold the financial institutions

Japan's financial industry has become weakened and is unable to utilise effectively that vital social resource, capital. This is a serious problem. A new arrangement must be made to courageously tackle the objective of 'contributing to the regions and the world,' not just profits and efficiency. This can only start with availing the 1100 trillion yen in personal savings for free exchange. The computerisation of society will make this possible. Electronic money is just a foothold. The revolution will occur when capital is freely exchanged through trading between individuals on an equal footing. If one considers the rate at which Japan is ageing, competition with the world and the speed at which computerisation is moving ahead, we cannot wait anymore for the Japanese financial institutions to reform themselves.

I believe financing in Japan will be transformed by the efforts of its citizens. First of all, the awareness in the citizens will have to be changed. In Germany, banks don't work on the principle of collateral first; loans are granted according to the prospects of the applicant's business. Also citizens will sympathise with a business and make interest-free deposits, or act as guarantors. This is an example of how it is important that citizens have a readiness to commit themselves to enterprises that they support. When this happens, the citizens will, as a natural development, form their own judgements of the financial institutions' policies and management philosophies, and take these into account when depositing or with-drawing their savings. Hence the financial institutions will be forced to change their attitudes.

Needless to say, for this to be achieved, access to information is indispensable. The Citizens' Bank will soon establish a web site on the Internet. Information provided will include types of businesses financed, management know-how, as well as various ways of utilising funds, so that users will be able to mutually do business at their own risk. We hope that such an open platform will tie people's assets and communal objectives closer together. This is our challenge – a new breed of financing for the computerised society.

And that also is my vision of Tokyo, the future financial centre open to the world.

The 'financing gap': myths and realities

Paul H. Dembinski
(Executive Secretary of the Finance Observatory, Geneva,
Professor at the University of Fribourg, Switzerland)

In recent years the debate on the 'financing gap' has become increasingly contentious in numerous Member States of the European Union. The issue involved is nothing more or less than to know whether the world's financial system, both globally and through its national relays, allocates financial resources on the one hand efficiently and, on the other hand, equitably. To answer this question, each of these aspects has to be examined separately with regard to a different reference system. This paper is accordingly divided into two parts. As regards the system's efficiency, the question goes to the heart of modern economy, its principles of functioning and the dogma underlying such principles. As regards the equitable allocation of resources, that is more a question of social justice and the role of the institutions responsible for ensuring such justice.

Let us start by turning the question around: what could cause the financial sector to fail to allocate efficiently the resources with which it is entrusted? And, as a secondary question, what would be the consequences of such inefficiency? In a second stage, it is important to examine how the new approach to risk assessment adopted by the financial sector leads to part of the national economy being deprived of financing, with as a consequence certain sectors of the economy likely to suffer from chronic 'under-financing' whilst other sectors are 'over-financed'.

1. Efficiency: myth and reality

The body of economic theory and the political arguments justifying the belief that the market economy is superior to any other economic system are based on the premise of the efficient allocation of resources. Literally, the premise of the efficient allocation of resources asserts that the market will ensure that the resources entrusted to it are allocated in such a way as to ensure that the productivity of the marginal unit of a given production factor is not inferior to the rest of the economy. That is the sine qua non condition to enable the market to accomplish its main function, namely that of setting prices. Consequently, it is possible to guess the consequences that would result from a dysfunction of the market which would moreover prevent it from allocating resources efficiently. Part of these resources would be wasted because they would have been allocated to sectors where the productivity of the last unit employed is inferior to those of the rest of the economy. The same economic theory is distinctly less forthcoming on how, in a system where, by definition, the actions of the economic operators are uncoordinated, the 'invisible hand' can have a vision of the economy as a whole. The question that must be answered in this connection is whether the accepted characteristics of an economic model can a priori be considered as realistic given the concrete problems and contingencies to be faced in implementing a purified, idealised theory.

Adapting a theoretical blueprint to the actual functioning of the financial system is not easy, in particular on account of the extremely complex structure of the financial system itself. The growth of the financial system that we have witnessed over the last twenty-five years has been accompanied by two distinct developments which, on first analysis, would seem to be contradictory. On the one hand, the financial system has become even more complex, in particular due to the specialisation of individual institutions, while on the other hand there has been a standardisation of the public's expectations and requirements with regard to the remuneration of their deposits. We are only just beginning to measure the consequences of this twofold and paradoxical evolution.

Access to financing has become an area where companies from all over the world, all sizes and sectors taken together, are in fierce competition. Every company tries in its own way to attract investors and to convince them either to place their funds with the company directly, as in the case of a loan or share issue, or to 'bet' on the company by acquiring its shares or bonds that have already been issued. In this race to attract financing, companies find themselves increasingly in competition with governments that are also looking to raise capital to finance their deficits.

At the other end of the market, among depositors of funds, there is a growing standardisation of the public's expectations and requirements with regard to the yield on the funds invested. In concrete terms, this means that depositors with funds placed on a savings account with a regional savings bank are amazed to see that the remuneration they receive is far less than the return that they hear or read about in respect of stock-market investments. Faced with such a situation, they will be tempted to switch their savings to unit trusts, for example. This reaction will be a warning for the savings banks and will in the future, in all likelihood, affect their investment strategy.

The essential function of the financial system is to act as an intermediary between the demand for financing and the supply of funds. In this respect, financial institutions play a leading role in matching supply and demand: they direct funds to one use rather than another. But, contrary to what is implied in the underlying economic theory, intermediaries are not neutral, since their actions introduce a new element into the process, which from the point of view of the recipients of the funds can seem to distort the process. This 'distortion' is caused by the fact that each institution has its own cost structure. Thus, for customers of two different institutions, an identical investment will be more or less interesting, depending on the cost structure of each institution. Consequently, cost structure considerations, as well as existing methods of remunerating funds, will have an undeniable – and sometimes decisive – effect on the type of projects that the institution prefers to finance with its customer deposits. In a final analysis, taking an extreme scenario, an investment that is relatively unattractive in itself can appear more interesting to the customer and to the intermediary than another more profitable investment, but for which the intermediation costs are considerably higher.

The inescapable conclusion is therefore that – all other things being equal moreover – the intermediation cost structure of a specific financial institution influences the way in which it allocates the resources under its management. In fact, financial institutions endeavour to use their resources in such a way as to equalise the return on these resources. In doing this they pursue a policy of productive efficiency. However, productive efficiency at the level of a single financial institution is not enough to guarantee an efficient allocation at macro-economic level.

On the basis of current economic knowledge, it is difficult to assess the gap between an ideal and reality. On the other hand, it is possible to identify the characteristics of financial transactions which provide the intermediaries with a good return. These are either standardised large-volume transactions which generate commissions that are small in terms of percentage but produce large amounts in absolute terms, or very sophisticated transactions which involve interesting commission levels despite the relatively small amounts involved. In their determination to maximise profits from the two types of transactions, financial institutions are more and more clearly turning their back on certain types of operations, for reasons linked not to the profitability of the projects themselves, but on account of their insufficient 'net profitability', that is to say profitability after deduction of the intermediation costs.

At the present time, there is a lack of empirical studies that explicitly take into consideration the effects of the cost structures of intermediaries on the pertinence of the allocation of resources. Such a lack of studies helps to perpetuate the premise of the efficient allocation of resources. However, it should not be forgotten that the intellectual appeal and formidable resistance to criticism of the premise of 'efficient allocation' rely more on the fact that the premise is based on a syllogism rather than on empirical demonstrations that support it.[1]

The conceptual analysis carried out here allows us to conclude that the structure of costs at financial intermediaries, their preference for such and such a type of transaction rather than for another, is effectively likely to introduce a bias in the allocation of financial resources. It is impossible to quantify the importance of this bias. However, it is not absurd to fear the worst and to assert that the world's largest companies – which directly do not produce more than 20% of the world's GDP – absorb a disproportionate share of world savings. If that were the case, the rest of the world's economy would – in relative terms – be under-financed. Thus, having regard to the growing role of the market in providing financing, the situation where 80% of savings is apparently allocated to the 20% of GDP produced by companies having direct access to the stock markets is perhaps not that far away. When these imbalances come out into the open, it will be too late to make adjustments. It will be time to take full stock of the wastage produced by 'efficient allocation'. The correction will come by way of a massive investment switch when confronted with the reality. Such a correction has a name: a major financial crisis.

2. The risk and the market's shortcomings

In the second part of this paper, the aim is to review the focus of the debate on the 'Financing gap' and to look at different means of resolving the problem. The difficulty lies in the fact that the debate is being conducted on at least three very different levels: with regard to the role of financial market operators, in terms of social considerations and, finally, from the point of view of whether a political intervention would be appropriate.

What price for what risk?

Among the professionals of the financial sector, the debate is a question of price and risk. To be more precise, the question is what price for what risk. To answer that question, increasingly sophisticated methods are being developed. At the root of these efforts, there is the barely concealed determination on the part of banks to make each customer pay the price that corresponds exactly to that customer's specific risk level. In reality, this determination to achieve transparency is the first step towards risk de-mutualisation.

However, the determination to put a price on the risk faces two major difficulties which stem from the very nature of financial risk. In fact, contrary to the risk of illness or death which can be quantified statistically for a given population, the same does not hold true for a specific investment project. The latter is calculated on the basis of a projected distribution of future earnings. Thus, assessing the financial risk is related more to forecasting than calculating probabilities. Contrary to an insurance company which seeks to increase the number of similar policies to cover itself against an homogeneous risk, finance institutions want to diversify risk. In other words, whereas in the case of insurance companies the increase in the number of contracts of the same type increases the financial soundness of the contracts as a whole, the opposite is true for a bank which by increasing the concentration of its exposure with regard to an homogenous population reduces its soundness. Thus, the risk of a given institution with regard to a specific credit comprises two potentially conflicting aspects: customer risk and portfolio risk.

By their ability to assess the two risk aspects described above, notably thanks to new evaluation methods, banks are able to manage rigorously their overall exposure. Thus, it is not unusual for banks to set quantitative ceilings on their exposure, or purely and simply to exclude certain sectors or certain types of credit from their portfolio. In such circumstances, the question 'what price for what risk?' is meaningless. The bank simply rules out certain projects, irrespective of the economic viability of the project.

Empirical data confirm that the gap in terms of interest rates charged is widening between 'AAA' borrowers that have access to the global market and self-employed persons who simply want to borrow a few thousand francs to provide their business with working capital. Nevertheless, the situation in Europe is very diversified. Globally, in the Northern European countries, even small firms do not complain over much about the problem of access to credit, whereas in the Southern European countries, the situation is considerably more divergent.

The strict application of these risk management principles to all potential customers can easily lead to the exclusion, purely and simply, of certain categories of 'customers' from access to credit. The same is true for innovative and recently created businesses. These considerations highlight the relevance of the questions raised in the first part: are there any guarantees that this way of assessing credit risk contributes to the efficient allocation of resources at macro-economic level? Is it still a question of market forces, or rather a question of 'market shortcomings' which can – even from a theoretical point of view – justify an intervention, for example by the public authorities? (see below).

Market shortcomings

This question on the existence or absence of the 'financing gap' has an undeniable social dimension. According to an idea advanced with increasing force by part of the associative movement, access to financing is a social 'right', derived from human rights principles. The question of credit to unemployed persons who are no longer entitled to receive unemployment benefits or to self-employed people, forced by the circumstances of life to build their own professional future, is becoming a question of fairness in the same way – or almost – as access to social security. To rectify such 'market shortcomings', people are inevitably looking to the public sector or the para-public sector to provide a solution, and this in turn inevitably displeases the financial institutions which see 'special' competitors gaining a foothold in their market.

Inevitably, at some point in time, the question becomes political. Is there a need to set up specialised institutions? Is there a need to regulate, subsidise, guarantee or give tax breaks to encourage the financial sector to adopt a more supportive approach to the parts of the society that they are increasingly neglecting? Is there a need to reverse the prism of the structure of their internal costs? Is there a need to correct the distortion referred to above? The replies vary according to the moment, and also depend on the economic and social context. There are three major challenges at the heart of this debate and the public and private sectors must meet these challenges in one way or another:

(1) The challenge of the conflict of interests: the globalisation of financial markets – whether one wants it or not – means that unemployed persons who borrow 20,000 francs to set up their own business are in direct competition with a company such as Nestlé when it floats a loan. Nowadays, for reasons of cost structure at financial intermediaries, the Nestlé transaction would be preferred. Is this choice in the interests of the depositor and the community to which the depositor perhaps belongs, or does it benefit only the intermediary? The conflict of interests that this example highlights can have an adverse effect on the financial sector's role in ensuring that resources are allocated in a pertinent way.

(2) The challenge of increasingly 'contractualised' savings: the development of finance and financial products that are draining the traditional reservoir of informal finance. Consequently, one of the natural sources of financing for very small business is in the process of drying up. In time, the demography of these businesses could suffer. This is an aspect of the more general problem of the allocation of financial resources that has not really been studied.

(3) We must not refuse to face up to the facts – the cost of processing a dossier is high – and small borrowers will not be able to bear such costs if there is no cost-sharing on a mutualist basis. Banks will find themselves facing a dilemma: on the one hand, some of them have to protect their 'local' image which guarantees them a certain volume of savings, whilst on the other hand they are tempted to tarnish this image by excluding certain categories of customers.

NOTE
1   See Paul Dembinski and Alain Schoenenberger, 'A Safe Landing of the Financial Balloon is not impossible' in *Finance & Common Good*, Autumn 1998.

Chapter two

New banking pioneers

The poor are creditworthy: the experience of FIE, S.A. (Bolivia)

M. Pilar Ramirez
(FIE, Bolivia)

To argue that banking cannot be done with the poor because they do not have collateral to offer, is the same as arguing that men cannot fly because they do not have wings. Men have the singular distinction…of being extra-ordinarily innovative… Now to argue that this innovative animal cannot design a banking system which does not rely on collateral is simply an insult to human ingenuity.

Professor Muhammad Yunus, Bangladesh 1978

The ability of these institutions to lend effectively beyond the 'frontier' of those who have collateral to offer, when those safely behind the frontier make much bigger losses lending to more prosperous people, is one of the most extraordinary achievements of development policy in our time.

Paul Mosley, University of Reading, England, 1995[1]

Introduction

Who would have thought 10 years ago that lending money to 'poor' people for their economic activities would be good business? Who would have imagined then, that 10 years later the business world – namely bankers and financial managers – would be discussing credit to low-income sectors as an 'industry' and one as a very profitable one? Or hearing government officials and banking regulators question some very basic banking practices in order to accommodate the large sectors of society – those living in situations of poverty? Very few indeed, seriously, but this is exactly what is happening today in many parts of the world, and it makes for fascinating storytelling.

The story begins anywhere, really, and in fact it did so almost everywhere, especially in the so-called developing world, the South. Anywhere and everywhere where there were individuals – usually members of non-governmental organizations – willing to challenge unacceptable situations in the living conditions, the lack of access to basic services and in institutional practices that affect the livelihoods of millions of people classified as 'the poor'. A defiant position at the time, which sought to reverse those conditions in manners that went beyond what the current development policies professed, farther than what the international cooperation community was proposing and financing, or what governments were willing to adopt as economic or social policy.

The individual pieces of this story are located in countries as diverse and far removed from each other as Bangladesh, Indonesia, the Dominican Republic, Colombia, Kenya, Bolivia. They are all parts of a whole today, different each in method and content, but all pointing in the same direction: the provision of sustainable financial services directed at those most in need and proving, time and again, that doing so is feasible and profitable.

Unveiling microfinance

How did all of this start? A quick review of the beginnings and its initiators shows two similar concerns:

- a preoccupation on the part of some individual or organization about the lack of access to capital, by way of loans, of low-income groups, and
- the determination of commercial sources of credit to deny this access on the grounds that 'the poor' have no collateral to show and are, therefore, not creditworthy.

In every case these concerns led individuals and organizations to seek ways by which to go around the collateral requirements, designing a variety of alternative forms of collateral and credit delivery methodologies, to provide the needed service: *microcredit*. The examples are numerous: the Grameen Bank's *group lending* in Bangladesh, the *solidarity group* method of Accion International first tried in the Dominican Republic and then expanded to many other countries, *village banking* and *savings schemes* or '*caisses villageoises*' in Africa, the *individual lending* methodology of Bank Rayat in Indonesia and of FIE in Bolivia. In doing so, microcredit has become an ingenious and alternative way by which the poor of the world now have access to affordable financial resources for their economic activities.

All of these programs started on a small-scale basis, supported usually by some international donor funding which allowed for a process of trial and error to test and perfect the credit delivery method. The motive behind many of these early experiences was to 'prepare' the clientele and the formal financial institutions in order to gradually transfer the better clients to the commercial banks. It was quickly seen, in all cases, that when the method suits the client and his or her economic activity, no matter how poor the client is, the loan is repaid and is done so on time. 'The method suiting the client' simply means that the evaluation process of the client – and/or the activity – has been correct, the loan amount and repayment time defined are adequate, and that the activity being financed is economically sound.

Despite the differences, each of these credit services have proven to be very effective and very successful. The element that is the same for all is their adherence to very basic banking practices, such as: weighing heavily on the economic activity, charging market based interest rates, following strict loan collecting procedures, etc. By providing access to cash that is needed in this manner, each of these programs has shown dramatically that the poor are creditworthy, that they repay the loans received, and that they do so, surprisingly, at interest rates that are usually higher than those available at commercial banks. A 1996 World Bank survey found that 206 institutions had about US$17 billion in outstanding small loans to more than 13 million individuals and groups as of September 1995.[2] In addition, it is documented fact that the levels of arrears for the more successful programs historically do not exceed 5%, with some programs reporting arrears as low as 2%!

Access to loans results in thriving microenterprises and other economic activities managed by 'the poor', increased incomes, new sources of employment, and improvements in the families' living conditions. From the point of view of the organizations behind the programs, successful financial services have resulted in growth for the organizations themselves, increased amounts of financial resources, growth in equity and investment capacities, expansion of outreach and operations, self-sustainability, and yes, profits!

Success and growth

Once programs reach levels of self-sustainability the growth and expansion have been impressive. From hundreds of clients serviced to hundreds of thousands and millions, with portfolio growths of 20% or more, a year. A significant element in this growth pattern is the increased use of commercial sources of funding, from local sources, once the initial donor funding has proven to be insufficient. In addition to being successful as lenders, these microcredit programs have had the capacity to attract local commercial banks' financial support, by way of loans, to increase their operations. This interface with the formal banking world was a natural next step in the financial systems approach to microfinance[3] that many programs have now adopted. The idea of transferring the better clients to the commercial banks was dropped. Why lose this clientele to others when we can continue servicing them successfully and grow too in the process? Why not become regular financial intermediaries ourselves specializing in this market we know so well?, became the new trend.

Attracting the financial system

Governments and the international community following this process have initiated – and successfully completed in some countries – serious regulatory changes in the banking laws and financial policies governing financial intermediation activity. The changes provide for the incorporation of NGO initiated microcredit and savings programs into the financial systems through the establishment of specialized categories for microfinance. These create a regulatory framework for such institutions that limits their functions compared with those of commercial banks, but that generate appropriate standards for those organizations to enter the formal financial system. Such is the case of the Private Financial Funds[4] in Bolivia and the EDPYMEs in Peru, for example. Banking authorities in other countries – Kenya,[5] for example – are also looking into special legislation for microfinance institutions. As part of the financial system, microfinance, has become serious business and a new market for investment opportunities. It is not too bold to expect that, not far off in the horizon, rating standards[6] of microfinance institutions (MFIs) will be common practice, as it is today in any growing industry.

None of this would have been possible if there was any doubt on the creditworthiness of the clients these institutions service. There can be no stronger statement that 'the poor' have proven to be among the best clientele a financial institution can have.

The case of FIE in Bolivia

Bolivia prides itself today with having the most successful microcredit institutions in the world, and in showing how different types of institutions and credit methodologies can coexist, compete with each other and reach impressive levels of growth. As of June 1998, 43% of the borrowers of the entire financial system of the country, were being serviced by formalized microcredit institutions.[7] Not only that, but Banco Solidario, the first commercial bank in the world dedicated to microfinance, ranks today as the top financial institution of the country.[8] So much for 'the poor' not being creditworthy.

Founded in 1985 by five professional Bolivian women as the first non-profit organization offering microcredit services to the so-called 'urban informal sector', FIE was initially supported with small grants as seed money from Northern NGO donors. Having successfully drawn interest from the Interamerican Development Bank, FIE in 1987 was approved a first soft loan for the equivalent of US$500,000 with which to launch the credit program on a broader scale. Between 1988 and 1990 the organization dedicated itself to institution building activities such as perfecting its *individual lending* methodology, preparing and upgrading the software for loan portfolio control, getting to know its clientele, improving loan officers' performance indicators, expanding the loan portfolio and planning for sustainability. In 12 years as a non-profit operation the organization grew from a staff of eight in La Paz to a working team of 136 in 14 branch offices present in seven of the nine departments of Bolivia. The final figures of FIE, the non-profit, were: over 100,000 loans disbursed, more than

23,000 outstanding clients, the loan portfolio totaled $12.7 million US dollars, having disbursed in total close to $70 million US dollars, with an average loan size of $550 US dollars. In addition, the NGO was able to increase its equity to $2.9 million US dollars.

FIE's clients have always been small manufacturers of a variety of consumption goods, merchants, and artisans of Bolivia's economic poor sectors, of which 60% are women. The clients' average monthly income lies between the equivalent of US$150 to $200. In general, microcredit programs in the world service this economic stratum. A clientele no commercial bank had ever dealt with, and one that was perennially subjected to living without the opportunities that access to small amounts of cash, provide. Their small businesses are started at enormous personal sacrifices or, worse, an endless cycle of indebtedness to moneylenders and other very costly informal sources of cash.

Effective management of the FIE loan portfolio, with increased improvements in information gathering, and of the credit technology and loan collection practices and incentives, showed a financial growth that could qualify FIE for market rate loans from commercial banks. Furthermore, it became increasingly clear that the combination of increased outreach and sustainability could only be possible through a courageous move towards working with funds from the local commercial market. Courageous because this required not only an excellent performance on the part of FIE's loan program, but also because it would have to fulfill the guarantee requirements of the commercial banks. The historically low rate of arrears (never more than 4%)[9] was one of those guarantees which the banks looked at.

This show of confidence in the low-income clientele and the risk-taking entrepreneurial capacity of the NGO, proved successful in another front. The Ministry of Finance of Bolivia and the Superintendency of Banks began accepting the fact that microcredit NGOs are part of the broader financial system and that laws and public investment policy must reflect this.[10]

FIE began its transformation into a formal and fully regulated financial institution in 1995. This required forming a Limited Liability Company of which the NGO is only one shareholder. Others include one other NGO, the Swiss Development Cooperation and three private investors. It also required a strict adherence to the regulators' requirements and supervisory expectations in order to obtain the Operating License as FIE, S.A. Private Financial Fund, on February of 1998.

As a Private Financial Fund, FIE S.A. has continued to grow providing the same quality financial services to its traditional clientele, including savings. The new legal framework which places it within the banking community, has given the business added prestige and credibility. The fact that FIE S.A. now reports to the Banking Authority of the country like any other financial institution, establishes 'the poor' as a highly attractive market for private investments, directly or through the capital market.

As of March 31 1999 what began as a small non-profit operation in 1985 has disbursed $97.2 million US dollars in 135,348 loans, with an outstanding loan portfolio of $16.8 million US dollars and 25,838 active clients. Of this loan portfolio, 69% are loans for manufacturing activities, 31% for trade and service activities. In terms of men and women serviced, 61% of the loans have gone to women. In addition, FIE S.A. has mobilized $8.2 million US dollars in savings from the public. Impressive results, indeed, and coming from individuals and families that live and work in the lower income levels of our society.

ENDNOTES

1   Paul Mosley and D. Hulme, *Finance Against Poverty*, Routledge, 1995.
2   World Bank, 'A Worldwide Inventory of Micro-finance Institutions', in *The Sustainable Banking with the Poor Study*, Washington, DC, July 1996.
3   Maria Otero and Elizabeth Rhyne, eds., *The New World of Microenterprise Finance: Building Healthy Financial Institutions for the Poor*, (West Hartford, Conn.: Kumarian Press, 1994).
4   To be explained in the case of FIE, S.A. presented below.
5   This is the case of K-REP, Kenya Rural Enterprise Program.
6   Private Sector Development Corporation, of Washington, DC. has already begun the rating practice of MFIs in Latin America.
7   Banco Solidario and the Private Financial Funds: Caja Los Andes, FIE, FASSIL, ACCESO. As reported by the Superintendency of Banks and Financial Entities of Bolivia, September, 1998.
8   1998 CAMEL financial evaluation of banks in Bolivia, *Nueva Economia*, April, 1999.
9   Due the following day on the loan's indebted balance.
10   The Law of Banks and Financial Entities of Bolivia (1993) provides for the creation of Private Financial Funds (FFPs) to allow NGO credit programs to become financial institutions authorized to offer credit and savings services to the microentrepreneur sector.

An example of micro-finance in the North: Fundusz Mikro (Poland)

Rosalind Copisarow
(Fundusz Mikro/Street UK)

Introduction

How many people are lucky enough to be offered $24 million of starting capital to design and create an entirely new financial institution, especially one dedicated to a market generally considered unbankable? I will always be grateful to the Polish-American Enterprise Fund for giving me this exceptional opportunity. Not only did it push me into rethinking from first principles what banking really ought to be about, but it also allowed me to test in practice the validity of some growing convictions that had gradually taken root in my mind over the course of my career in commercial lending.

It is now only four short years since Fundusz Mikro made its very first micro-loan. Nevertheless, we have managed during that time to disburse over 25,000 loans worth $25 million and not only obtained a consistent 98% repayment rate but also built a scale of operation large enough to fully cover its running costs and become a self-sustaining institution. Although these results are hardly sufficient to draw any generic conclusions about the legitimacy of the Fundusz Mikro approach across the whole of Europe, I hope they do at least indicate the need to re-evaluate the widely held view that micro-finance cannot work in the North, however successful it may be in South.

I firmly believe it can work in the North but, to do so, must be approached with quite a different attitude from that adopted by either charitable community loan funds or commercial banks. Not only do the operating companies' attitudes need to be radically different but so also do the community's at large. The concept of giving people a hand-up instead of a hand-out is much talked about but has yet to be widely adopted in concrete action. Also, the legal and regulatory environment, including tax and accounting issues as well as definitions of charity and business, all need urgent review and reform if the micro-finance industry is to be encouraged to develop on the one hand and protected from failure on the other.

These are all issues, however, which, though difficult, can be addressed, for they may all be regarded as externalities in relation to the two central issues of (i) whether or not micro-enterprises in industrialised, richer countries need 'Southern-type' micro-finance, and (ii) whether or not they have similar propensities to repay unsecured loans to the levels seen in the best micro-finance institutions worldwide. If there is indeed the demand and the repayment basis is sound, then surely we have a secure foundation for the building of an industry.

In this paper I will try to address some of the underlying principles of micro-finance which make it just as appropriate in the North as the South and show how here too, there is every reason to expect high demand and repayment. (These are what one might term 'client issues'). Next, I will discuss some institutional design issues which are crucial to achieving at minimum financial sustainability. Finally, I will look at the implications of these issues for the wider environment – what are the current obstacles, how might they be addressed and what specifically can the public, private and voluntary sectors each do to help build a healthy micro-finance industry? First, however, it is worth reflecting on why and for whom we need a micro-finance industry in the North.

The case for micro-finance in the North

The Southern view is clear: micro-finance is a very important tool for poverty alleviation and in many countries is needed by the majority of their citizens because unbankability is the norm not the exception. Nevertheless, it should be stressed that not one Southern micro-finance institution that I have ever visited serves the absolute 'poorest of the poor'. Below a certain threshold of energy, determination and morale, a person cannot make proper use of a commercial interest rate debt instrument. He or she first needs relief-type help, such as counselling, food, shelter, donations, etc.

The same is true in the North. Thanks to a welfare system, relief programmes are available and appropriately provided to the needy. They are also, however, provided (in the form of soft loans and grants, income support, counselling and training) where funds permit, to people who do not qualify as 'mainstream' but neither do they need to be candidates for relief. What they really need is a hand-up but it is generally not available. Meantime, as commercial financial institutions de-mutualise and merge and globalisation has created higher minimum thresholds of profitability for credit transactions to be deemed worthwhile, the community of potential bank clients who do not qualify has increased substantially over the past decade. This has stretched the public purse to the limit and left the majority of the potential micro-finance market in a no-man's-land: too rich to qualify for relief, too poor to qualify for mainstream credit.

Some micro-enterprises may be able to take personal bank overdrafts or borrow on credit cards. But this often creates more problems than it solves because the unstructured nature of the debts is inappropriate for inexperienced borrowers and leads them frequently into default. The majority borrow from family, friends, loan sharks or do without. Again, this comprises unstructured, one-time assistance, very expensive and/or totally inadequate for the needs of a growing business. A small proportion obtain public sector- or voluntary sector-supported soft loans or grants for start-ups. These do little, however, to ensure their transition into the financial mainstream if they cannot be supplemented by further 'development' capital. Many micro-enterprises operate in the grey market because the bureaucracy and tax regime create too high a threshold for them to cross in one step into officaldom. What these businesses need is transitional support which incentivises them into the formal economy.

The micro-finance market in the North therefore encompasses start-ups, grey market activities and fully registered small businesses that still lack the collateral for mainstream credit. It may not be as large or as poor a market as in the South, but it is nevertheless substantial; it is largely hidden from measurement by appearing to be served by other means or by being outside of the formal economy; and it could well grow in the future if minimum thresholds for mainstream credit continue to rise. What micro-finance offers in the North is not so much classic poverty alleviation as a means of supporting small business survival and development; incentivising start-ups; motivating people out of welfare who have the desire and capacity to become financially independent; stimulating in an organic, unsubsidized way the creation of thousands or even millions of jobs; and re-attaching to mainstream society a whole segment of unnecessarily excluded people.

Client issues

Let us look first at what micro-enterprises actually need from their financial institution:

1   Small amounts of capital, (£1000 on average for a first time borrower in Poland; likely to be £3000 in the UK); the amount structured by an expert to match precisely what they can afford without undue risk of default, i.e. to protect as well as support their development;

2   Minimal waiting time for the loan to be approved – the fragility of the business might well not survive the cashflow consequences of a one month processing period; and minimal bureaucracy and time taken to complete the application process;

3   A high probability of receiving a loan. The reason banks do not have higher rejection rates is that people do not bother to apply for a loan if the chances of success relative to the processing time and the paperwork involved are too low. It is therefore essential to maintain high acceptance ratios in order to encourage people to apply;

4   Reasonable interest rates – these do not need to be below standard bank lending rates to small business clients but they cannot be anything like as high as money lending rates;

5   Immediate subsequent loans for the further development of the business, assuming timely repayment of the previous loans;

6   Friendly, professional lending officers who understand the client's business, can advise where required, treat the client truthfully, efficiently, fairly and with respect and are therefore in turn respected by the client;

7   Clearly pre-explained terms and conditions including all costs, all small print in the loan agreement, all requirements which, if met, will ensure the client's future access to larger loans, etc;

8   Other tailored financial services, especially including a bank current and deposit account with lower transaction charges in reasonable proportion to the (small) average balances;

9   No training requirements in order to obtain a loan. Training, consulting, mentoring services available for purchase by the client at reasonable cost;

10   Opportunities to network with other micro-enterprises for mutual support purposes as well as to explore business development opportunities.

This list of requirements may look obvious, reasonable and not too difficult to respond to, that is, until one examines the extent to which existing financial institutions are in fact failing to meet them.

Banks fail on many points, especially: 1, 3 and 8. As mentioned earlier, unstructured credit is fatal for inexperienced borrowers and the reason banks do not structure it (in the form of a business cashflow-based loan as opposed to a personal loan or overdraft) is because it is more labour-intensive and therefore theoretically less profitable. A low probability of having the loan application accepted disincentivises a large proportion of the market from even trying, just as the high transaction costs on bank accounts detract a considerable potential deposit base from being brought into the financial system.

Most credit unions also fail on point 1, i.e. to provide loans tailored to the businesses' cashflows. They are also unable to support a micro-enterprise's growth (point 5) if the loan requirement exceeds their fairly restrictive limits. Further, with credit limits related to the deposits first made by a client, the waiting time for a first loan can be months (point 2) and the deposit requirement may exclude many potential borrowers. In addition, marginal and excluded populations may not be eligible to join a credit union.

Money lending companies such as Provident Financial, Cattles, Scottish London, etc. score very well on many points. Their biggest problems for micro-enterprises are the 40-160% p.a. interest rates (point 4) which are prohibitive for businesses and, again, consumer loans which are neither structured to the businesses' cashflows nor likely to be big enough for their future development (point 5).

Finally, public sector and voluntary sector loan schemes, though well-intentioned, are frequently poorly designed with unstructured loans, a low probability of application acceptance especially for the better (i.e. less disadvantaged) clients, low or no chance of any further loans, sometimes required pre-training and, worst of all, a confusing message which undermines a loan instrument with a 'grant culture' that does not press delinquent cases nor incentivise timely repayment.

Although Fundusz Mikro was modeled on the leading micro-finance organisations in the South, in Northern terms what it represents is a response to the micro-enterprises' needs described above, by encompassing the relevant elements of many different kinds of already existing financial institutions.

It therefore has a similar mission and focus on non-financial support (points 9. and 10.) to those of public- and voluntary- sector programmes; its personal risk assessment methodologies are more like those of credit unions i.e. based on mutual trust; its business risk assessment methodologies are adapted from those of banks for larger companies (i.e. based on cashflow); it has a highly mechanised back office like that of a credit card company; an organisation structure similar to that of a money-lending institution (combining the best of bottom-up grass roots loan officers with top down financial systems and economies of scale); and a financial objective which lies roughly between the most grant-dependent and the most profit-seeking.

Its goal is at minimum to be fully self-supporting, i.e. to cover its total operating costs and maintain in real terms the value of its loan capital. Whatever return it can achieve above that, should then be subservient to its strategic goal to offer credit as widely as possible.

Regarding client issues in general, three key points are worth making:

1. There is nothing fundamentally new or untested about micro-finance in the North; it has all been done before, though in bits and pieces within different segments of the financial services industry. Micro-finance should therefore not be treated as simply the newest fashion in development economics which could well be discarded within a decade. Rather, it should be understood as a revival of a centuries-old system of trust-based lending. This is proven by the derivation of the word credit (*credo, credere* – to believe or trust) which, together with the equally important concept of mutuality, is at the very root of lending.

It works because it taps into the natural predisposition of all animal species to co-operate with each other for reasons of enlightened self-interest. Benefits and obligations must be balanced to produce a water-tight system of 'metaphysical' collateral. Defaults generally arise from poor programme design or implementation, not from any essential problems with the borrowers.

2. It is important to remind ourselves of why trust-based lending is no longer the norm in the North. This is not due to repayment problems but to the need by financial institutions not only for profits but for year-on-year growth in profits. This precludes small transactions, however safe, from being attractive. (Those institutions still using a trust-based methodology, such as credit unions and money lending companies, still have excellent repayment results).

What has happened therefore is a shift in the meaning of the word 'credit-worthy', from 'being able to repay the loan' to 'being able to offer a minimum profit to the lender'. Muhammad Yunus (Managing Director of Grameen Bank) has declared credit to be a human right, i.e. a universal right. I would not agree – I believe one must be creditworthy to take on credit. However, my definition of creditworthy is the original one and includes anyone who can repay a reasonably-priced loan, however small a profit it may generate for the lender.

3. The upper and lower limits of micro-finance need to be recognised:

At the upper end, micro-finance breaks down when the loan sizes reach the level at which, with all the will in the world, borrowers are unable to raise the sums needed to repay the loan from their own savings as well as from all their friends' and family's contributions, if their businesses collapse. Peer group guarantees are better than physical collateral only when the combined resources at the group's disposal can provide an effective back-up repayment source. After that, physical collateral-based lending should take over.

At the lower end, micro-finance cannot be based on thin air! There must be a business, however tiny, which generates net cashflow surpluses. Some public sector and voluntary sector programmes incur large defaults because they do not observe this rule when they finance start-ups. When interest-bearing debt is used as a substitute for seed equity, it inevitably puts a huge burden on fragile, uncertain cashflows. Fundusz Mikro will lend to any micro-enterprise with at least three months' net cashflow surplus, however tiny – this is our definition of a creditworthy start-up and we have found that while it does not preclude anyone with a serious idea from starting and returning in three months, it does effectively screen out businesses that people are only prepared to try with someone else's money – most failures are from this latter group.

Institutional issues

If we approach the institutional requirements of micro-finance organisations by reviewing the main obstacles to be overcome, the two problems most frequently cited by banks (as to why they do not engage in micro-finance) are those of high credit risk and high transaction costs. I hope the previous section has sufficiently addressed the credit risk issue to conclude that, just as it is not a problem in the South, neither should it be one in the North. It just needs a specific approach.

As regards transaction costs, these have been addressed in the South partly by highly streamlined procedures, partly by vast economies of scale and partly by charging substantially higher interest rates than bank rates (although still significantly lower than those of money lenders). In the North it is equally possible to streamline the procedures and to create economies of scale – in Fundusz Mikro for example, we had three loan processing clerks looking after a 1000 client portfolio in 1995 and now, with 10,000 clients, we still only need four such people. Interest rates, however, are another matter.

(a) Rates of return

The interest rate affordable by a micro-enterprise is a direct function of its gross profit margin. The poorer the country, the higher this margin is likely to be, especially on exported products. In the North, not only are markets tougher and more competitive but so also are micro-enterprise owners' expectations of what constitutes a fair interest rate on a loan. Whereas in the South, they do not consider bank rates a relevant marker, in the North they do. Hence Northern micro-finance organisations can only partly address the transaction cost issue, but in Fundusz Mikro we have shown that this can be done sufficiently to become at least self-sustaining. If we compare some example interest rates being charged today in the UK, this throws further light on the potential levels of profitability of Northern micro-finance organisations:

Lender/Borrower	Interest rate (example APR)	Nature of transaction costs
Structured bank loan to small business	14%	Tailored business risk assessment
Personal credit card to individual	20%	Computer-driven, credit-scoring assessment
Money-lending company making consumer loans	100%	Tailored personal risk assessment/ collection process
Credit union consumer loan to member	12%	One-time personal assessment; costs frequently subsidised by volunteer/ donated administrators
Fundusz Mikro interest rate (zloty) (average Polish inflation during period charged: 15%)	30%	Tailored business risk assessment
Potential UK micro-finance institution rate	20%	Tailored business risk assessment

What we see is that in order to maintain their required rates of return, banks can only charge 14% if the transaction size has a certain minimum value. Below that, they have to offer cheaper products such as personal overdrafts where no business assessment is involved. Credit card companies and money lenders both offer micro-size loans and their rates show what needs to be charged in order to obtain a commercial rate of return involving, respectively, computer-based and tailored/manual assessment processes. Credit unions' rates are neither fully costed nor intended to provide a commercial return to investors. In comparison with these institutions, if we agree that business risk assessment involves more work than personal risk assessment, which is in turn more work than a computer-driven process, Fundusz Mikro's (real) rate looks cheap, even after taking into account the low rate of return to investors. The reason for this lies in the simplification and elimination of administrative procedures.

In the UK, though the nominal interest rate needs to be lower than Poland's, the real rate may be similar, indicating that investors in the two countries can expect a similar rate of return. Since the Polish and UK rates reflect their respective countries' typical gross profit margins for micro-enterprises, they are probably the maximum rates generally affordable. This then more or less caps the returns the industry can generate in the North, barring some further streamlining of procedures in the future.

Therefore, despite this book being about the social responsibility of banks, micro-finance is not, in my opinion, the responsibility of the banks alone. This is both because of its low potential returns in the North and because of the quite distinctive nature of the business which suggests that it is far better undertaken by specialist institutions. These reasons are also to some extent connected, in that asset-driven lending methods (used by banks) minus the assets are bound to create default problems.

On the other hand, micro-enterprises represent the next generation of small business clients for banks and an additional market for non-credit products. Banks should therefore have an interest in supporting their development. Also, though their lending approach may be completely different from that of microfinance institutions, commercial banks have a great deal of experience that they can share quite cheaply with microfinance organisations e.g. in the areas of governance and supervision, asset and liability management, internal financial control and audit systems and software programmes to fully integrate the treasury, accounting and loan administration records. (These are areas in which most microfinance organisations are particularly weak).

What is therefore needed is a partnership approach which enables banks to contribute funding and know-how on a wholesale basis, i.e. to independently-managed micro-finance institutions, with support from the public and voluntary sectors to cover a major portion of the shortfall in banks' rates of return. The concept of partnership is, of course, already familiar and accepted amongst UK banks, government and the voluntary sector. However, it has yet to result in prompt action on a much larger scale.

(b) Development methodology

So far I have reviewed the key institutional issues only with respect to full-grown micro-finance institutions. Another set of institutional issues, however, revolves around the optimal method of growth and development for a brand new micro-finance institution. If financial sustainability is the goal, one of two alternative approaches can be taken: to minimise costs or to maximise revenue. The cost minimisation approach may be seen in those local community loan funds and credit unions which are volunteer-run or have part of their operating costs donated in kind. Their advantages are that they require low investment and can rapidly become self-financing. On the other hand, because their outreach is small, their impact is limited, and growth beyond the local level is prevented by both the vision of those involved and the lack of contractual agreements against which to secure funding for growth.

The revenue maximisation approach which makes impact and outreach the top priority involves building a large organisation in order to benefit from economies of scale. Most people taking this approach have done so by starting small and gradually adding local branches as each one in turn becomes profitable. This has enabled the initial loan capital investment to be kept as low as possible. However, it has created a much longer lead time to sustainability (i.e. the point at which there are enough branches to fully cover the central overheads as well as the local costs) and until that point is reached, the institution has remained grant-dependent. Grameen Bank took at least 20 years to reach this point and Banco Sol (in Bolivia) 11 years.

The challenge we set ourselves in Fundusz Mikro was to find a way of combining the best of both approaches: i.e. the speed to sustainability of the cost-minimization model with the outreach and impact of the revenue-maximization model. If we could achieve this, we felt it would ultimately be the cheapest (i.e. least draining on grants during the years of operating deficit) as well as provide financial support to the maximum number of micro-enterprises within the shortest possible timeframe. The method we therefore adopted was to design the full-scale institution upfront, to hire the future senior managers immediately and, after an initial pilot testing period of a year, to open as many branches as possible. Whilst this involved greater financial exposure by creating higher short term operating deficits, over a five year period it was a much cheaper, shorter and surer way to the sustainable state we have since achieved. For future micro-finance institutions in the North, I now feel convinced this is the optimal development route for anyone whose goals are wide outreach and rapid impact at the cheapest ultimate cost.

Wider issues

In the course of my efforts to promote the Fundusz Mikro model for the UK, I have come to experience at first hand the main obstacles which such a project must overcome and therefore feel uniquely qualified to write about them! Firstly, let me list them:

- A problematic definition of charity under British law;
- The lack of any public-sector or voluntary-sector commitment to the concept of 'optimal project funding';
- The lack of an internal organisation structure in today's financial institutions, companies, charities and government bodies capable of evaluating and

responding to proposals which fall between profit-maximising and charitable in the conventional sense;

• Difficulty for commercial banks to fund the start-up phase of a lending business which uses alien methodologies to its own and potentially serves a market which they themselves have rejected or with which they have incurred high defaults;

• Lack of fully integrated welfare-to-work incentives;

• Lack of any appropriate legislation, regulation and supervision for the micro-finance industry.

To take each of these in turn:

Definition of charity

The story is told of a father who was trudging home through the forest with his young son. The son says to his father, 'Father I am tired. Please carry me' and the father replies, 'Walk on as far as you possibly can and when you can go no further, then I will carry you'. Anyone hearing this story nods wisely and agrees with the father's response. According to the law, however, 'self-help' and 'charity' are placed in diametric opposition to each other such that, if a person does something for him or herself, (s)he cannot by definition be a recipient of charity. An unemployed person may need a large amount of external support but can still manage to do something for him- or her- self. Similarly, an employed or self-employed person with a lower than subsistence income, though mostly self-reliant, still needs some external support.

At an institutional level, a school for disabled children for example, may be able to raise some revenue from parents' contributions while the rest must come from charitable sources; and a sustainable micro-finance organisation may be able to generate enough income from its lending operations to cover its operating costs, but not enough to also cover the commercial cost of its capital. The point here is that if we agree with the father-son basis for helping people, or institutions which help people, then 'gap-filling' support should become eligible for charitable status and for tax-exemptions for the donor.

Optimal project funding concept

In the same way as we think about how best to help people by first requiring, incentivising and empowering them to do whatever they can by themselves, so too may we think about how to appropriately allocate public or donor funds to charitable projects. Micro-finance has (rightly, in my opinion) been criticised for 'using up precious grant monies' intended for poverty alleviation, thus leaving the hungry, sick and destitute with inadequate support. If one assumes that pure grant funding is the most limited form of funding available and commercial capital the most unlimited, the concept of optimal project funding is simply about allocating funds with the highest affordable cost of capital to any given project.

This means that if a project only needs partial grant funding and the rest can be equity or debt, then it should not take grant funding for the whole. It also suggests the need for a measurement tool to help investors/donors equate e.g. a low-yield 10-year loan to a commercial 10-year loan plus a grant of £X in present value terms, and obtain a tax-exemption for the grant-equivalent provided. Projects requiring funding would then be evaluated and compared along a 'subsidy spectrum' for any given funding level, as well as in relation to their goals, achievements or outputs. As a result, much more 'socially directed' funding should become available, requiring rates of return ranging from part-grant, part-capital-retention to 'ethical' investment rates, a few points below pure commercial rates.

Internal organisation structures

At present, neither the British government nor the European Commission, nor commercial financial institutions, companies nor charities are set up to properly evaluate and respond to requests for 'intermediate' funds. Private sector organisations either seek to maximize their profits or to 'minimize' them (i.e. give them away in the form of charitable donations). There is therefore no proper value ascribed to a sustainable project. Whatever does not generate commercial returns will fall into the charity department and with charitable funds being strictly limited, no high-impact sustainable project requiring economies of scale and therefore larger investment amounts is likely to be within their budgets.

As regards government money, only grants are so far possible for micro-finance. Within the charity sector, a few institutions do make investments or loans but this needs to be much more widespread. (The Program-Related Investment model pioneered by the Ford Foundation in the USA is an excellent reference point). As for other potential providers of intermediate funds, I believe, both at an institutional level (e.g. the Church of England's investment portfolio) and at an individual/community level, there is a vast potential untapped market of would-be investors in socially directed projects, who understand the superior value of recycling their funds again and again vs. making one-off donations, but are not incentivised by the charity and tax laws to do so.

Specific difficulties for commercial banks

In respect of micro-finance specifically, what we are asking of commercial banks is quite a tall order: not only are they required to admit to the scale of population they are failing to serve, but also to agree that a brand new organisation with no track record and a set of intended practices in direct opposition to their own, is more likely to succeed than they are. So much so, that they are willing to fund its start-up, conditionally commit future success-based funds for its development and agree to a social rate of return.

If micro-finance were not about an activity (i.e. lending money) at which banks feel they ought to be the experts, it would probably be easier to approach them for funds as they would not be tempted to assume at least as high a level of industry knowledge as the applicants' own. Even then, however, as the funding required in the first instance would really be for start-up venture capital, it should rather be requested from socially-directed venture capital funds. Banks could then lend or invest the major portion of the loan capital in the post-pilot phase, once a track record had been created from the pilot loans.

Welfare-to-work incentives

At present, anyone on welfare who starts a business (officially) will immediately start to lose their benefits despite the lack of subsistence level profits from the business. This clearly needs to change but, meantime, if there is an implicit understanding that a reasonable amount of grey market income fulfils an important role in helping people through the transition phase to the formal economy and is a necessity until the laws change, then micro-finance can act as a useful tool to encourage the transition process. In Fundusz Mikro we do this by tying the loan amounts for which borrowers are eligible to the percentage of their undeclared income which will be recognised in the cashflow calculation. The higher the loan amount, the lower the percentage of undeclared income that will be recognised. Thus the borrower always has the choice of how much to declare but the less (s)he declares, the smaller the loan for which (s)he is eligible.

Micro-finance legislation, regulation and supervision

What kind of licence does a micro-finance institution need to properly serve micro-enterprises?

1   The ability to use up to 100% of its loan capital on unsecured lending
2   The ability to start lending with a very small capital base
3   The ability to take client deposits
4   The ability to lend out of borrowed funds as well as out of its own capital or grant monies.
5   The freedom to make loans or take deposits without the restrictions imposed on e.g. credit unions or mutual credit societies.

If such a licence were to be created, what measures could be taken to protect the health and safety of the micro-finance industry?

1   The deposits of micro-enterprise owners need to be safer than those of average (richer) bank depositors. There should therefore be a lower cap on the micro-finance institution's capital-asset ratio and perhaps a graduation policy such that, for brand new organisations it is lowest and then rises with the track record of consecutive years' lending with a minimum repayment rate.
2   There should perhaps also be separate ratio requirements in relation to client deposits (only) vs. total risk assets, based on the size and track record of the organisation.

3   The national deposit insurance scheme covering bank clients should also include clients of micro-finance organisations, or a separate scheme established.

4   An industry-specific set of institutional risk assessment measures should be formulated.

5   Standardised definitions of e.g. delinquencies, defaults, operating and financial sustainability, should be created.

6   Standardised performance measures to compare asset quality, operating efficiency, etc. between different institutions, should be introduced.

7   Incentives should be provided for banks to offer their know-how to micro-finance organisations, to strengthen their governance, internal control functions and back office systems, for example.

8   There should also be incentives for insurance companies to develop an institutional insurance product for micro-finance organisations to protect them from systemic risks in the portfolio. Whereas banks tend to collapse because of problems in or over-exposure to a particular industry sector, this is much less likely to happen in a micro-finance institution, unless it is badly managed. The main risk in (well-managed) micro-finance institutions is that of flood, drought, acts of war, etc. which, if they occur, can affect a substantial proportion of the total loan portfolio. This, however, should be insurable and must become so if the industry is to survive.

Several countries, including South Africa, Peru and, in the North, Bosnia have enacted or, at least drafted, specific microfinance legislation. Both the legislation itself and the practical experience of operating within it should be very useful to other countries considering the introduction of similar legislation.

Conclusion

Micro-finance in the North is at present hardly existent, and certainly not in a way that is capable of making a significant impact within a short period of time on an affordable, long-term basis. Yet for millions of Northerners, it is a more appropriate tool to help them become self-sufficient and move towards mainstream bankability than any means of support currently on offer. If it is to become widely available, it must be affordable. This means that it needs to be provided by self-sustainable institutions.

As far as I am aware, the worldwide microfinance industry currently comprises about 7,000 institutions, out of which no more than 100-200 are both profitable and serving tens of thousands of clients, and none of these are in the North. Within the 300-500 programmes in the North, Fundusz-Mikro has come considerably closer to profitability and scale than any other, and it is for this reason that its methodologies are described to such an extent in this paper.

A simple recommendation for the creation of many Fundusz-Mikro-style organisations in the North is not, however, the answer. This is because there is no-one in whose interest it entirely falls to take up such recommendation. The social rates of return that the industry can offer in the North therefore require a partnership approach to be taken by the banks, the government and the voluntary sector. In addition, a whole set of legal, regulatory, organisational and attitudinal changes in the wider environment must accompany these partnerships in order to make them truly effective.

Communities are creditworthy: Shorebank (USA) and Bumblebees

Lynn Pikholz and Ronald Grzywinski
(South Shore Bank, USA)

'Now here you [Shorebank] are, flying like a bumblebee – which has mathematically and scientifically been proven NOT to be able to fly, and yet it flies'

'So are you [Shorebank] an exception or is there something systemically pertinent about what you have been doing for the past 25 years that policy makers cannot just push aside like a mere curiosity?'[1]

Everyone, except the bumblebee itself, knows that a bumblebee can't fly. Its wings are not large enough. Aerodynamics declares it is scientifically impossible. The greatest computers in the world all come to the identical conclusion; it cannot fly. But what does the bumblebee do? It ignores the great minds, the skeptics, the computers... and it just goes ahead and flies.[2] A statement like this is easily used as a springboard for many lessons: Why not one on community development lending?

Shorebank Corporation is a bank holding company that invests in and works at restoring markets in underserved communities. With assets of $900 million and $79 million in capital, Shorebank invested over $100 million during 1998 through its own commercial banks and other subsidiaries in five U.S. locations to demonstrate that lower-income communities are worthy of additional private and local investment, even by stringent private sector standards. Shorebank's investments generate external awareness of untapped market potential in less affluent communities. Shorebank is committed to a business-driven approach to community economic development. We base it on our belief that alleviating poverty requires creating wealth, and that wealth is created best when businesses identify and invest in neighborhood assets. Too often, we undervalue assets in economically distressed neighborhoods which offer sound business opportunities to businesses and banks willing to look for them.

Four undercapitalized, overleveraged and idealistic individuals acquired South Shore Bank

Shorebank's founders, a group of four bankers, began seriously questioning the conventional wisdom that bumblebees don't fly in the late 1960's.[3] They began a successful minority small business loan program at a bank in Chicago. The program out-performed similar large bank programs and Shorebank's founders began exploring the potential of broader private sector approaches to urban problems. In 1972, the Federal Reserve Board observed that Bank Holding Companies, 'possess a unique combination of financial and managerial resources making them particularly suited for a meaningful and substantial role in remedying our social ills.'

We believe this is true. Banks have a large number of attributes that make them particularly attractive as the core of a community development institution. As a regulated, large-scale institution, a bank is known, trusted, legitimate, well capitalized and self-sustaining. A bank possesses unusual capacity to be continuously knowledgeable about the neighborhood economy. And a bank can convert ordinary deposits into development loans; through doing so, it leverages its capital approximately 14 times! As a regulated business, the bank is forced to work to a bottom-line discipline that ensures a focus on being effective and efficient.

Shorebank's founders decided to translate their beliefs into a banking institution. Undercapitalized, overleveraged, and idealistic they acquired South Shore Bank with $800,000 in equity capital and a $2.5 million equity loan. Shorebank began operations in 1973 in South Shore, a community of approximately 80,000 people on the south side of Chicago which had virtually gone from all white to all black within the prior decade, a familiar scenario at the time in many areas of urban America. At the time the founders took over the bank, almost everyone had stopped investing in the community, and the last remaining bank, South Shore Bank, was trying to move out.

For the first four years, the best and the brightest bankers ignored us

Like the bumblebee, everyone believed Shorebank would fail. For the first four years the best and the brightest bankers ignored us. We could not hire anyone with banking experience because no one believed a job with us had a future. Since Shorebank's humble beginnings, total assets have grown 15 times to $900 million and total capital has grown 95 times. Shorebank today consists of 22 affiliated organizations in five locations with 500 employees. Our four commercial banks in the U.S. are all fully regulated institutions. Shorebank's other subsidiaries and affiliates include for profit real-estate companies; not-for-profits that do higher risk enterprise lending and labor force development; and venture capital funds. Shorebank also has a consulting company, Shorebank Advisory Services, which works with for-profit and non-profit organizations both locally and abroad and has been instrumental in assisting conventional banks, both domestically and internationally, tap into new market opportunities which have both profit and development-impact potential.[4]

Since 1973 Shorebank's assets have grown 15 times and capital has grown 95 times

From the early eighties until our recent expansion into three new states in the nineties, Shorebank's return on common equity averaged 25% and the return on total average capital for the same period averaged 13%. Mostly as a result of our three start-up bank holding companies, Shorebank Corporation ended the most recent five years (ending on December 31, 1998) with consolidated earnings averaging only $0.2 million, and the return on shareholders' equity averaged 0.002%.

South Shore Bank, our oldest commercial bank in Chicago, has been the 'earnings engine' of the Corporation throughout the history of Shorebank. Since 1973, the Bank has produced cumulative profits in excess of $36 million. Nearly $15 million, or 40%, of those earnings were generated during the past three years.

South Shore Bank is our earnings engine

In 1998, South Shore Bank (SSB) generated record earnings of $6.2 million – a 21% increase over 1997. In 1997, South Shore Bank's results were similarly impressive at $5.1 million – a 45% increase over 1996. South Shore Bank's lending in economically distressed neighborhoods in Chicago has increased around 15% over each of the past two years. The majority of this lending is in multi-family rehabbing, and small business lending. The bank's loan loss reserves to total loans ratio is 1.7% (peers are at 1.4%) and charge-offs are at a historic low of around 0.37% (peers at 0.3). Historical average charge-offs for the past 12 years have been 0.56% (peers are at 0.5%). For the past 25 years, average charge-offs are around 0.6%. The leverage ratio of the bank is 6.2% and the loan to deposit ratio is 66%. South Shore's return on equity (excluding goodwill, which distorts the number because of our recent acquisitions) is 18.98%. Including goodwill it is 11.78%.

South Shore's lending portfolio is split more or less equally between commercial lending, which is almost exclusively to small businesses (over 99.9%), and real estate lending. South Shore Bank's small business and real estate portfolios have been consistently profitable. How do we do it?

Certainly, for the bumblebee, there is a lot of weight for such little wings. So, how does it do it? The most compelling theory we found (with some application to community development banking) lies in the fact that static objects are governed by different stability laws than dynamic objects. For example, take a bicycle. As a static object it is not stable (like a tricycle would be). Leave a bicycle standing without support and it will fall over. However, a moving bicycle is perfectly stable, and it is easy to explain why with basic physics. The bumblebee is the same, as a static object it is not aerodynamically stable, it cannot glide. But when it is flapping its wings, we're into a whole new ball game for how air moves around it.[5]

Shorebank achieves its development goals on a sustainable basis

Sitting statically at a desk, it is very easy to call community development lending unprofitable and not the domain of 'good business'. When we start flapping our wings a little and examine real opportunities that exist in less-affluent neighborhoods, our language quickly changes from charity and subsidies, to investment and market opportunities. The numbers on South Shore Bank's lending and financial performance clearly suggest that it is possible to transcend the worn out and superficial contradiction between business and charity, between development and profit. Shorebank is achieving development impact on a sustainable basis. The switch in Shorebank's capital base over the years is further evidence of the shift in private sector perceptions that development banking can generate returns and 'do good' at the same time. Common equity has grown to 98% of total capital. Today, a diverse group of investors including a growing number of major banks, insurance companies and other businesses make up the majority of our shareholders.

Shorebank's founders were convinced that the goal of development banking is to attract and combine the resources necessary to build a critical mass of permanent development activities sufficient to restore community and investor confidence, changing the dynamic of spiraling decline into a self-sustaining process of renewal. Our experience and the experience of other major banks in the United States now confirm several core beliefs about this process:

Many ordinary residents in distressed areas are creditworthy

First, many people in distressed communities desire to improve their own life conditions and, although they may lack conventional credit histories, many of these ordinary residents are fundamentally creditworthy.

Second, local development capacity, whether in the form of small scale, locally based entrepreneurs, fledgling business entrepreneurs, or community development corporations, need to be supported in a disciplined, business-like fashion. Positive community development is a long-term partnership between residents who care about their communities and financial institutions with similar motivations.

Third, market forces can be restored in under-invested communities if the level of institutional capacity is sufficient to the task at hand. Permanent, self-sustaining institutions must be created. The problems occurred over decades, and require long-term, permanent solutions. This cannot be a 'quick fix'.

Fourth, an array of complementary interventions is often necessary to reverse disinvestment. The multiple, complex, mutually destructive problems confronting disinvested communities regularly require an equally comprehensive set of mutually reinforcing tools. These allow synergies to be achieved, such that activities, which would not be viable in isolation, can succeed together.

Fifth, successful restoration of market forces requires that revitalization be targeted to clearly identified geographic areas and markets with the potential for renewal. Targeting allows an institution to develop the necessary specialized market expertise, allows controlling risk and transaction costs, and assures that investment will be concentrated in order to achieve critical mass.

A bank must be responsive enough to allow it to generate and broker development deals

Finally, to succeed, the institution must be close to and driven by its markets. It must be innovative, flexible and customer driven, based on relationships of mutual discipline and accountability. A bank must be close enough, specialized enough, and responsive enough, to allow it to identify, generate and broker development deals with manageable risk; and it must have the credibility to build partnerships and leverage outside resources.

The bumblebee is one of nature's most adaptive creatures. They are excellent pollinators because many parts of their body have become adapted for this purpose. They can fly at much lower temperatures. They have longer tongues to reach flowers with long, narrow corollas and their hairs are branched and are perfect for picking up and transferring pollen. Bumblebees would die without flowers and many flowers would be unable to breed without bumblebees.[6]

South Shore Bank (SSB) was our first bumblebee and the local entrepreneurs in South Shore were the flowers that needed juices to produce. In every society, these small and medium sized businesses make up the sector which creates jobs and is the fertile soil from which entrepreneurial innovation and expansion sprouts. Without these businesses, many banks in the long run, would die. Shorebank saw that the profitable provision of financing services to this sector as a great market opportunity.

Local rehabbers risked their own savings to purchase buildings using loans from SSB

Shorebank's best-known enterprise support program that it operates profitably through its commercial bank in South Shore, is its multi-family mortgage loan program which finances residents in the business of rehabbing apartment buildings in economically distressed areas. This unconventional approach to entrepreneurial development created a profitable lending niche for South Shore Bank; it also created successful businesses, and resulted in visible development benefits. The local residents realized real estate appreciation and improved, secure, affordable rental housing. The primarily African-American building owners realized an increase in wealth.

The stage for a successful credit program in South Shore was set in 1975 by a consortium of savings and loan associations who — at Shorebank's aggressive urging — undertook a 300 unit, publicly financed, scattered site rental housing rehabilitation project in South Shore. The project demonstrated strong market demand for the highly attractive rehabilitated, secure and affordable rental properties. Local investors then proceeded to invest without subsidy, risking their own savings to purchase other buildings, with South Shore Bank financing them.

Local rehabbers succeeded by acquiring under-valued assets (apartment buildings in a neighborhood that had undergone racial change) and investing in their upgrade cost effectively through shrewd purchasing of materials and use of their own and other available labor. They took advantage of the strong market demand for safe and affordable housing. In essence: the market was right; they had the skills and drive; and they matched their motivation with a huge time commitment (true sweat equity) and dedication to their business of rehabbing.

South Shore Bank tailors its loans to meet customer needs

Two other factors were critical to their success. First, rehabbers were able to manage their unsubsidized finance because of the way South Shore's lenders creatively structured their loans. This was very different from the technician-style asset-based approach of many other commercial banks. Second, rehabber learning took place through informal information sharing and as well formal meetings among fellow entrepreneurs.

South Shore lenders tailored the loans to meet customer needs. The loan program operated simply, without construction escrows, lien waivers for contractors or much paperwork. The financial economics of most of South Shore's customers would not have allowed them to abide by these rigidities. Payment arrangements need to be more flexible. This approach fits the pragmatic style of most borrowers, the deal's inability to afford much in soft costs, as well as with the personality of South Shore Bank's chief lender, Jim Bringley. Jim and most of Shorebank's lenders have a disdain for bureaucracy and a passion for interactive customer contact, both in meeting the borrower's financial needs, and 'collecting hard and fast' when the borrower slips on a scheduled payment.

If a borrower comes in with promise, we make the deal work

South Shore's mandate to its lenders was simple: 'If a person comes in with promise, make it work.' Loans were structured to fit the borrower's cash flow. This sometimes meant an initial six months moratorium of principle payments; approving loans with an additional amount for working capital to fund early bank repayments, or offering a line of credit to buy a property quickly and cheaply from a desperate seller.

South Shore Bank's lending department also facilitated the sharing of information among rehabbers. This took place through rehabber networks started by a modest bank effort to aid information sharing. The local rehabbers in South

Shore knew of one another's skills and reputation but did not meet with one another on any structured basis.

Entrepreneurs learn best from other entrepreneurs

South Shore Bank's chief lender understood that the rehabbers could benefit from interacting with one another. He knew the local rehabbers since many had taken loans at the Bank. He offered them the bank's boardroom as a place to meet on Saturday mornings to talk about issues of common interest. He knew the fundamental truth that entrepreneurs learn best from other entrepreneurs. They believe someone who has already done something that has worked.

Half the attendees at these meetings were proven operators; half were novices. The rehabbers who had done well had credibility. So if one of them said 'hey, don't get that type of boiler or use Jack's Boiler Company to fix that specific problem, or get this particular part,' the others listened and learned. In more recent years, the rehabbers run their own meetings at a local Mc Donald's restaurant. We never served hamburgers.

South Shore Bank's lenders also assist borrowers by advising them when they might be overpaying for a property. Assisting a borrower not to overpay means the loan will be better able to fund needed rehab work. The lenders also gave advice on alternative and incremental rehabbing options, especially if borrowers did not have much extra cash on-hand.

Our real estate department likes to grow with its customers for as many decades as possible. It prefers first-time rehabbers to start with a small building which is a good fit with their existing capacity and then to grow with them as they develop more competencies in the real estate business. If, for example, a rehabber has never done a project, we would want to finance a less sophisticated rehab scope (e.g. repairing job; redo floors; put in new mailboxes or new windows and frames) on a six flat. For bigger apartment buildings with large rehab needs, South Shore's lenders prefer rehabbers to show that they will devote significant time to the project. If they are not already working on the rehab full-time by the time they are doing 36 unit rehabs, they should demonstrate that it is their intention to do so in the future.

Large U.S. banks now compete to make loans to local rehabbers

Shorebank's rehabbing initiatives contradict the traditional banker's 'bigger is better' idea of business. The cumulative impact of rehabbing has resulted in: job creation; safe and affordable housing; and presumably a better quality of life for residents. It has brought more mainstream investors into the area. Large banks now compete to make loans to rehabbers. And local rehabbers have built up both equity and skills to undertake larger scale rehabilitation. Today, dozens are engaged in extensive rehabs of large 3 story, 24-36 unit brick buildings. Without a penny of subsidy, the finished product is a truly beautiful building that is safe and affordable at between $450 (one bedroom) to $550 (two bedrooms) to the typical tenant, a young woman with two children.

Two full-time equivalent loan officers currently finance the rehabilitation of 75-100 buildings a year in South Shore alone. That's about $10 million/year/lender with an average loan of $250,000 and with some rehabbers getting loans in the $1 million plus range.

South Shore Bank now operates in 13 designated neighborhoods of the Chicago City, home to nearly half the city's African-American population. Demand remains strong in our initial neighborhood 25 years later and is growing in the neighborhoods closest to the lenders. In 1998 we did around $50 million in real estate housing deals, $21 million in single family and $30 million in multi-family. Cumulatively, our real estate entities have done over $500 million in our target neighborhoods company-wide. The loss rate on these loans is low by bank industry standards and the portfolio contributes substantially to the bank's profitability.

Shorebank began doing its first mortgage on single family rehabs five years ago. And, only two years ago, as a result of our expansion into a new locality with huge tracts of vacant land, we began lending for new construction. Our total real estate portfolio is around $200 million in Chicago, of which single family deals make up 35%. Like for our multi-family lending, we do not use much subsidy or insurance for our single family deals. Mostly, private mortgage insurance companies' dictates like the restriction that a borrower cannot have more than 30% of the purchase price of the first mortgage allocated towards rehab, simply don't make sense for us or our borrowers.

We cover our increased exposure with a 1% fee to borrowers. This is the same price that the insurance company would charge borrowers. The average single family rehab deal is $85,000. This price includes purchase and renovation. Borrowers usually put down 3%, but this is flexible. Our loans are usually fully collateralized and we generally do progress payments and advance only a portion of the money upfront. For first-time borrowers this is especially true.

Our lenders take the deal the whole way through

We differ from conventional banks in that our lenders take the deal 'the whole way through'. At Shorebank, the lender is the one who meets the customer for the first time, goes to visit the property, does the application, the underwriting, and manages the property appraisal. He or she also goes out for progress payment checks and follows up immediately on any late payments. Conventional banks often have three people doing different parts of the same deal and the underwriter may never meet the customer. Each of Shorebank's lenders has underwritten lots of differently structured deals in our selected neighborhoods. As a result, they are better able to make judgements for each new deal that walks through the door.

The same appraisers do all our deals for similar reasons. They know real comps (comparable property prices) and are able to give meaningful and valid appraisals. They know how the value will change on a particular street corner if the floors are sanded and a gate is installed. They are able to advise us, and we, in turn, advise our borrowers. Our deals are incredibly customer intensive with a lot of face-to-face contact.

You become a paper pusher instead of a deal maker when you rely too heavily on subsidies

It may seem strange to some that we choose not to take advantage of available credit enhancement products and subsidies available for the Bank's real estate products. Abiding by the restrictions and bureaucracy of government require- ments would require that we push paper the whole day (adding to our cost structure), rather than doing deals. There would also be controls on South Shore Bank's borrowers, for example, who they are allowed to hire to do the job. This adds to their cost structure too. Even if these subsidies did not have all the nega- tives, it is doubtful that they could have ever been provided at the rate and scale that we would have required them. Since the early eighties the work of these local entrepreneurs has affected well over a third of our first neighborhood's 24,000 units of rental housing in South Shore. Subsidies are simply not ever generated on this scale – a scale that we believe to be necessary to achieve an impact at neighborhood level.

A logical question, then, is how South Shore Bank makes these housing loans for poor people living in distressed neighborhoods without subsidy, and still makes a profit. First, we do not have all the higher costs that often accompany government subsidies. Second, we assist our customers in getting good prices for their deals. They may buy a typical abandoned building for $5,000 a unit and put in $12,000 for rehab. This makes a quality product affordable for really low- income residents. South Shore Bank does not usually finance more than $25,000 of debt in a unit. In other cases, the housing stock is in relatively good shape and a small investment adds substantially to the value. Third, South Shore's borrowers use highly skilled contractors who get the job done at below market cost. Sometimes, for example, these are plumbers who may be working for the City by day, and moonlighting at a cheaper price at night. Fourth, we structure the deals to fit the cash flow of our borrowers. And fifth, we structure correctly for the risk because we know our neighborhoods really well. We are probably one of the only banks that does not stick by any debt-service ratio rule. But we are careful and realistic in our projections about the future profitability of the buildings that we finance.

It may sound like Shorebank is anti-subsidies. To the contrary, much of our development work would not have been done as profitably without government programs. Our real estate housing development affiliate uses low income housing tax credits. Our not-for-profit companies use job-training funds. And our banks have deposit insurance and use Small Business Administration (SBA) guarantees and the State's Capital Access Program.

We are cash flow lenders

South Shore Bank's small business lending niche is with neighborhood businesses that are often poorly capitalized and who are vulnerable to economic downturns. Many have sales below $1 million and the vast majority of South Shore's borrowers have annual sales below $5 million. The remainder almost all have less than $10 million in sales. Clearly, these are not mom and pop micro deals.

We are cash flow lenders. Shorebank's borrowers sometimes do not have much collateral or management experience and their earnings history is often short or non-existent. Yet, they are capable entrepreneurs who we believe will succeed. They are creditworthy and fully bankable if the deal is structured to fit their cash flow and their ability to manage debt.

But lending is more people-intensive and risks are higher; both because of the lack of sufficient collateral and a long earnings or management track record. This is especially true for start-ups. This means that losses may be higher, and banks, like us and like you, want some protection. It is for this reason that the government credit enhancements are so important.

But many of our small business deals wouldn't have been done as profitably without subsidies

The US government's credit enhancements do work. And they work because they are smartly structured to provide enough incentive for banks to do small business lending deals, and enough disincentive to ensure that the deal make sense. In the case of the federally funded Small Business Administration (SBA) subsidy program, banks are insured up to 75% with a cap of $750,000. In the case of a default, banks will pay a 25% loss on a pro rata basis. Although individual losses may be small, they add up. If South Shore Bank does approximately $10 million a year in SBA guaranteed small business deals; even with a 75% SBA guarantee we would still have 2.5 million dollars at stake. We thus have an incentive to 'lend smart.' On the other hand, we can make a $1.5 million loan to a single small business in our target area and we are still guaranteed for 50% of that amount just in case things go wrong and the business suffers a loss. SBA's historical average loss rate is 7%. This is reasonable given the market that it is catering to. After all, if we expected the SBA to have a 2% loss rate like any other bank, there is no need for SBA to exist at all.

South Shore and the experience of other banks show that profits can be made making SBA guaranteed loans. Surprisingly though, seven out of the fifteen largest SBA lenders in the country are non-banks like General Electric, AT&T and the Moneystore. These businesses do SBA lending purely to make profits. This begs the question of why traditional banks, who are under pressure to do community development lending are not using it more. One guess is that there is often a fundamental mistrust between government and banks. Often a misplaced and misguided mistrust. Second, there is an assumption that borrowers, who look 'different' on paper, are less creditworthy. Third, SBA and similar subsidies require lots of paperwork and bankers need to invest time to understand all the intricacies. Bankers do not naturally have any inclination for this type of effort. A more recent government incentive program in the U.S. called the Capital Access Program overcomes many of SBA's shortfalls and has been favorably received by an increasing number of major banks.[7]

We may know derivatives, but we have been left in the dust by bankers in developing countries

Jane Jacobs, a well known North American urban development specialist once said at a small business symposium in Canada that: Westerners like us have no difficulty creating sophisticated financial products like derivatives, but that we have been left in the dust by the Latin Americans and Asians who have figured out how to deliver loans of several hundred dollars to uneducated entrepreneurs who cannot present credit reports or financial statements, profitably. The point Jane Jacobs and many others have since made, is that smaller deals at market interest rates to less affluent people in less affluent markets *do* work if they are structured to suit the borrowers, their cash flow, and their ability to manage the loan. Not only do they work for borrowers, but they are profitable for traditional banks and are the fodder of far more lucrative business deals for banks in the future.

And now, to end our bumblebee session... We are not saying that lending in economically distressed areas is easy. But for those bankers that are open to seeing the business opportunities for making sound investments in economically distressed areas, the potential for both profit and development impact is enormous, and there is increasing evidence from players worldwide that this is the case. Bumblebees (in the plural) do fly. And as the economist John Maynard Keynes would have said if he was around at the time that the first bumblebee took its flight, 'in the light of the evidence, I have changed my mind.' May all serious bankers do the same.

Post Script[8]

If you should ever find a grounded bumblebee early in the year, just at the start of the first warmer days, then it is probably a queen. She may have been caught out in a sudden shower or a cold spell. If the temperature of the thorax falls below

27°C the bumblebee cannot take off. The best thing you can do is to pick her up using a piece of paper or card, put her somewhere warmer, and if possible feed her. When she has warmed and fed she will most likely fly off. You can feed her using a 30/70 mixture of honey and water in a pipette or eye dropper or simply by putting a mixture of honey and water on the table, but be careful not to wet her hair or get her hot and sticky. By saving a queen you may have saved an entire nest.

ENDNOTES

1   Comments received by the authors from Christophe Guene of INAISE in February 1999.
2   Adapted from an electronic reprint of Entomology Notes # 10, Michigan Entomological Society.
3   Ron Grzywinski, a co-author this paper, is one of Shorebank's four founders and is currently serving as the CEO of Shorebank Corporation.
4   Lynn Pikholz, a co-author of this paper, works as a Corporate Analyst at Shorebank Advisory Services, Shorebank's international and domestic consulting company.
5   Adapted from an electronic reprint of Entomology Notes #10, Michigan Entomological Society.
6   *ibid.*
7   For more information on the CAP, see 'Capital Access Programs: A Summary of Nationwide Performance,' Department of U.S. Treasury October 1998.
8   Adapted from an unsourced internet site.

The environment and social justice are creditworthy

Bettina Schmoll
(Ökobank, Germany)

Protecting the environment, stepping in for peace and social justice, promoting sustainable economic activities, taking responsibility for the future – these are the principles of the German Ökobank. In practice this means promotion of projects in the fields of environment, social commitment and emancipation, for which Ökobank offers special, low interest loans.

The conventional banks regarded the founding of the ecological and social co-operative bank in the banking capital Frankfurt eleven years ago with scepticism. That a business policy could be based on profit optimisation rather than profit maximisation seemed to be a sheer contradiction to the 'natural' operational principle of banks. The underlying principle of Ökobank was to operate in a way that not only the return on capital, but also the service to people and the environment be part of the return calculation. This striving was also expressed by the slogan heralding Ökobank's 10th anniversary in 1998, 'your money and your life' rather than 'your money or your life'. Ökobank's business is therefore extensively determined by the will to have no money to go to the nuclear industry, the armament industry, chlorine industry and projects abusing human rights.

The result after 10 years: the Ökobank-idea is successful, not only in its socio-political aims but also economically. In the financial year 1997 Ökobank grew by over a third (31.9%), the balance sheet as at 31.12.97 was 319.3 million DM, which corresponds to an absolute increase of almost 77 million DM in comparison to the year before. Loans to Ökobank's special target sectors amounted to 60 million DM. Today Ökobank is considered as an expert in ethical-ecological investments.

The roots of the 'Eco bank'

The idea that committed people should be allowed to take responsibility for what is done with their money emerged at the beginning of the 80's out of the peace and environment movement. For those who did not want their money to serve armament, nuclear power, environmental destructive or human rights abusing projects, a financial alternative had to be proposed. At the same time money should be invested for a sustainable, environmentally and socially sound economy. In 1988 things were ready, Ökobank obtained its co-operative bank license and launched its business with headquarters in Frankfurt.

Ökobank serves private persons, organisations and enterprises that are close to the bank's objectives. Furthermore, it does not want to exclude people on low income and weak economic influence, such as those who are on social security, migrants and the unemployed.

Participation out of principle

The organisational form of a co-operative was a deliberate decision. It left much scope for democratic principles through participation in policy shaping and decision-making. It is the members who are to decide which way Ökobank goes. Next to the statutory bodies, such as the general assembly, there are additional forums in which members and employees discuss business policy and strategies. Ökobank regards itself also as a self-help organisation that offers its members the opportunity to organise their own financial activities in accordance with their political and social commitment and ideas.

Transparency is another basic work principle of the bank. Members and customers should be aware of what is being done with their money and, correspondingly, beneficiaries should know where the money comes from. Likewise, savers are informed comprehensively about the chances and risks of their respective investments. In 1998 Ökobank had about 24,000 members and 33,000 customers.

Money for a good cause: the target projects

The duty of Ökobank is to promote members in their economic, ecological, social and cultural undertakings and to create and support forms of environmental, social and equal opportunity promoting businesses. In the daily banking business this means that money is invested e.g. in the building of solar factories, car sharing, self-administered carpentry businesses, health food trade or housing projects for single parents. Parallel to the usual bank services such as current accounts, savings accounts and monthly saving schemes, Ökobank has developed special promotion fields. By underwriting so-called 'promotion savings bonds', customers can forego the payment of interest in favour of specific projects. This interest gift enables low interest loans in favour of target projects that fall into the categories of Ökobank philosophy.

Presently, Ökobank offers such 'Promotion Bonds' with topics such as energy, environment, women, self-management and mental disability. A specific savings bond for 'social commitment' is divided into education, development, culture, migrants and common housing. Depending on their specific interest and commitment savers determine what kind of project their savings and foregone interest will go to. The interest rate on such 'promotion loans' is usually 1 to 3 per cent lower compared to usual market rates.

The contact relations between savers and borrowers are particularly close in the case of so-called 'Project Savings Bonds'. In this case savers allocate their money into one particular project, such as in the case of VCD, the German association for improving traffic management (Verkehrsclub Deutschland VCD e.V.). Ökobank provided the association in 1988/89 with the start-up capital of over 200,000 DM through the 'VCD Project Savings Bond'. VCD had not had any chance at other banks where it was not seen as creditworthy, its know-how in road policy being its only capital and guarantee. Ökobank also provided start-up capital in millions to Gepa, a company involved in fair trading with developing countries. Today both these organisations have become successful enterprises with an extensive set of goods and services that have become indispensable for the development of their respective markets.

While during the first years demand for (low interest) promotion loans had been considerably lower than supply, they have been rather in balance these last couple of years. The demand for promotion loans is highest in the energy and environment sectors. Particularly private persons who intend to build a house show a great interest in the possibility of support for their energy saving and ecological buildings. Those who build for example a low or passive energy house, using environmentally sound building materials such as native wood, eco-textiles or recycled wallpaper and do without PVC materials obtain a promotion loan covering up to 60% of the total building costs. It is in the building activities in particular that Ökobank sets up signals for environmental conservation through its promotion funding. Eco-houses, built with the help of Ökobank, demonstrate publicly that alternatives to the conventional, energy hungry and environment polluting building do exist.

Ökobank succeeds again and again in helping businesses that work for a sustainable living to a breakthrough. This was the case for Alb Natur, a natural textiles correspondence seller; Davert Mühle, a wholesaler importing and exporting biological cereals, or Union Gewerbehof, a coalition of 50 environmental and social enterprises lodged in a common former industrial building which includes a print shop, a company commercialising ecological building materials and a training project. Each of these enterprises received promotion loans of more than one million DM without which their start-up or structural development would not have been possible.

In its promoting business, Ökobank also distinguishes itself through an evaluation committee which is rather unique in the banking sector. Indeed a panel of independent experts checks on the basis of specially developed criteria whether a project is in conformity with the aims of Ökobank and whether it is promotion-worthy. The members of the panel are not remunerated. Employees have no vote in the committee. The bank as such only examines the economic factors falling in line with the credit approval process.

The service range of Ökobank

Ökobank is a direct and universal bank. The greatest part of the banking business is done electronically or by telephone. The main branches are in Frankfurt and Freiburg and subsidiaries in Berlin and Nürnberg. In addition to the ecological and ethical business policy, Ökobank aims to offer a good quality service to its customers. Both these aspects form the basis of success for the bank.

Ökobank offers all typical bank services ranging from savings accounts, savings bonds and various savings contracts to time deposits at normal market conditions. It provides also investment insurance, pension schemes and life insurance, it grants mortgage and building loans as well as investment loans and other credit services for businesses. On the equity market, it offers the ethical-ecological investment fund 'Ökovision' and mediates direct risk capital, e.g. into wind funds.

Customers can make all their financial transactions through Ökobank and are not dependent on any other bank. With the credo 'no money for nuclear power, armament and apartheid', and for some time also 'no money for chlorine industry', it was important to extend the offer to the largest service range possible.

New products – investment funds and direct investments

Ökovision

Eight years after its founding, in1996, Ökobank together with Versiko AG introduced the investment fund Ökovision. It was a response to the many customer demands, who did not want to miss this type of investment.

The ethical-ecological criteria of Ökobank are also valid for the Ökovision investment fund. It invests particularly in the equity of enterprises that use environmentally friendly technologies, produce or trade environmentally friendly products such as renewable energy, and develop or use technologies that reduce or get rid of environmental pollution. Also considered are enterprises valuing a culture of corporate democracy, participation, equal rights and human working conditions.

The selection process of each enterprise is labour intensive and time-consuming. A non remunerated investment committee assesses whether the shares envisaged by the fund managers match the investment criteria. For this, the expertise of the committee members, acquired through working with various environmental and social organisations, is essential. Transparency towards the shareholders is respected through half year reports containing information on products and work methods of each enterprise selected and the decision process of the investment committee.

This complex procedure is worthwhile. In the profession, Ökovision is reputed as being the strictest ethical-ecological investment fund with high investor confidence. The fund's notoriety increases continuously.

While sticking close to the ethical-ecological criteria, the shareholders' return expectations are not lost out of sight. After two years of existence Ökovision ranked among the best traded eco-funds on the market. In February 1999, the fund capitalised 35 million Euro. Since the start of the fund the average performance was at 6.6% per year; with a high of 21.4% in 1997 and a low of -2.1% during the turbulent year of 1998. The main sectors represented in the portfolio are the service industries (13%), consumption & health (11.4%), capital goods & engineering (9.5%) and capital goods & energy systems (9.4%).

Direct investments

Innovation is a key element for Ökobank. The development of new products is to increase competitiveness on the market and also to reach out for new customer groups. Furthermore, in line with Ökobank's will to offer up-to-date services to its customers and members, new developments such as in the field of tax law, are seriously taken into account.

Since 1996 Ökobank offers direct investment opportunities in the form of closed funds. Here too the financing of innovative and social enterprises is a priority. Through these investments they obtain the necessary capital to secure a bank loan. So far (as at 2/1999), Ökobank set up two wind funds and a property fund. The essential advantages for the investors are that the money directly benefits an enterprise that complies with the ethical-ecological expectations, they obtain a share of the profit, and losses – occurring especially during the starting years – are tax deductible. When offering these investment opportunities, Ökobank takes great care however in informing frankly and comprehensively all potential investors on the economic risks and the realistic returns to be expected from such investments.

Ökobank is particularly keen on offering investment opportunities that help to build up wind farms as it is an important step towards ending the dependency on nuclear energy by extending the supply of renewable energies.

In 1997 Ökobank broke into new ground with the property fund 'Rommelmühle'. Nearly 13 million DM of capital was necessary for transforming a corn mill into the first green warehouse in Germany, including space for living, recreation and apartments. Only ecologically made goods are sold in the 8,500 square meter retail area, ranging from furniture, building material, clothes, to gifts and food. The whole project was planned ecologically from the outset by Archy Nova, a specialised construction business, taking care that the wellbeing of people (room climate, short distances, atmosphere) is thought through and respected. The Rommelmühle is well connected to the public transport network and is supplied in energy by its internal hydroelectric power plant. Investors are guaranteed a good long-term return thanks to the rents that the building earns.

An idea grows – the Ö enterprise group

Soon after establishment it appeared that the customers of Ökobank, particularly small businesses in the targeted promotion areas, had a considerable demand for advisory and accompanying support beyond usual bank services. In 1989, Ökonsult was founded as a company for organisation consulting and enterprise development. It is a subsidiary of Ökobank. Its task is advisory support for promotion-worthy projects with the aim to facilitate successful and sustainable business. Good ideas are often there, however experience is often lacking especially in starting up projects and in business administration. Its service spectrum therefore includes advice in business management, development of human resources, leadership, strategy, ecology and conservation of resources. Ökonsult works for private businesses as well as for associations and not-for-profit organisations.

Secondly, as introduced earlier, Ökovision is an international investment fund, founded in 1996 by Ökobank, Versiko AG and Investiko GmbH. Ökobank is member of the management board and is majority shareholder.

Ökofinanz Frankfurt finanlly, is a project development organisation for ecological and social investments. It has developed the wind funds and the Rommelmühle property fund for Ökobank. Other closed funds are planned, particularly in the area of renewable energies.

Together with Ökobank, these organisations make up the Ö enterprise association. As a quality sign, 'Ö' stands for the criteria by which the Ökobank's work is guided: sustainability, emancipation, environmental soundness and social responsibility.

The future

In order to accomplish Ökobank's development purpose further, the establishment of an Ö foundation is currently under discussion. With its funds, projects could be supported that are dependent on donations and subsidies, such as social, cultural and research work.

Ökobank is attentive to evaluating itself regularly on its self-imposed yardstick. Hence, from the year 2000 on, an ecological and social audit is to examine over a couple of years where exactly the bank stands in respect to sustainability, conservation of the environment, democracy, equal opportunities and emancipation. With the ecological and social audit Ökobank once again hopes to break new ground. While there are numerous examples of ecological audits, no standards exist yet how to define and develop social compatibility of an enterprise. The ecological and social audit should therefore be designed to lay down new yardsticks, which other, interested enterprises can compare themselves with.

The quality of its services and the composition of the product range are a permanent challenge for Ökobank and the Ö enterprise group. New and innovative investment products will therefore continuously be developed, especially in regard with the turnover target of one billion DM which Ökobank has set itself.

New forms of ethical banking for an increasing social demand: Banca Etica (Italy)

Laura Foschi and Francesco Bicciato
(Fondazione Choros, Banca Popolare Etica, Italy)

1. Introduction

B anca Etica is the first alternative bank in Italy. It was constituted (as a bank) in May 1998 and it started banking activities in February 1999.

Some of Banca Etica's key characteristics are:

* To give credit to organisations founded on values such as solidarity, helping the disadvantaged, the conservation and development of the environment and the promotion of enterprise linked to the respect of human rights;
* Strong partnerships with organisations such as third sector enterprises, local authorities, religious associations, environmental associations, trade unions, local committees;
* Strong member participation in the Bank activities, the members being grouped in local volunteers associations (GIT: Gruppo Iniziativa Territoriale) to organise promotional activities;
* Assessment and selection of enterprises (or projects) through a set of economic, but also social and environmental criteria which guarantee their ethical qualities.

The following text will give a view on the larger setting in which these specific characteristics are articulated and some tools that help to enact Banca Etica's strategy. In particular, the role of the third sector for Banca Etica, the synergy that can be created with local authorities and the evaluation methodology to finance social enterprises will briefly be reviewed.

2. Welfare state crisis and the role of the Third Sector in Italy

Neither the Government nor the Market seem to be able to give an answer and to provide those services necessary for the improvement of the quality of life, culture and leisure time. This willingness to meet a growing spectrum of unsatisfied needs is one of the reasons that motivated the European Union to support the Third Sector, specifically in view of creating jobs (*Third System and employ-*

ment, working programme of European Commission for employment, industry and society, DGV, 1998).

A large debate about the definition of the Third Sector has been going on for some time, but once again we can use the European definition saying that the word Third Sector defines whole organisations that belong neither to the public nor to the private for-profit sector [*Ibid*].

Third sector organisations are co-operatives, associations, charities, foundations that provide goods and services or develop an economic activity. They differ from traditional enterprises in that profit is not their primary goal. Their private sector framework differentiates them also from the public sector.

The presence of unsatisfied needs and the opportunity to satisfy them through new forms of economic activities, give room for a wide growth of the Third Sector. Several experiences mixing social and economic goals have emerged to satisfy an increasing social demand, and at the same time, have been creating concrete employment opportunities.

Some data on the Italian Third Sector
- 418,000 employees = 1.8% total national employment
- 39% growth rate of employment during the '80s (general growth rate of employment was 7.4%)
- 4,000,000 people engaged in social activities
- 16,000 conscience objectors
- 52,000 social enterprises:
- 1.1% of GDP
- 52.7% of public financing (30% contracts, 17.5% grants)
- 46.7% of private financing (about 32% from selling goods and services)

The interest for the Third Sector is strong at the level of the European Union institutions. Several interesting programs – mainly concerning employment – reveal the importance of this sector in terms of employment and welfare creation (and also diversity).

Recent analysis (Eurostat, 1996) confirm that the Third System enterprises:
- comprise between 6% to 6.5% of the total number of European private enterprises;
- employ 6.4 million people (5% of total employment) of which 59% are in the association sector, 34% in the co-operative sector, 7% in the mutual sector. The percentages may of course vary from country to country, for example the Third Sector organisations providing social services represent 29% in France, 23% in Germany and 25% in Italy. Moreover, although the number of associations is higher than that of co-operatives, it is the latter that create proportionally more employment (53% of the sector) and higher turnover

(79% of the sector).

* have proportionately created more jobs in the '80s than the economy as a whole, i.e. 11% against 3.7% in Germany, 15.8% against 4.2% in France and 39% against 7.4% in Italy.

3. Social demand and social investment supply: the birth of Banca Popolare Etica

3.1. Banca Etica: the first social bank in Italy

In 1994, a widespread movement involved in social co-operation and protection of the environment launched the Banca Etica project. The aim was to provide a tangible instrument for a new school of thought for finance and economics. Unions, social co-operatives, local authorities, associations and NGOs (all organisations with strong territorial roots and with a relevant social dimension) participated in this ambitious initiative. They built on the experience of the Mutual Self Management initiatives (MAG) in Italy, and of the alternative banking system in the rest of the world.

In May 1998 the Cooperativa Verso la Banca Etica reached the amount of social capital required by the Italian legal system to become a bank. An extraordinary meeting of the shareholders changed its statute and its legal framework transforming it from a co-operative structure to a bank (specifically a Banca Popolare). On 8 March 1999 Banca Etica, the first ethical bank in Italy, became completely operational and opened its door to the first customers.

The main products of Banca Etica (on the fund raising side) are ethical certificates of deposit and ethical bonds (in the long term other services may be offered such as a current or savings account, ATM services, etc.). It is also forecasted that the saver will be given to choose the level of interest rate, which he can forego partly or completely to allow for lower interest levels for the enterprises financed.

Banca Etica finances enterprises that develop activities in the following sectors:
* Social co-operation and other social activities
* International solidarity
* The environment
* Culture, civil society and sports

Some figures on Banca Etica
➢ 7,500,000 Euro of capital stock
➢ 13,000 shareholders:
➢ 1,800 non-profit organisations
➢ 169 local authorities
➢ 17 banks
➢ 11,000 individuals

Internationally, Banca Etica is involved in the development of microcredit, notably through the participation at Microcredit Summit activities and Microcredit programmes carried out by the World Bank. Banca Etica is also a member of INAISE (the International Association of Investors in the Social Economy).

3.2. The Third Sector as the main market of Banca Etica

Banca Etica is mainly directed towards the market of non-profit enterprises – also called social enterprises.[1]

The Italian legal framework for Social Enterprises

Social Co-operatives

According to law 381/91, social co-operatives have as an objective the pursuit of the general interest and of social integration as:

cat. A) social health and educational services;

cat. B) agricultural, industrial, commercial or service activities that employ at least 30% of disadvantaged people.

Associations (ONLUS)

It is the recent reform act on the non-profit system that rules the association status. Associations are defined as social voluntary organisations that do not have for-profit goals. They have to pursue a non-economic objective (art.12-42 cod. civ.). They can be instituted e.g. for sports, culture, nature conservation.

Co-operatives

Co-operatives in general can also be considered to fall within Banca Etica's target group, on the basis of their mutual goals – which is their main distinguishing characteristic from ordinary companies according to the Italian legislation. Co-operative activities have to consist in providing goods, services and employment directly to members of the organisation at more advantageous conditions than those prevailing on the market. Several kinds of co-operatives are covered by the Italian law, ranging from production activities (agriculture, industry, handcrafting, etc.) to service activities. An important particularity is the limitations falling on profits, which may only be distributed in proportion with the legal interest rate (art. 1026 Civil code, law 31 January 1992, n.59).

A social enterprise is an organisation able to link management plans with social intervention while operating in a competitive market. It is indeed so that between the market and State, there is an increasing room where this new sector of social enterprises can play a substantial role. Social enterprises promote a fairly new organisation model able to satisfy the increasing social demand, particularly in the social services sector, with the possibility for employment creation.

Some features of social enterprises are:

- Their aim is to maximise social utility. For these enterprises profit is a constraint to respect and not a goal to maximise.

- They achieve this by developing a range of activities such as providing employment opportunities for disadvantaged people, health care, environmental conservation, cultural initiatives, etc.
- The organisational structure is non hierarchical. They promote sharing of responsibility and management among employees, the involvement of customers, and stakeholder participation in general. Moreover, social enterprises can rely on a network of volunteers that promote and support the enterprise's activity.
- Their production activity is based mainly on services and goods with a high social impact. The goods and services produced usually have a low added value. This is due to the high labour costs involved in employing disadvantaged people as well as in the limited economies of scale.
- They have particular legal frameworks, which allow them to provide goods and services in a better way and sometimes to get funding and fiscal advantages.

4. A new model of welfare finance: some projects of collaboration between Banca Etica and local authorities

Among the partnerships that Banca Etica developed with a range of different organisations, the collaboration with Local Authorities is particularly interesting.

The policy of Banca Etica is oriented towards a mixed welfare society where the public sector collaborates with the third sector. In practice, collaboration with a decentralised administration does not always guarantee participation. Yet Banca Etica wants to promote horizontal (non hierarchical) subsidiarity, which means full participation between citizens, social organisations and local authorities in the decision making process.

In a context of welfare state crisis, public and third sector organisations have a mutual interest in cooperating. The third sector is able to produce a high level of social welfare and to substitute itself in part for the public administration in providing social services.

However there are some difficulties for local authorities to get involved with the Third Sector. Firstly, local authorities often do not know much about the third sector, whether in terms of its dimensions, its structures, or its mere presence on the territory. Secondly there is a lack of standard tools to evaluate the capacity and social efficiency of the delivered social services. Thirdly, there is no appropriate legislation for regulation of the Third Sector.

Banca Etica can represent an interesting link between Local Authorities and the Third Sector. Presently, 6 Regions and 190 Municipalities are shareholders of Banca Etica and have underwritten about 800.000 Euros of its capital stock, thereby creating a strategic partnership to be developed through common tools:

Cash advances:

Banca Etica will for instance finance social enterprises which receive funding from public institutions (such as the European Union, Italian Government, Regions, etc.). Because of bureaucratic reasons, public support is often late and social enterprises often risk to go bankrupt in consequence.

Stock capital for Social Enterprises (Cooperative di Capitalizzazione):

Under-capitalisation is a structural problem among Social Enterprises, in particular among those involving disadvantaged people in their production process (type B co-operatives). The lack of stock capital is one of the main causes of difficulty in accessing credit, which is why a new organisation, a capitalisation co-operative (cooperative di capitalizzazione) will be set up. Local authorities, Banca Etica and other stakeholders will provide the needed capital, with the Local Authorities (and Regions) as the main shareholder.

Banca Etica's role and competence in collecting the funds for the capitalisation co-operative is an important one, as it will carry out a territorial campaign to collect stock capital and donations – similar to the 3 year campaign it carried out to collect its own capital. This mobilises a strong network of social co-operatives, families, volunteer associations, trade unions, churches and individuals.

Banca Etica will also assist the capitalised social co-operatives in assessing their financial needs, will help them implement their business plan and will complement the capital with short and medium term credit on a one to one basis.

Municipal bonds (Buoni Ordinari Comunali, BOC):

Municipal bonds are a new financial tool in Italy to collect funds from citizens for public projects. Banca Etica will orient local authorities in choosing projects of common interest. In a context of welfare state privatisation, it is indeed important that the new partnerships be set up strategically to serve and respect the most disadvantaged people. Ethical Finance as understood by Banca Etica, working across the full range of partners from welfare state to social organisations, must play a significant role in those upcoming scenarios.

5. New criteria for enterprise assessment

Banca Etica's way of selecting enterprises worthy of funding is one of the features that makes it unique in the Italian banking context. It is interesting to describe the principles employed by Banca Etica in its investigation process.

The main goal of Banca Etica is to provide credit to economically reliable enterprises that demonstrate attention to the social utility they produce. In addition to standard economic analysis, Banca Etica analyses the consequences that different production activities can have on human health, public welfare and the environment. This means that the Banca Etica staff needs new tools to investigate values that have not been examined so far by the existing banking system. The objective is to work towards a system of indexing and parameters that must eventually be as objective and clear as possible.

5.1. Social and Environmental Evaluation of Social Enterprises (the VARI model)

Banca Etica has created an innovative assessment tool, the VARI model (Values-Requisites Indicators), to evaluate social enterprises. The assessment of a credit demand, from an ethical finance point of view, must and can be based on a relatively simple system, to provide a tool that must be easily usable both by the bank staff and the credit applicant. It must be simple also because it adds an ethical assessment to the economic analysis. Moreover, as well as being a formidable instrument for Banca Etica to achieve its social mission, it can also be so more generally for the financial instruments of the social economy.

The VARI (Values Requisites and Indicators) method developed by Banca Etica mainly refers to social-environmental aspects. It is a simple tool that allows the bank staff to have wider information on the investigated enterprises. It allows to consider the whole project, the coherence with its mission, its structure and its long term soundness. The valuation model VARI (Values Requisites Indicators) requires two essential steps:

First, each funding request must be preceded by an application-form in which the enterprise is described in its essential lines (type of organisation, human resources framework, main activities, further economical information). It is also required at this stage to pass the admission threshold (negative criteria) below which the ethical financing cannot be granted. Banca Etica will refuse to finance all enterprises whose activities are in opposition with its scope. For this reason each enterprise or association will provide a self-certification document confirming the adherence to some minimum criteria and declaring that it has not been involved in a series of negatively defined activities (see below)

The Admissibility Threshold: Exclusion Criteria

Banca Etica will exclude all the enterprises that produce:
- ➤ Health hazardous products (such as genetically modified plants and food).
- ➤ Environmental hazard and exploitation (pollution; intensive exploitation of soil, underground and natural resources; animal experimentation; nuclear energy production; highly energy consumption activities).
- ➤ Lack of respect for the human dignity (abuse and discrimination of workers; no guarantees on health and safety in the work place; sexual, religious, political discrimination; pornography, drugs, alcohol, tobacco, gambling).
- ➤ Abusive political relationships (direct or indirect links with dictatorships; economic activity for political interests or vice versa).
- ➤ Shipping industry.

The second step, after passing the admissibility threshold, is then to proceed with the valuation based on the VARI model as such. This model is based on nine

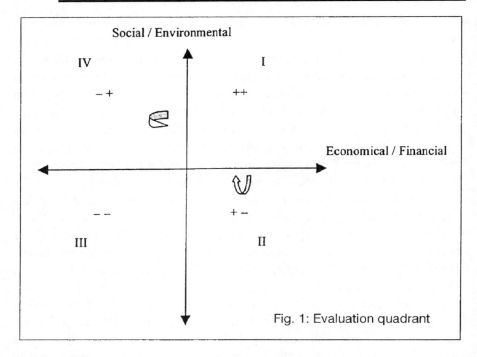

Fig. 1: Evaluation quadrant

basic 'Values' which are of importance to Banca Etica and to which the loan applicant must demonstrate respect to. For each value there are some essential 'Requisites' that guarantee the respect of those values. For each requisite a set of 'Indicators' have been identified to see whether the requisites are respected.

For example the indicator 'Number of women present on the board of directors', is one of several indicators that identifies the fulfilment of the essential requisite 'No gender discrimination'. This requisite is one of those referring to the value 'Equal Opportunity', the respect of the requisite could mean the fulfilment of the value. Another example is the indicator 'Periodical pollution control' that refers to the requisite 'Respect of the environment', that is one of the requisites belonging to the value 'Eco-sustainability'.

5.2. The evaluation quadrants: a 'political problem'?

One of the problems of such an investigation system is the correct balance between economic and social-environmental valuation and, inside the VARI system, the weight given to each single value and its indicators.

In particular, it is important to establish, looking at fig.1, in which quadrant the Social Enterprise is situated in. While quadrant I represents an optimal valuation (economic and social-environmental valuation are both positive), quadrant III represents a totally negative valuation, and thus the impossibility to provide any financing.

Quadrant II and IV constitute the real problematic knots, with situations that are neither totally positive nor negative: in one case (quadrant II) there is positive economic evaluation and a negative social-environmental one, in the other one (quadrant IV) the social-environmental valuation is positive while the economic one is insufficient.

In these two cases, it will be necessary to take actions to reward the 'orientations' that lead from quadrants II and IV to quadrant I.

To conclude, as a pioneering ethical bank in Italy, Banca Etica explores new ground in a) the extent of its partnerships with regional government, local government and the third system and b) the efforts it makes to clearly assess the social and environmental impact of its lending decisions.

ENDNOTE
1   The Italian case is particular: at the moment Banca Etica is mainly oriented towards providing funding to the non-profit sector. Nevertheless, as occurs at the European level, there are no constraints to extend Banca Etica's activities also to Social Enterprises with a for-profit framework.

New monies – old ideals: monetary innovation and the local economy

Christophe Perritaz
(Financial Observatory / University of Fribourg, Switzerland)

It is difficult to find common ground amongst economists when you speak to them about money. It has to be said that the latter is constantly evolving, in relation to the changing needs of the economy. Whether starting out with a grain of wheat or a grain of rice, it turns up later in the form of coins made out of precious metal, then banknotes and even plastic. Each transformation puts back on the agenda issues which we thought we had clarified. Today, it is technology which is disturbing the picture. For the past twenty years or so, money has increasingly been operated without any physical medium: it has become electronic, virtual or even cybernetic.

Technological advances open up new perspectives. The customer loyalty schemes set up by the airlines, the supermarkets and other telecommunications operators clearly constitute new methods of payment – which certainly do not yet have all the characteristics of a currency – but the widespread use of which have serious implications. Originating from their marketing departments, these products enable large global groups to develop networks which extend across the world. When I fly with my favourite airline, I collect precious points, which I can then use to pay for another flight or my hotel bill without worrying about the price in local currency and without having to use this currency to pay. The transaction is cleared internally by whichever group I have chosen to be a customer with.

Against these global 'money' developments, structural unemployment and social exclusion put back on the agenda the creation of exchange networks in addition to those organised within the framework of traditional monetary trade. The Systèmes d'Echanges Locaux (SEL), as they are called in France, have the same objective as their Anglo-Saxon counterparts, the Local Exchange Trading Systems (LETS). Some of these networks fight openly against the globalisation of the economy, others respond more pragmatically to a need not met by traditional routes.

What is money for?

Money measures and registers value, and allows us to make payments. The metre measures distance, money gives an account of value. Just as the metre can take the form of a length of wood or metal, etc., money can come in several forms (metal, paper or fiduciary)

The analogy goes no further. The strict definition of distance was given for the first time at the first general conference on weights and measures in Paris in 1889. According to that definition, the metre was equivalent to the distance which, at a temperature of 0 degrees centigrade, separated the axes of two parallel lines drawn on the international platiniridium prototype held at the Breteuil pavilion in Sèvres. Today, the metre is equal to the length light travels through space in 1/299,792,458 of a second.[1]

Economists have tried to apply the same model to define the unit of account, but value, unlike distance, is a matter of subjective appraisal and, furthermore, can vary with time. The value of a tool can be zero to someone who does not know how to use it, but to the craftsman it can be very high. Years later, when better tools have been invented, that same tool could become useless and so of no value even to the craftsman. Conversely, if this type of tool is no longer produced, the craftsman might be willing to make great sacrifices to obtain it, because he needs it. Value is a subjective concept which can vary with time.

In order to make sizeable purchases, you have to be able to save. But savings can also be used for a 'rainy day' or more usually, savings finance a quiet retirement following a busy working life.

At the macro-economic level, businesses also choose to save, in order to make important timely investments. The life cycle of products show that businesses reap significant returns when a product reaches its maturity. On the other hand, during the launch of a new product, a business pays out a great deal of money. In order to invest, a business can borrow either from the bank or on the financial markets. Therefore the business uses a value which other players (businesses or private) are saving in the meantime.

The value reserve function is very important in a market economy, since it allows the allocation of resources to whoever needs them at any particular moment.

Value reserve brings us face to face with the concept of interest. For a long time the Church condemned interest bearing loans, because it considered that money could not of itself create value. Today, we consider that interest is justified in two ways:

- Interest ought at least to cover the rate of inflation. In this way, the creditor gets his money / investment back at the end of the period.
- Equally, interest should cover a risk premium. It is, in fact, by no means certain that a debtor will be in a position to repay his creditor at the end of the period. It can happen – risk is an integral part of economic activity – that the debtor's business fails and the creditor will carry a part of the loss, since he will not recoup his outlay.

Value reserve money allows surplus buying power to be held back for the time being in anticipation of a future purchase.

The intermediary of exchange function is commonly put forward by reference to barter. Thus, according to André Chaineau 'the essential role of money is to ensure that barter is broken into two separate trading stages.'[2] For Françoise Renversez: 'The use of money allows the exchange to take place without being conditioned by the existence and coincidence of two co-exchangists as required in a bartering process.'[3]

The impracticality of barter had already served as a starting point in the analysis of the role of money by Adam Smith in 1776. In Book 1 of *The Wealth of Nations* he wrote: 'In his shop the butcher has more meat than he can use; the brewer and the baker would willingly buy some of it, but all they have to offer in exchange are the various products of their trade, and the butcher already has all the bread and beer that he needs....' This is what we call the problem of matching supply with demand: the agent who wants to give A and receive B, has to find someone who wants to give B and receive A, which is not obvious.

Global corporate monies

The customer loyalty programmes operated by big businesses do not yet qualify as parallel 'monies'. In no case do they constitute a measure of value, since the price of airline flights or hotel stays are still expressed in national currency. Their value reserve function is very limited since the points accumulated lose their validity beyond a certain time limit. However they represent an exchange intermediary, since they are accepted as payment for certain transactions.

The legal monopoly to issue money still held by national central banks acts as a brake to the development of these mechanisms, although this monopoly is being eroded. In the current context of liberalisation, it seems unlikely that the issuer of new monetary instruments would be put under the supervision of the central bank. The development of 'global corporate monies' would therefore mark an extra stage in the process of the disappearing of physical money. In the past central banks were able to keep a certain control on the issuing of money, by means of obligatory reserves imposed on the banks, or by the rates of interest which the banks were liable to pay when they restocked with new money. The issuing of money was always covered, partially and as a last resort, by the central bank, which pledged as security its infallible reputation.

Nowadays big businesses benefit from total public confidence. It is in this context that virtual money steps in, defined as 'computer money with no immediate interface with conventional money. Virtual money is money that isn't there in any real monetary sense. It is not – and cannot be – measured as part of the permanent money stock'.[4] The businesses in question can cut themselves free totally from the central money stock and issue their own monetary devices, secured solely by the confidence which the public grants to that business. The central bank would no longer have any control over economic activity which used this instrument for its trade purposes.

In concrete terms, with loyalty programmes, the member businesses participating in the loyalty scheme can pay their employees – at least in part – by means of this new method. Thus the businesses are assured of a return from the salaries paid, in compensation for which the employees get preferential conditions.

This new method of payment reveals interesting characteristics. It is free from national boundaries, but it is confined within a network of businesses. It allows holders of this money to obtain goods and services which they need. Wherever they are in the world, this method of payment certainly responds to a need. We are witnessing a redrawing of monetary boundaries. Equally, it is worth noting that if national money becomes obsolete, economic policy in the service of the common good is losing one of its tools – monetary policy – to the benefit of private business strategies.

'LETS money'

The promoters of LETS often quote as a point of reference the example of Wörgl, which has interested economists such as Gesell and Irving Fisher. LETS (Local Exchange Trading Systems) seems to have developed in the English speaking world in the mid-eighties, then in France. Today, there are 300 SELs in France, totalling 20,000 to 30,000 members.

'A prime example of a LETS'
In 1932, the mayor of Wörgl (in Austria) – in order to address the problem of an unemployment rate of 35% – decided to issue specially printed banknotes, which were designed to be stamped to show a depreciation of 1% per month. They were secured by the same sum in formal money deposited in a local bank. Two years later, Wörgl was the first Austrian town to achieve a return to full employment. Lots of works were able to be carried out (water supply network, road maintenance, replanting in the surrounding forest....). This town became a focal point of interest for numerous economists. Apparently, within the community, the money carrying a negative rate of interest circulated forty times more quickly than the formal money.[5]

Each LETS maintains an up to date catalogue listing the availability of, and requests for, the goods and services of members. This enables members to meet and agree on the terms of the exchange (type of service or good involved, amount in local money units...). Once the details of the exchange are decided, the two parties sign an IOU (an exchange form). This form is in three (tear-off) sections: one is sent to the administrators of the LETS, and the other two are for accounting purposes for the two participants in the agreement. This allows the two members' local money unit accounts to be credited and debited, these accounts having a limit in terms of overdraft and credit. It is easy to understand that this in no way represents a return to barter which some people wanted to see, rather it is a system of multilateral indebtedness.

'A more elaborate example'

The WIR bank in Switzerland is one particular example of an exchange system. In the first place it extends beyond the local community, because it covers the whole country. However, it offers services to a well-defined group, SMEs. The co-operative nature of its banking differentiates it from pure LETS, which are often associative.

Founded in 1934, the bank's objective brings it close to LETS. It attempts to ease SMEs' access to credit by issuing its own money, WIR. The member businesses of WIR can benefit from credit at especially advantageous rates, despite the fact that the bank applies classic criteria in the granting of loans. To limit risk, the bank grants only between 10 and 20% of the total investment sum in WIR. With the credit obtained, the business can pay its suppliers.

LETS are in fact monetary systems because of the exchange balancing and their accounting systems; the philosophy of LETS rests on the dynamic balancing of debts, along with the maintenance of a debt relationship. The specificity of 'LETS money' lies in its socialising character, and you can find in it the essential role of money as a social bond. As its name indicates, 'LETS money' is a pure exchange intermediator.[6]

As a general rule, 'LETS money' is not a unit of account: its benchmark most often remains the national currency. Nevertheless a large number of systems use hourly units in their trading.

The objective of LETS clearly promotes a medium of exchange which serves as a means of payment for exchange which is excluded from an economic system based on national currency as intermediary. On the other hand, in the absence of a developed banking system, 'LETS money' can only marginally serve as value reserve. When a LETS member saves 'LETS money', he would have to be able to deposit in a bank, so that the sum can be invested, otherwise the saving is only a non-consumption. It means then that someone has excess income available, more than enough to meet his needs. The traditional solution to this problem lies in the investment of this excess so that its value might be preserved.

'LETS money' is therefore essentially a means of payment, with its subsidiary role as a unit of account, but it is difficult to see it as a value reserve.

Local money vs. global money

The emergence of 'local monies' on the one hand, and on the other the visible emergence of a global money is a paradoxical situation which reflects a duality reminiscent of the old gold standard system.

In those days, the overlord made available to the population banknotes, guaranteed by gold reserves, which could be used as a means of payment within the community. Actual gold was used between the regions. Unlike banknotes, gold has an interesting quality, because its weight alone counts (in terms of value). The overlord could easily accept coins from neighbouring regions, even if they did not bear his image.

The overlord can use these 'foreign' coins in two ways. Building up capital allows him to retain a certain purchasing power on foreign products. But he can choose to recast the coins with his own image and use them to make purchases within his own country. The nuance is not unimportant: it is a question of investment decisions, in order to retain and create value.

The important thing is to gauge correctly the need for investment. If the overlord invests in a less than successful local venture, he will receive a poor return and the preservation of his homeland capital will be affected by it. Conversely, if the population happens to take advantage of such investment, the community will benefit. The reasoning – in reverse – is valid for neighbouring communities.

The metal monetary system bestows a serious responsibility on the holder of the right to mint money: that of deciding the allocation of resources for the benefit of everyone.

The problem of offsetting balances exists as much in the LETS system as in a corporate monies system. What do you do with the 'LETS money' which is building up because its owner cannot find – within the network – the product he needs? By enlarging the LETS you could increase the range of products offered, but LETS would then lose its 'raison d'être'. You could choose to convert the 'LETS money' into national currency, but then it would in turn cease to have a 'raison d'être'.

The reasoning is similar in the case of the corporate monies system. It would be an illusion to think that a network of businesses – apart from becoming monopolist – could offer all the goods which its staff might require. The system limits the economic freedom of the member to purchase, or becomes fundamentally altered by opening itself up to other monies, whether national or corporate.

The key lies in controlling the convertibility of one means of payment into another. Today the authority of the overlord of times past has been entrusted to the currency exchange markets, supervised more or less well by the national central banks. It is clear however that the market does not necessarily work towards a better allocation of resources amongst the different economies. LETS on the one hand, and corporate monies on the other, are renewing their efforts to establish a balance between the necessary universality of a value reserve and an intermediary in more local exchanges/trading. But who would have the insight and wisdom to judge the degree of convertibility of monies amongst them?

ENDNOTES

1   Source: Larousse Bibliorom
2   Chaineau, André, *Mécanismes et politiques monétaires* ('Mechanisms and monetary policies'), PUF, 1974
3   Renversez, Françoise, *Eléments d'analyse monétaire*, ('Elements of monetary analysis'),

Dalloz, 3rd edition, 1995

4   *ibid.*

5   Lietaer, Bernard, *Beyond Greed and Scarcity* (awaiting publication)

6   This description of LETS is taken from an article by Denis Bayon, Jerome Blanc, Isabelle Guérin, Gilles Malandrin and David Vallat, published under the leadership of Jean-Michel Srevet. The article itself appeared in a report entitled *Monnaies locales et lien social: l'emergence des Systeme d'Echange Local* ('Local money units and the social linkage: the emergence of Local Exchange Trading Systems'), written by the authors and sponsored by the Banque des Dépôts et Consignations, Paris, in October 1997.

Chapter three

Learning from past (mutual) banking pioneers

The structural erosion of the co-operative principle and the chances of reversing the trend

Josef Stampfer
(Raiffeisenbank Kötschach-Mauthen, Austria)

A. The idea of the founders F.W. Raiffeisen and H. Schulze-Delitzsch

In the context of the 19th-century Prussian economic centralism, co-operatives were founded to counter political, confessional and economic dependence. Trade, small enterprises and agriculture were not able to find lenders for the financing of necessary investments. The co-operatives operated as risk-communities – each member guaranteeing to the extent of his full belongings, thus enabling purposeful economic activities. Prof. Oswald Hahn called the co-operatives 'the inventors of the modern service enterprise'. Basic co-operative principles were free will (it is each member's choice whether or not to engage with the co-operative), subsidiarity (what the individual can do on his own will not be taken over by the community) and the principle of regionality (allowing a clear perception and quick decision making). The founding of the co-operative banks solved three problems: they offered bank services locally, they had the ability to examine the credit-worthiness and economic potential very rapidly thanks to the personal knowledge of the borrower and, finally, they offered bank services at a low cost.

B. The significance of co-operative banks from an economic point of view

The basic pillars for the co-operatives' success are the cultivation of personal relations, customer proximity and, as a result of that, a good comprehension about local problems. The large number of motivated staff and engaged shareholders and high competence for local decisions enables co-operative banks to exploit market opportunities optimally. The bundling of the production of services on country and regional level supports the efficiency of the primary co-operatives and produces excellent results. Co-operative banks have a market share of over 30% today and rank among the most profitable banks in Austria; there are 720 Raiffeisen-banks with 1,733 branches and 80 Volksbanken (popular banks) with 484 branches. In Germany there are 2,600 co-operative banks with 17,200 branches. 3 million members in Austria and 12 million members in Germany see the co-operative as 'their enterprise' for the improvement of basic economic conditions.

Because of fundamental differences in co-operative objectives and the unavailability of data sources from other countries, I will confine myself to Austria and Germany. To my knowledge, the obligation of each co-operative member to directly contribute to the promotion and development mission ('Förderauftrag') exists in this form only in Austria and Germany.

C. Recent developments

The market has changed considerably: the 'supply-driven market' has turned into a 'consumer-driven market'. It is no longer output that determines local productivity but rather the increased quality exigencies of the customer. Through technological developments (Internet and Intranet), distances become less and less relevant and ever more market partners compete for customers. This requires that we question our own identity and analyse the roles of the secondary and tertiary co-operative levels. Possibilities for local primary bank co-operatives to take stakes in regional and national co-operative businesses shall ease a reallocation of functions within each sector level and promote required co-operation.

An updating of the development mission to the contemporary necessities has not been done; the identification of the members with their bank has declined during the course of the years. The expansion of non-member business – through the fiscal neutralisation of member and non-member activities – and the abolishing of the price reductions on goods for members have watered down the specificity of the co-operative self-help system and facilitate the management's abandoning of the development mission ('Förderauftrag').

The secondary and tertiary co-operative levels are also increasingly interested in the profit potential and the capital of the primary co-operatives. The delegation of decision making, out of convenience, to the secondary and tertiary levels leads ever more to a loss of the primary co-operatives' autonomy. Important decisions are thus often made without direct influence of those concerned; information deficits arise, making effective control more difficult. Questionable ties between senior positions and an alienation from the idea of the founders cause that it is not the primary co-operatives as parent companies that determine the events but the powerful 'federations'. These federations have become independent within many areas and control the network under the pursuit of their own objectives (e.g. through strategic information policies or through cumulating posts and mandates). To protect the interests of the members of the primary co-operatives a compulsory audit was introduced. But because of position linkages and collisions of interests the audit does often not work in a way it should.

80 primary banks have joined forces in the 'Association for the Promotion of Austrian Primary Banks' (Förderungsverein Österreichischer Primärbanken) to ensure their independence, exchange information and experience, to reflect on the core principles of free will, subsidiarity and regionality and finally to define and carry out an up-dated development mission.

D. Corporate orientation or member orientation? Shareholder value or human value?

The restructuring and downsizing of primary co-operatives led to a strong delegation of tasks and functions to the secondary and tertiary levels. The people responsible of the secondary and tertiary levels of that time were committed to the co-operative ideal of the founders. This fundamental attitude however has changed; power motives and economic interests of their own led to the conflict of interests prevalent today. The differing views among the co-operative levels on the independence and the future of the primary co-operatives have become evident on different occasions:

- *The judicial ruling against a statute dictation:*
  The Raiffeisenbank Kötschach-Mauthen wanted to change its statute in order to expand its business scope. This required the consent of the audit department of the secondary level. Because of the linkages between this department with the Landesbank within a 'mixed federation', an agreement was denied out of the self-interest of the latter. The Raiffeisen bank turned to the Highest Court of Justice (OGH) and achieved a ruling in their favour. The OGH decided in 1991 that the highest legislative body of a co-operative was its general assembly. The latter may decide on any business of the co-operative on its own initiative and with binding effect for the other organs of the co-operative (decision 6 Ob 6/91).

- *The rejection of price dictations:*
  On the basis of statute regulations, the Raiffeisen federation of Salzburg intended to commit the primary banks by majority decision to payments of non-ordered services. An arbitral tribunal declared the ruling as illegal and thus it was withdrawn.

- *The prevention of a consolidation regulation in banking law (BWG):*
  A proposed ruling in the banking law (Bankwesengesetz, BWG) would have given the general sector institutions the right to direct primary banks. The consequence would have been a transformation of the independent primary banks into mere branches. Through the initiative of the Association for the Promotion of Austrian Primary Banks this regulation was successfully prevented.

- *The rejection of federation treaties:*
  There were attempts in several federal states to replace the single-contract regulations between the primary co-operatives and the secondary and tertiary co-operative levels by general regulations voted on majority rulings.

- *The rejection of country-wide joint liability:*
  It was also attempted to have the primary banks guarantee with their own capital the total deposits of all sector levels through an unlimited guarantee declaration.

- *An active involvement in the reform debate of the co-operative law:*
  A current draft for discussion intends to replace the present law – ensuring

strong protection of the primary banks and its members – with regulations to protect the overall sector institutions.

The fact that the primary level had rediscovered its members and their interests led to conflicts with the secondary and tertiary levels. The representatives of the secondary and tertiary levels see the primary banks as tools for sales, the member as marketing instrument for customer loyalty and as buyers of products and services. The primary banks see the members as owners, as partners with whom the services are co-ordinated with and directed at, to the benefit of the region. The secondary and tertiary levels, however, set up structures with central control of production and sales. But if the co-operative is turned into a 'conglomerate-like' enterprise, it will lack important checking authorities. Results like the huge bankruptcy of 'KONSUM' (a large retail co-operative) could then not be ruled out.

The co-operative banks in the Association for the Promotion of Austrian Primary Banks see a different solution, which they consider better for the co-operatives, their members but also for society.

Human value in the co-operative as an alternative to shareholder value in joint-stock companies.

It is not capital that should be the focus of the co-operative, but the individual member. The objective of co-operatives should be to offer their members services that are otherwise not available to them. Opportunities for co-operatives to promote their members are various. They can offer services that are qualitatively superior to those of other suppliers or have price advantages. Every co-operative fulfils at least one 'market balancing function!'

Publications by Anneliese Fuchs, Stefan Gross, Gertrud Höhler, Christian Lutz, Rudolf Mann, Helmuth Muthers, Julia Stahl, Peter Stahl and many other experts, trends and futures analysts show quite new chances and opportunities for the co-operative. Considering the clear trends and individual observations, it can be seen that due to an exaggerated profit orientation (in which too often only short term results or size considerations count) a vacuum emerges on the personal relationship level. Through the gigantic corporate mergers, numerous market gaps appear that call for initiative-minded enterprises. Humanity, interpersonal competence and the social culture in enterprises of a human scale with clear tasks grow into new chances and challenges. Technological changes, the speed of changes (above all, however, the enormous increase in knowledge of Internet and Intranet) cause new fears among people. More than ever people, as social beings, need the community, need to be accompanied through the processes of change. Here appears another outstanding chance for co-operatives!

The vision of a modern co-operative bank is that of a financial and know-how service provider in the region. The co-operative bank is a network hub of knowledge and abilities in the region. The human and spatial closeness, the technological standard of the bank and also the know-how of employees form a symbiosis and are important building blocks of a regional economic community.

Since the co-operative bank belongs – through their members – to its customers, it cannot reject joint responsibility for the region's continuous development. Only if the members prosper will the bank also prosper!

'Economic feasibility and humanity are each other's condition. Without the one we cannot do it – without the other one we cannot bear it.' (Roman Herzog, former president of Germany)

The co-operative history is proof that economic aims are attainable, provided the human being is at the core of co-operative services. It is indeed for the freedom and self-determination of its members that co-operatives have been founded.

E. Chances for member-oriented, human co-operative banks

For the member

Members of a co-operative bank have, independent of the underwritten capital, one vote, each member thus is of equal importance. The member decides in the general assembly about the use of profits and elects the bodies. Development funding programmes, which are developed with the members, can be passed by the general assembly and carried out with the members. The co-operative offers, as know-how and network hub of the region, support to the people on their way to economic success, self-responsible and self-determined activities.

For the bank

Member and employee orientation are closely linked in a co-operative bank. A corporate culture, in which the benefit for the customer counts more than profit, in which the people and their needs are met by the service potentials of committed, entrepreneurially thinking employees provides for quick and efficient problem solving. The constant dialogue between the co-operative bank and its members creates consciousness of problems and guarantees a timely adjustment of bank services to changing demands.

For the region

The co-operative bank can act for the benefit of its members in the region independent of regional borders, political circumstances and election deadlines. The expert knowledge of well educated employees and also technical devices are available beyond the mere bank activities to the people in the region. Whether through sports, culture or education, on many levels the employees of the co-operative bank are even in their leisure time active for the people. Information events and member forums create a 'common spirit' in the region and help to dissolve fears. The co-operative bank can contribute to a climate of self-responsibility in the region. *Regionalisation means quality of life!*

What a co-operative bank can initiate and accompany in the region:

- job fairs for young people
- youth forums
- intensification of cultural life (e.g. through innovation prizes)
- bank services adjusted to old people's needs
- old people forums
- accompanying support at business start-ups
- mediating business supplies and demands (black board for the region)
- and many other things

Why not ask the members what they need? Let us establish ourselves as promoter of our members and promoter of our region! If the region blossoms, the co-operative bank will blossom. It has nothing to do with publicity but to take the people and their problems seriously, it is about attentive member dialogue!

The necessary economic success will also take place because the co-operative creates an inimitable 'monopoly' in the market through member orientation and interpersonal competence within the region. The co-operative bank does not need to be anxious about its future. As long as it looks for solutions of problems jointly with its members, they will also commit themselves through self-responsibility and self-determination for the survival of their co-operative.

'The objective of a co-operative is quality of life for everyone!'

(Dr Anneliese Fuchs, economic psychologist and author)

BIBLIOGRAPHY
Blaich, Dr. R. (1995), *Der rote Riese wankt*, Vienna: TOSA Verlag-Edition Zeitgeschichte
Brazda, Dr. J. / Schediwy, Dr. R., *Strukturprobleme von föderativen Verbundsystemen*, Wien: Forschungsinstitut für das Genossenschaftswesen.
Fuchs, Dr. A. (1999), *'Social Feeling' Gefühl für Menschen*, Vienna: Böhlau Verlag.
Gross, Dr. G. F. (1989), *Beruflich Profi, privat Amateur*, Landsberg: Verlag Moderne Industrie.
Gross, Dr. S. (1998), *Ausbruch aus der Servicewüste*, Landsberg: Verlag Moderne Industrie
Gross, Dr. S. (1997), *Beziehungsintelligenz*, Landsberg: Verlag Moderne Industrie.
Höhler, Dr. Gertrud (1989), 'Virtuosen des Abschieds' *Neue Werte für eine Welt im Wandel*, Düsseldorf: Econ.
Lutz, Dr. C. (1995), *Leben und Arbeiten in der Zukunft*, Munich: Wirtschaftsverlag Langen Müller Herbig.
Mann, Dr. R. (1996), *Netzwerk zum Erfolg*, Mannheim: Korter Verlag.
Mann, Dr. R. (1995), *Das ganzheitliche Unternehmen*, Stuttgart: Schäffer-Poeschel Verlag.
Mann, Dr. R. (1990), *Das visionäre Unternehmen*, Wiesbaden: Gabler Verlag.
Muthers, H. / Haas, H. (1996), *Vom Mitarbeiter zum Mitunternehmer*, Offenbach: BABAL Verlag.
Muthers, H. / Haas, H. (1994), *Geist schlägt Kapital*, Wiesbaden: Betriebswirtschaftlicher Verlag Dr. Th. Gabler.
Schuster, Dr. L. (1997), 'Die Genossenschaftsbank im Spannungsfeld zwischen Ideologie und wirtschaftlichem Erfolgszwang', in: *ÖBA* 4/97.
Stahl, J. (1997), *Die Renaissance des Förderauftrages als Konsequenz von Qualitäts-management in Genossenschaftsbanken*, dissertation at Berufsakademie Villingen-Schwenningen.

Popular credit: original ideas and recent applications in France

Thierry Groussin
(Confédération Nationale du Crédit Mutuel) and
David Vallat (Centre Walras, Université de Lyon 2) France

Introduction

The first wave of industrialisation called into question traditional forms of solidarity, which were typically based on family and village communities.[1] At the same time, it created favourable conditions for the formation of a new social class, namely the working class, and thereby the emergence of a class solidarity (which took the form of craft unions, workplace solidarity, cooperation etc). This class solidarity thrived on the strong impulse towards integration through work.

The Industrial Revolution was accompanied by mass impoverishment. This 'new poverty' differed from the 'backward' regions, where poverty was absorbed by the networks of primary socialisation (family, religion, community). This situation was not discussed publicly at the time, because no structure had been envisaged to address this poverty and people were aware that it constituted a threat to the social order. Poverty became stigmatised as degradation or danger (there was talk of the 'dangerous classes').[2] Pauperism undermined the optimism of the 18th Century and crystallised the social question. There therefore had to be a way of assisting the poor to gain access to work, without at the same time calling into question the principles of state liberalism.

A possible solution was credit. The history of credit and that of poverty have been intertwined for a long time.[3] Throughout the Ancien Régime, most social groups of modest means, and the peasantry in particular, could only survive with the help of credit because regular outgoings could only be met from income which was contingent upon the availability of work or the state of the harvest. Poverty frequently gave rise to recourse to the usurer, because no banker would agree to lend to the poor. A debt was repaid through a loan and, as a last resort, IOUs accumulated with the usurer. To combat poverty, it therefore sufficed to provide access to credit in such a way that the poor were able to create their own employment.

This issue of the availability of credit to the poor arose from time to time when the State considered itself unable to address the spread of poverty on its own. At an interval of 138 years, credit was depicted as a way of combating poverty. Thus, in 1859, the Academy of Moral Sciences proposed the following subject for an award:

'Credit institutions. Sources of credit in their relationship with work and the welfare of classes of limited means. Research and make known the history of institutions with the object of facilitating the application of the means of credit, in particular the mont-de-piété, the banks of Scotland and the lending banks of Prussia (*Vorschussbanken*).'[4]

More recently, the first Microcredit World Summit took place in Washington on 2–4 February 1997. The preamble to the plan of action began as follows:

'We have assembled to launch a global movement to reach 100 million of the world's poorest families, especially the women of those families, with credit for self-employment and other financial and business services, by the year 2005.'[5]

Popular credit in the 19th century was, especially in France, a means of giving autonomy to the peasant and working classes. The former were directly in conflict with abuses by usurers, while the latter were trying to defeat the alienation of wage labour, which took the form of the worker's cashbook and the regulation of the workplace through the arbitrary power of the employer.[6] Access to cheap credit transformed workers into small capitalists, particularly through producer co-operatives. Apart from the particular conditions of individual nations or individual institutions, a fundamental distinction must be highlighted. Popular credit can be directed to individuals or organisations. In the former case, it gave a helping hand to a small farmer, an artisan or a small businessman. In the latter, credit was often made available to a worker organisation of a co-operative or community based type. This second form of popular credit was particularly prevalent in France until 1871, which is a date which marked a long interruption in the initiatives for the emancipation of the working class.[7]

We shall see at an early stage (section 1), through an history of the development of popular credit, who were its principal founders. From Germany, the practice of popular credit spread to several other countries, to France in particular (section 2). We will attempt to relate the original principles of popular credit to current practices in France, in particular those encountered in the experience of the Crédit Mutuel (section 3).

1. Germany, the birthplace of popular credit

At the beginning, credit was perceived by German workers and peasants as a means of freeing themselves from usury.

The growth of popular credit in Germany was rapid in the second half of the 19th century. It evolved independently of the State as a result of the accumulation of popular savings. The experience of popular credit can largely be distinguished according to whether its application was urban or rural. The juxtaposition of the two conceptions of popular credit is also that of two men: Friedrich Wilhelm Raiffeisen and Franz Herman Schulze-Delitzsch.

Agricultural Mutuals

On 1 December 1849, Friedrich Wilhelm Raiffeisen founded an agricultural mutual credit organisation in a small village in the Rheinland (Flammersfeld), where he was the local mayor, in order to combat usury. Farmers frequently had to have recourse to usurers in order to finance their undertakings. The latter, by lending a first cow, then a second and a third etc, captured most of the income from the agricultural enterprise. In order to meet the due date for payment, the peasant had to sell either a few head of cattle or a little land. In that way, the usurer took control of the enterprise.

Having witnessed this abuse, Raiffeisen founded an association which bought the required cattle and leased it back at a moderate rate over several years. However, in order to purchase the first animals, the bank had to find a source of capital which it then had to borrow. The problem of guarantees then arose. The founding members stood surety. They guaranteed with their possessions that the borrowings would be repaid to the bank. As a result of the success of this venture, the inhabitants of Flammersfeld invested their savings, in return for interest, into the association and its activities grew.

Raiffeisen was later nominated at Haddesdorf and, encouraged by his initial success, he founded the Charitable Association of Haddesdorf with the aim of making loans to small farmers and artisans in order to ameliorate their moral as well as their material conditions.[8] Because of lack of support, the organisation soon collapsed. The fund for loans to those who were unable to obtain credit elsewhere, on the other hand, survived. Raiffeisen converted it into an association (the Association of Lenders of Haddesdorf), so that the debtors were linked with each other. Little by little, the function of the fund evolved until it reached its final principle, 'All applicants for credit must become members of the association; his loan must be guaranteed by a surety who is known to be solvent.'[9] The first objective remains: this type of association thrives on mutual aid. The members provide deposits or security in order to assist their neighbours.

Associations of the Raiffeisen type, which obtain very cheap credit in a restricted field, have several characteristics. No capital is accumulated to found the organisation (if the law requires it, a minimum level of capital is obtained). As a result, the members do not have a stake in the organisation and do not take dividends. The profits are used to constitute a fund which is indivisible and permanent which, when it attains a critical size, is able to avoid calling on external sources of capital to finance its loans and thereby to lend without charging interest. The members are collectively liable to the extent of all their assets, which guarantees their good moral conduct. The functions of the organisation are carried out benevolently. The strong cohesion of the group rests on a shared faith which, on the one hand facilitates the acceptance of reciprocal commitments and, on the other hand, presents a moral guarantee. The fact that the Raiffeisen associations evolved at village level was a further guarantee that the credit obtained would be well used. Effectively, the members of the village were witnesses to the uses for the credit at the same time as being members of the bank. This regional organisation on a parish by parish basis was founded in the main on confidence which depended on geographic and confessional proximity.

The Raiffeisen model, aiming at facilitating access to credit and freedom from usury, was not unique. Charles Gide observes[10] that, of the 18,000 associations for agricultural credit which existed in Germany in 1930, two thirds did not originate from the Raiffeisen model, but resulted from other initiatives, of which the most significant was the Popular Bank.

The Popular Banks

In contradistinction to the numerous initiatives providing mutual credit (of which that of Raiffeisen was one), Franz Herman Schulze-Delitzsch, a magistrate and deputy to the Prussian Diet, favoured action in the urban environment which was targeted at workers. The first Popular Bank was founded in 1850 in the town of Delitzsch (Saxony). Schulze-Delitzsch[11] is to industrial co-operative credit what Raiffeisen is to agricultural co-operative credit. These two new forms of organisation began at a similar time and developed in conjunction with each other.

The fundamental principle underlying Popular Banks was close to that of the Raiffeisen associations. The worker was able to obtain credit if the actual guarantee was substituted by a mutual surety. As an individual, the worker would run the risk of being unable to meet his commitments to his creditor, when confronted by the vagaries of life (unemployment, accident, illness). On the other hand, if this risk were spread over a large number of people in solidarity with each other, it would become minimal, which could only serve to reassure the creditor. Here too, loans were made openly. It was not a question of discounting the effects of commerce, but simply making a loan. The public which benefited from these loans explicitly comprised those who did not have access to ordinary banks. Loans were made from funds provided beforehand by the members of the bank or borrowed from financial institutions on the basis of the guarantees provided by the members. As in the case of Raiffeisen, liability was unlimited.

The route taken by Schulze-Delitzsch departs from that of Raiffeisen in the sense that the popular banks were not like associations, but rather incorporated organisations, owners of capital and remunerated for their investments. For that reason, loans were made at a discernibly higher rate of interest than by the Raiffeisen associations. Moreover, the shareholders shared any profit and the administrators were remunerated for their work. In this system, unlike that of Raiffeisen, the lender was distinctly favoured over the borrower.[12] It is true that a specific objective of these banks was to encourage saving amongst the popular classes. In that way, the shares of these banks (amounting at the time to in the order of 1,000 marks each, according to Gide[13] a considerable sum), could be acquired by subscribers of modest means, because they were payable little by little in phased instalments. The shareholders were attracted by the profits, which thereby facilitated the constitution of a capital fund.

These two approaches can be clearly distinguished, even if they shared the common goal of making credit accessible to those who were ordinarily deprived of it. Friedrich Wilhelm Raiffeisen appealed to the faith and the solidarity of the members who constituted the mutual credit associations. Franz Herman Schulze-Delitzsch promoted banks which followed more the capitalist model. The Schulze-Delitzsch model also diverges from that of Raiffeisen in the little importance it attached to activity based on geographical proximity.[14] It is true that, in the urban environment, it is far more difficult to delineate individual communities than in the rural context. However, the principle of unlimited liability – which both approaches had in common – implies of necessity the cooperation of the members. Group pressure had to be sufficiently strong to discourage deviant behaviour which risked ruin for the membership as a whole.

Despite their immediate success, the mutual credit associations of Raiffeisen have been criticised above all for the fact that these financial institutions are founded on solidarity and Christian love without profit for the members. Thus, Schulze-Delitzsch, proponent of the famous *Selbsthilfe*[15] rather than Christian charity, characterised Raiffeisen's initiatives as 'the castle of the co-operative card'.[16] He could well make the point that his capitalistic model functioned just as well in the rural environment.

Dissemination of the initiatives

The principles of the agricultural association of mutual credit and the popular banks spread more or less successfully throughout Germany. While in Great Britain co-operative initiatives surged forward, essentially in the form of consumer co-operatives, in the wake of the movement begun by Robert Owen and taken forward by the Rochdale Pioneers,[17] credit co-operatives were more or less non-existent. Charles Gide offers the interpretation of this phenomenon[18] as indicative of the unequal struggle, in that country, between small proprietors and big capital. It appeared that no reform was capable of weakening capital and the struggle led nowhere. Only Scotland proved the exception to the rule, ordinary banks developed in place of the popular banks thanks to the existence of widespread branches, which attracted a local clientele.

In Italy, the statesman Luigi Luzzatti founded in 1864 the first popular bank in Milan[19] on the German model of Schulze-Delitzsch. The savings banks joined the movement, founding popular credit associations using the models of both Raiffeisen and Schulze-Delitzsch. Among these associations, there were some which even made loans of honour with no other guarantee than the signature of the borrower (Wollemborg associations).[20]

Before we look at the spread of co-operative ideas in the field of credit in France, we should point out that the powerful co-operative movement begun in Quebec by Alphonse Desjardins is still relevant but goes beyond the frame of reference we have set ourselves in this study. His analysis has been the object of numerous studies.[21]

2. Popular credit in France – a belated arrival

The co-operative movement in France developed strongly between the revolution of February 1848 and the restoration of control to the 'party of order' leading to the coup d'état of 1851. After 1860, co-operatives entered a period of renewal with the liberalisation of the Empire.[22] It is in this context that the successive initiatives of Pierre-Joseph Proudhon, Jean-Pierre Beluze and Leon Walras[23] were taken, three illustrations of the organisation of credit in the service of the emancipation of the working class.

The repression which hit the workers after the Commune* set co-operative organisations back and with them popular credit. Moreover, while Germany was the cradle of co-operative credit and a potential source of inspiration, it was not good form to mention it after the debacle of the 1870 war (i.e. the war between Prussia and France, which was lost by the latter). No doubt these factors explain why the organisation of popular credit took time to form in the last quarter of the century. It was not until late in the century that a series of experiments (in which worker initiatives were in the minority) saw the light of day. These constituted the foundation of three financial organisations, still belonging to the co-operative and mutual sector: the Crédit Agricole, the Crédit Mutuel and the Banque Populaire.

The Popular banks

In 1897, there were only 23 urban credit associations.[24] They suffered from competition from the multiplicity of agencies of the large banks (Credit Lyonnais, Société Générale, Société Générale de Crédit Industriel et Commercial – CIC) and, deprived of legal status, popular credit could only obtain sufficient financial

---

* The so-called 'Commune de Paris' was a worker-based revolutionary government set up from March to May 1871.

support from the Banque de France. The intervention of the State enabled the institutionalisation of the movement of popular banks and its expansion.

A law passed after the first World War, on 24 October 1919, made available credit amounting to 100 million francs in aid to demobilised artisans and traders demonstrates the involvement[25] of the State in the popular banks. It was the time of reconstruction. In order to manage State credit in a centralised fashion, a syndicalised union of popular banks was formed in 1919, to which about 30 popular banks were affiliated. This foreshadowed the birth of the Caisse Centrale des Banques Populaires (20 June 1921).

'State' Agricultural Credit

As an agricultural country, France in the 19th century had financial networks which were structurally poorly adapted to agriculture.[26] The Crédit Foncier, which was created in 1852 did very little. The cadastre was not sufficiently well managed to give the peasants reliable title to the land. Moreover, this institution had the objective of consenting to long term loans for the purchase of land. The returns offered by land are frequently lower than those of interest on loans. It is a short step from there to the comment of Charles Gide, referring to the Crédit Foncier, that 'credit supports the proprietor as the rope supports the hanged man'.[27] Moreover, the Crédit Foncier can only help those who own land, which is not the case with all farmers. Finally, the main preoccupation of all farmers is financing their working capital and not the purchase of land. Better adapted to the latter than the former, the role of this institution seems to have been, at best, secondary: 'All in all, what is known as the 'Crédit Foncier' only operated on the margins of lending'.[28]

This weakness in the financing of agriculture explains the creation in 1861, under the orders of Napoleon III, of a Society of agricultural credit. This organisation took excessive risks and disappeared in 1876. To combat usury, there was no option but to look to the examples created on the other side of the Rhine.

Although the influence of Raiffeisen was common to both, agricultural credit financed by the Catholic Right (operating in the pure tradition of social Catholicism, a tradition which was affirmed and expanded in the papal encyclical of 1891, *Rerum Novarum*) and the agricultural credit of the left, supported by the State, stood in opposition to each other.

Jules Meline[29] and the Republicans promulgated a Raiffeisen type model in the Act of 5 November 1894, which introduced a law favouring future agricultural credit associations: tax exemption and reduced administrative formalities. The required syndicalisation of the members established a further link between them[30] moving in the direction of a shared responsibility which is a characteristic of credit co-operatives (of which the operative principle is 'one man, one voice'). Furthermore, recourse to syndicalism provides for reliance on existing networks, thereby facilitating the growth of the movement.

However, without the philanthropy of social Catholicism, the 'Republican funds' developed slowly.[31] The Catholic funds had the advantage of the confidence and the investments of the wealthy.[32] The latter were wary of co-operative organisations. Meline decided on financial intervention by the State in order to inject dynamism into their rate of growth. The Banque de France, which was then independent, was only permitted to renew its charter on condition that it made an advance of 40 million francs in gold and that it effected payment of its annual dues (both of which were due to the State) to financing agricultural credit societies. If the State was able, by intervening in this way, to exercise a right to inspect accounts, it limited its role voluntarily to a supervisory one and avoided undermining the mutualist nature of these organisations. In order to take regional characteristics into account and to avoid a centralised fund reminiscent of the imperial Société de Crédit Agricole, the State voted in the regional funds law of 1899. The regional funds stood as intermediaries between the Ministry of Agriculture and the local funds. Following criticism for its heavy handedness, the State entrusted the management of the funds as a whole to an administrative body, namely the Caisse Nationale du Crédit Agricole. The specific values of this organisation endured: bottom-up organisation, mutual aid and cooperation.

Mutual Credit

Unlike 'official' or 'state' agricultural credit, there were a number of original initiatives, and they were by far the most numerous (at least at the beginning). In 1885 the Banque de Crédit Agricole was formed in Poligny (Jura), a product of a right wing agricultural syndicalism. Louis Milcent established this model and very quickly over 300 associations could be identified of the Poligny type. In 1882, in Wantzeau (Alsace) an agricultural credit association appeared on a Raiffeisen model. At the end of the same year, there were about 15. This strictly Raiffeisenian current separated quickly from the Centre Fédératif de Crédit Populaire of the liberals Reyneri-Rostand.

The refusal of the State to intervene coincided with the strong religious involvement which characterised the associations which bore the name of the lawyer from Lyon, Louis Durand (1859-1916). The features of the 'Durand funds' were as follows. Their members were not compelled to syndicalise, unlike in the case of the 'State funds'; they declined to use advances from the State in order to avoid submitting to State control; credit was obtained for a stated and guaranteed purpose;[33] the signature of a surety was required; religious characteristics predominated; finally, liability was unlimited, which suggests to Gide that, unlike the 'State funds',[34] they alone 'practised the principle of solidarity'.[35] These associations drew from the Raiffeisen model the restriction of their sphere of activity to the level of the village, with the result that the members all knew each other.

Durand found it all the more easy to adhere to the Raiffeisen model because his hostility to the Republican State drove him towards the principle of mutualisation. What was persuasive for this Catholic lawyer was the reduction to a minimum of remuneration from cash investment. In the tradition of *Rerum Novarum*, the papal encyclical of Leo XIII on the condition of the working class (1893), he edited a manual on rural funds, which he published in 1893. Durand thus conformed to the will of the pope to 'wrest (the workers) from poverty and procure for them a better lot'.[36]

A large number of rural funds were born at the instigation of clerics (above all in the Pyrenees, in the Indre and the Landes) which drew their inspiration from Durand's book. In July 1893, Durand founded the Union des Caisses Rurales et Ouvrières Françaises. About 500 funds affiliated to it. The agricultural funds which did not wish to submit to State control kept their distance. They were mainly situated in Brittany and Alsace. A descendant of the Union des Caisses Rurales, the Crédit Mutuel kept its Catholic identity for a long time.[37]

3. The current state of popular credit in France

In a complex and changing world, all ideas, actions and innovations finish by taking the libertarian route, going beyond the restricted vision from which it was born. Whatever its field, an invention comes to life when it escapes from the hands of its creator and on its way forward, brushes with the spirit of the age, stimulates other intellects, inspires unexpected possibilities, provokes resistance, modifies mind sets and behavioural patterns. If its life is long and vigorous, it will be found after successive generations, facing situations which its originators would never have imagined, having undergone a metamorphosis over the years in conjunction with a reality to whose transformation it had itself contributed, adding to its history unexpected chapters. The logic of life is a logic of combinations, pregnant with offspring which it is pointless to attempt to predict and human enterprises are no exception to that rule. Popular credit, in its generic meaning, is part of that adventure.

Thus, when Raiffeisen founded the first deposit and loan fund, his objective was clear. He wanted to address a social situation which his personal value system told him was intolerable. For him, the aim was: to eradicate usury, which multiplied spoliation and crisis before his eyes; the economic purge of individual, professional and family circumstances, which would otherwise worsen endlessly; and to restore permanently the dignity of individuals and social classes in need, substituting the logic of the loan for that of the gift.

On the other hand, did he realise at the time of the early tentative steps of his enterprise how big and influential those banking organisations would become in most countries one century later? To appreciate today the trajectory of popular credit is a difficult, if not ambiguous question. In other words, what should we appreciate and on which criteria:

- a special type of organisation confronting, in market forces, competition from capitalist enterprises?
- performance of an economic, financial or social nature?
- the source of the motivation of present day players?
- the current relevance of popular credit in the context of the turn of this century?
- the permanence or the evolution of the values and the purposes which constituted its initial objective?

The answers to these questions can only be plural and qualified, all the more so since the organisations which inherited the legacy of 19th century popular credit did not adopt the same solutions or favour the same methods of adaptation. Globally, popular credit presents today a very different image from that of its origins. But the environment itself has changed considerably. Did the confrontation of the initial experiences of popular credit with the profound transformations of our societies end in a 'faithful' adaptation, or, as the detractors of popular credit would claim, in a diversion which took it into areas where it did not belong and where it failed to respect the rules of the game?

The first point to make, and the most simple, is that the great beneficiaries of the experiments of Flammersfeld and elsewhere are still very much alive. Not only are they alive, but they have secured a place and an image which have not left the banking world indifferent. Proof of that is the repeated assaults and the multiplicity of procedures employed, by the commercial banks in France, to meet their challenge. A further proof is the manoeuvres deployed with increasing intensity throughout the world to encourage 'demutualisation'. And to put the little upstarts of popular credit back in their place, the interests of the members, the need for healthy competition or the stimulation of consumer spending are invoked in turn.

This debate can be interpreted as one of conformism – 'mono-culture' – as opposed to 'biodiversity'. Beyond that and above all, is the question of the place for democracy at the heart of economic and financial mechanisms where power, inexorably, becomes more and more proportionate to retained assets instead of the quality of human life. In a sense, from this point of view, the popular credit sector is perhaps a carrier of stakes which are much higher than those which are blown up out of all proportion by its detractors.

To take on these stakes, without doubt, raises the issue of legitimacy. Are the present characteristics of the descendants of popular credit sufficiently deep, relevant and authentic to enable them to take on their adversaries on a battlefield which is much greater than the one to which attempts are made to confine them in the name of market forces?

To answer this question would require an in depth study. In reality, these specificities manifest themselves in various ways within the organisations in question and the underlying processes are rarely explicit. By way of example, a project carried out by Boltanski's team at the heart of the Crédit Mutuel of Brittany made visible the role and the idiosyncratic nature of the values of that organisation. This project revealed the existence of a *plurality* of objectives. *This plurality is, in itself a primary factor of radical distinction*, while the dominant feature of many enterprises is that they are subjected more and more drastically to a unitary impetus, that of the *'shareholder value'*. Boltanski's team, as a result of its investigations, thus revealed not one but four objectives:

- an *industrial* impetus, being that of management and consisting of the minimum minimorum of all enterprise management,
- a *development* impetus which, in this case, had a militant tinge to it,
- a *civic* impetus, which took into account relations with the community and the region in which the institution had evolved,
- a *domestic* impetus, which took the form of consideration of the individual beyond purely financial and economic considerations.

This plurality had repercussions for the very organisation of the institution. It resulted from a dialogue which was stimulated by the creative tension of two categories of participants, the professionals and technicians on the one hand and the elected representatives of the members on the other. At the very least, it demonstrated a real social life and the continuing presence of the dynamic of cooperation.

It would be to go too far to suggest that this observation could be extended to all organisations originating in the 19th century tradition. But we will avoid the risk of making comparisons. It suffices to say that cooperation exists and there are places where it can be found.

In a study which is as partial as it is brief, we will try to take up its manifestations at four levels:

- that of the relationship with the member,
- that of the motivation of the staff,
- that of the organisation,
- that of its relation with social activity.

The relationship with the member

This has been designed from the outset by the 'democratic prejudice', which has long been a source of amusement for the 'grey suits', before becoming known as 'quality of access', a competitive advantage only belatedly discovered by other organisations. Marketing was able to articulate and generalise the demands of this area, but the descendants of the mutualist tradition were their precursors and some remain *leaders*, their brand name still benefiting as a result and it constitutes one of the lynch pins of their communication.

However, the relationship with the member is not only characterised by its form. Special attention to individual or collective needs has often stimulated the inventiveness of popular credit. Thus, the Crédit Mutuel has been a pioneer in different fields: bank-assurance, retirement savings accounts, simplicity of contracts, methods of payment made available to specific groups, to name but a few.

The motivation of the staff

At the second level, that of the motivation of the staff, it is convenient to take note of a cultural evolution on the part of both employees and volunteer administrators. The increasing pressure of competition, the professionalisation of its activities and the necessary diversification of its products which consumers expect, as well as the hardening of conditions of exploitation, which have forced some assimilation of the 'industrial objective' (see above). As far as the employees are concerned, over the past 20 years, they have had to add to the conviviality and simplicity of their customer reception the mastery of more complex products and services, the efficient use of new technology, more rigorous time management as well as a more commercial attitude.

As far as the administrators are concerned, the industrial dimension has also been imposed on them, rendering the decision making process more complex, compelled by multiple forces. This integration may have led some of them to think that the soul of the mutuals was in jeopardy. However, in all of the organisations which have taken care to conserve both their participants and the scope for the necessary debate, we have to observe the development of a particularly high level of originality and effectiveness. Thus the natural outcome would have been that the industrial impetus would have driven out the caring impetus. In certain cases, that is what happened. On the other hand, drawing on our personal experience, we can bear witness to the fact that a creative tension has developed – which is also highly innovative – which has resulted in the combination and the articulation of the two tendencies.

The organisation

At this level, the dialogical principle is clearly expressed. At the heart of those organisations which have remained the closest to their traditions, the organisation has preserved its local roots within a decentralised framework – which some would characterise as 'scattered', 'atomised' or 'multi-cellular' – and power, which continues to emanate from the base of the organisation and to rest with the representatives of the members, largely remains diffuse. In other respects, the distribution of professional staff at local, federal and central level makes it possible to measure the point at which the centre of gravity of these organisations is able to remain closest to the local dimension.

Simultaneously, at all levels of such an organisation, the areas of debate enable us, thanks to the joint presence of professionals and elected representatives, to confront and to differentiate the plural impetuses to which we have already made reference.

Social reality

What is the state of the confrontation of popular credit with society as we reach the end of the century? What debate is taking place within it in the face of the new problems mounting in society, as a phenomenon which was born of the refusal to allow other problems to endure in another time?

It seems to us that, despite an economic and financial success which could turn it away from its original values, popular credit demonstrates – to varying degrees, once again, according to the organisation – the capacity for initiative, involvement and questioning which is not present to the same extent in 'traditional' enterprises. A desire to be active on the social or societal stage is present which is not motivated by image politics or a political strategy.

For example, the Crédit Mutuel has signed an agreement with the Association pour le Droit à l'Initiative Economique (ADIE)[38] and distributes through this structure advances which are not adapted to the usual procedures under which loans are made (business start-up by the unemployed). In Africa, its International Centre has supported experiments in financial cooperation for years in areas which are often very difficult, conditions close in certain respects to those met by its sources of inspiration in the 19th century. It even involves itself in co-operative banks in Eastern Europe. Moreover, the multiplicity and the diversity of its activities which are referable to the local or regional level, especially in the area of associative life and of local development, is only explicable if there is a very lively 'mutualist consciousness', and activists who intend to put their value system into effect.

Conclusion

Credit has two faces. In the hands of the usurer, it is an instrument of impoverishment and dependence. It establishes a financial link which shackles the debtor. At the same time, when credit is envisaged within a reciprocal impetus it appears as a tool of liberation for those whose economic circumstances are precarious. Within a collective framework, whether in a co-operative, a community development corporation or a network of lenders, credit binds the members of the group into the collective and creates true financial bonds.

Making credit into a tool for development and emancipation is not a recent problematic. We have seen how the techniques of popular credit and the theoretical considerations which preceded them were initiated in Europe in the last century. It is also from Europe that the development banks spread into the countries of the South in the 1970s. It was thought then that mutual credit could prove to be a financial technique which would lend itself to the accompanying socio-economic development in those countries. The end of the 1980s saw these sources of inspiration topple. The financial techniques which have been the subject of experiments in the South have tended to become the models which the industrialised nations have attempted to adopt in the struggle against structural unemployment.

Quite apart from this cross fertilisation of sources of inspiration which has led to mutual influence, these experiences have destroyed any preconceived vision of credit and, more generally, of banking.

As an opening rather than a conclusion, we would like to put two questions.

1   Can the value system, which has endured until now having inspired the adventure of popular credit in the 19th century, inspire today the innovations which will exist for 21st century society and the problems which it will have to resolve, in the same way that for our predecessors invented the 'association of deposits and loans'?

2   Are activists in the field of popular credit today aware that, in addition to the services which it is their mission to bring to their members, their enterprises bear a democratic dimension which is all the more important for being particularly under threat from external forces, through the imperialism of financial thinking?

Perhaps Bergson has the answer: 'We should,' he said, 'marry the pessimism of the intellect with the optimism of the will.'

ENDNOTES
1   Cf Bernard Gibaud, 1986, p.16.
2   Cf Robert Castel, 1995, p. 218 et seq.
3   Cf Laurence Fontaine, 1999-09-25.
4   Cf Pierre Dockes and others, 1990, p. XII, note 11.
5   Note that a second summit took place on the 25-27 June 1998 in New York where the World Bank was involved. The International Labour Organisation has launched, also in 1998, a programme of research entitled, 'Micro-Finance in industrialised countries – enterprise creation by the unemployed'.
6   Giovanna Procacci, 1993, pp 238-239.
7   cf Edouard Dolleans, [1936] 1967.
8   Jean-Claude Gaudibert, 1980, p.169.
9   Jean-Claude Gaudibert, 1980, p.171.
10   Charles Gide, 1930, p.477.
11   Franz Herman Schulze attached the name of his town to his own name to distinguish himself from the politician Max Schulze.
12   With the qualification that borrower and lender both belonged, by definition, to the popular classes.
13   Charles Gide, 1930, p. 482.
14   Limiting financial activity to a limited environment may be seen as a brake on the development of the organisations.
15   In English, self-help.
16   Jean-Claude Gaudibert, 1980, p. 171.
17   Despite these different paternities, the 'official' and almost mythical date of the birth

of the co-operative movement coincides with the foundation in 1844, by 28 workers in the flannel weaving industry of a consumer co-operative: the Rochdale Equitable Pioneers Society (Rochdale being a suburb of Manchester).

18 Charles Gide, 1930, p. 483.
19 Luzzati adapted the German model by introducing limited liability within the means of the members and a restricted sphere of activity.
20 Louis Baudin, 1934, p.101.
21 Cf, for example Marie-Claire Mal, 1997.
22 The majority of the worker delegation sent by the Emperor to the Great Exhibition in London (1862) consisted of presidents of mutuals of professionals (Bernard Gibaud, 1980, p.33).
23 Cf David Vallat, 1998.
24 Among them were the Co-operative Bank of Worker Producers of France, founded in 1893. This co-operative society was run by an administrative council, consisting of representatives of worker producer co-operatives. The Co-operative Bank used the capital underwritten by the cooperators as well as gifts obtained to finance the development of worker co-operatives. For a history of the Co-operative Bank, see *1893 – 1993. De la banque coopérative à la banque d'économie sociale*, Crédit Coopératif 1993, pp. 31ff.
25 Belated involvement if it is compared to the founding Act of the Crédit Agricole: the Meline law of 1894 (see below).
26 Cf Andre Gueslin, 1985, p. 8. For an exhaustive examination of agricultural credit associations cf Andre Gueslin,1984, vols. 1 & 2.
27 Charles Gide, 1930, p. 469.
28 Charles Gide, 1930, p. 474.
29 He was Minister of Agriculture (1883-1885/ 1915-1916) as well as President of the Council of Ministers.
30 Syndical solidarity replaced here religious solidarity on the Raiffeisen model (cf Jean-Claude Gaudibert, 1984, p. 158).
31 In 1897, there were 75, as opposed to 500 Catholic funds (Andre Gueslin, 1985, p.12).
32 The dissolution of the Union Générale in 1882 however demonstrates the limitations, if not of the morality, at least of the competence of the Catholic banks).
33 A compartmentalisation of the use of the funds was imposed, which can be said, in a diluted way, to be: '[the associations] exercise a paternal control over the loans' (Charles Gide, 1930, p. 480).
34 The Act of 1894 made the local funds of agricultural credit into mutual organisations with limited liability.
35 Charles Gide, 1930, p. 479.
36 Encyclical *Rerum Novarum*, cited by Andre Gueslin, 1998, p. 161.
37 Moreover, right up to the mid 1950s, certain funds were run by country priests.
38 On ADIE, see also Maria Nowak in the last chapter of this book.

The difficulty and necessity of keeping the pioneering spirit: Rabobank

M.H.A. Jeucken and B.J. Krouwel
(Rabobank Nederland)

Introduction

This chapter discusses the origination, evolution and special position of the co-operative Rabobank Group. What is the Rabobank? Why is it different from other banks? Which guiding star does it have? Which special position does the Rabobank Group take between larger commercial banks and smaller credit unions? These questions are considered in detail, because they focus on the pioneering spirit. Also the question will be considered whether the original guiding star is still there. Is it possible or desirable that the Rabobank Group transforms to a shareholder-oriented company or will it stick to its original stakeholder-concept? Interesting to explore are the possibilities to shift from a socio-economic orientation to a sustainable business concept ('sustainable banking').

The origination of the Rabobank Group[1]

The existing Dutch co-operative banking system, consisting almost entirely of the Rabobank Group, has its origin in the rural communities of the Netherlands. One century ago the basis was formed by hundreds of local credit co-operatives as an answer to the lack of credit possibilities for Dutch farmers. Dutch agriculture had taken a turn for the worse in the second half of the nineteenth century (1875-1895), as the Netherlands started to import products on a large scale from the United States and other territories which had developed agricultural surpluses. Prices for Dutch domestic agricultural products fell. If they were to compete, farmers needed to borrow so that they could rationalise production methods. But they had no access to the commercial banks and were forced to borrow from moneylenders at exorbitant rates.

This situation called for an organised system of agricultural credit. The preference in the Netherlands was for the approach of Wilhelm Raiffeisen, a German mayor. He aimed primarily at 'uplifting' the rural population in his community which found itself in a poverty spiral from the combined effects of crop failure and usury by moneylenders. He founded in 1864 the first rural co-operative credit society. Farmers as well as small tradesmen and craftsmen who wanted a loan from this society had to become members. At the same time the local population was called on to deposit the little savings it had with the co-operative, so as to be able to lend the money against reasonable interest rates to the member borrowers.

In Holland the first local co-operative banks appeared in 1896. They developed rapidly and were mostly the outcome of local initiatives by conscientious dignitaries, farmers and small businessmen, with the encouragement of progressive churchmen and farmers' organisations. They had no government funding, so their capital base could be no more than their members' liability and the collateral on loans. By the turn of the century the local banks felt the need for an umbrella organisation for support and co-ordination, resulting in the establishment of a central co-operative bank in Utrecht and one in Eindhoven. Due to differences in ideology (religion) and ideas about the juridical structure, two central institutions were formed. One in the south (the so-called 'Boerenleenbank', Eindhoven) and one in the north (the so-called 'Raiffeisenbank', Utrecht). Until 1970, these different co-operative banks were competitors. Besides functioning as an advisory body, these 'central banks' were acting as an intermediary for the investment of the local banks' surplus funds, and as a financial reservoir for local banks, who lacked enough funds for their local lending operations.

The primary objective of the local Rabobanks is to finance their members, being local business borrowers, at the lowest possible rates and the most favourable conditions. The funds needed for member financing are allocated by tapping local markets for savings and time deposits. To facilitate this, the Rabobanks provide a wide range of financial services for both trade and industry as well as private individuals. Every Rabobank has a Board and a Supervisory Board, elected by the members. The board is responsible for the bank's local banking operations, which are exercised under the management of a professional banker.

The Rabobank Group today[2]

The present-day Rabobank Group is the product of a merger in 1972 between the two central institutions ('RA-BO' is an abbreviation of the two old institutions), with the local banks following their example shortly after. Today Rabobank ranks among the 40 largest banks in the world. In terms of balance sheet total – €250 billion – it is the second largest bank in the Netherlands (at Group level it ranks at the third place). In terms of market shares however, it is by far the largest bank in the Dutch domestic market. With some 1,800 branches it has the most extensive banking network of the Netherlands. The Rabobank Group consists of locally some 445 independent co-operatively organised Rabobanks, its central institution Rabobank Nederland, several specialist finance (home mortgage, ship mortgage, consumer finance, insurance, factoring and leasing) subsidiaries. In the hundred years of its existence the co-operative Rabobank became not only the largest bank in the Dutch home market, but also one of the strongest banks in the world. In fact it is the only commercial bank with the highest credit ratings (triple A) from the world's most important rating agencies: Moody's, Standard and Poor's and IBCA.

Rabobank's size and dominant position is clearly reflected in the following figures which are also proof of the fact that it is no longer mainly a 'green' (i.e. agricultural) bank. Although still covering about 85% of the bank credit require-ments of the Dutch agricultural sector, this is only about one fourth of its total loan portfolio. With a market share of 38% Rabobank now is also the Netherlands' leading bank in the sector of financing small and medium-sized (0-10 employees) companies. This sector largely dominates Dutch trade and industry in which more than one third of Rabobank's total loan volume is outstanding. The bank's share of the home mortgage market is about 25%. All these lending activities are mainly funded by the bank's 40% share of the Dutch bank savings market. This makes Rabobank also the largest savings bank in Holland. In addition, some 35% of the capital of investment funds in the Netherlands is entrusted to the Rabobank.

Rabobank Nederland has the legal form of a jointstock co-operative society, the local Rabobanks being both its members and shareholders. Rabobank Nederland's juridical position makes clear that it is not the local banks' head-quarters. It advises and supports its member banks, supervises their liquidity and solvency positions and acts as bankers' bank for the whole Group. In addition, Rabobank Nederland has a banking business of its own, which operates as the Group's professional wholesale bank. It specialises in financial services for major national and international corporate clients, as well as in money market and capital market transactions. For this purpose it offers a wide and comprehensive range of corporate banking and corporate finance products.

Rabobank's origins explain why the bank, for nearly 80 years, has been mainly domestically oriented. However, during the last two decades Rabobank's inter-national activities have been growing rapidly. This is the logical consequence of the bank's co-operative mission. In the last two decades of this century Rabobank's corporate members became more and more involved in international links. In order to be able to service members interest which does not stop at the borderline properly, Rabobank simply followed its corporate customers abroad. Consequently, its international strategy is primarily to be defined as servicing its Dutch business clients in those countries which are of most importance for Dutch trade. Rabobank International (a subsidiary of Rabobank Nederland) is respon-sible for the international banking operations. The still growing foreign network of meanwhile 150 offices in 39 countries (Rabobank Group) plays an important role in becoming a global player in agribusiness finance and health care, Rabobank's international 'niche' specialisation.

The Group's basic strategy of the 1990's, is directed at keeping its strong position in the Dutch home market and rooted in the so called 'All-Finanz' concept. This strategy aims at being a broad supplier of a wide range of integrated bank, insurance and investment products.

Fundamentals of the 'Raiffeisen system'[3]

To understand the Raiffeisen principle it is necessary to have a closer look at its basic fundamentals. These fundamentals are:

- Compulsory membership for (business) borrowers;
- Liability of members;
- Limited area of operation for the local banks;
- Allocation of profits to the reserve;
- Democratic and decentralised structure.

In a co-operative the basic assumption is that common interest also is in the interest of the individual members. For that reason individual membership is compulsory. Rabobanks' compulsory membership at the local co-operative level was to be limited to business borrowers in 1980. This was a logical decision because the articles of association were linking the co-operative objective exclusively to local businesses. In 1998 the Rabobank Group changed its strategy in accordance with its growing character of a broad financial institution. Membership is no longer compulsory and every customer can become a member and accordingly influence the companies policy. The only condition is that the customer has a certain commitment to the bank and it's ambitions, i.e. its primary objective.

As the first co-operative banks lacked own funds, depositors had to be given some other guarantee for the repayment of the money they had entrusted to these banks. This guarantee took the form of unlimited (personal) liability of the members for losses of the bank. Over the years however, the consolidated reserves had accumulated to such a level that unlimited liability was not reasonable any more. Therefore in 1980 liability was restricted to about €2,300 (NLG 5,000) per member.

A limited area of operation enabled and still enables the local co-operative banks to have a good view on the borrowers' business as well at his private circumstances. This was and is essential to prevent losses, to ensure a sound management of the funds entrusted, and to keep in close touch with the primary clients, being the members.

Allocation of the profits to the reserves is essential to prevent recourse to member liability. With visible reserves consisting almost entirely of own funds, which now are amounting to €10.4 billion (BIS-ratio of 11.3%), the Rabobank

Group is the strongest capitalised bank in the Netherlands. This and the fact that all parts of the Rabobank Group are liable for each other through a so-called Cross Guarantee System make it unlikely that a call would ever be made on member liability. Therefore, this liability was abandoned totally in 1998. To commit members to the bank, so-called (voluntary) member-certificates have been developed as an alternative. Since membership is essential, a democratic structure to ensure members' influence is also essential.

The social contribution of the Rabobank Group

Being a co-operative company and not a listed one with shareholders, Rabobank does not pay any dividends. As we have seen, all profits are allocated to the reserves. This is a big advantage for two reasons. Not only has the bank throughout the years always been able to finance the growth of its activities with its own funds, without being forced to resort to external capital suppliers. Moreover, this strong capital base is also to a large extent the reason for its AAA credit ratings, through which the bank is able to tap the professional financial markets at the lowest possible funding costs.

Co-operatives are not based on capital suppliers' interest, but on members' interest. So the Rabobank Group is not aiming at maximising profit, as do equity driven companies on behalf of their shareholders, but at maximising the economic benefit for its co-operative members. Profit is only an instrument to serve the continuity of the co-operatives, which is done by demanding the lowest possible price for loans and credits from the member borrowers, and at the same time by creating the most favourable lending conditions. Inherent to the latter is that if a member's business is in financial difficulty, a local Rabobank will give support as long as possible. This long term orientation is also characteristic for the way in which all other customers are treated. Although every bank will state this, in the 1970s en 1980s customers of other commercial banks discovered the difference: Rabobank does not give up as simplistically as other banks do. Another aspect of long term orientation is that Rabobank considers it to be its duty to stimulate businesses getting from the ground. It has raised a special Guarantee Fund to be able to stimulate (starting) entrepreneurs having promising plans but insufficient own funds with subordinated loans.

Rabobank's large market shares are not something to boast on, because they are the condition for being able to what every co-operative should do: influencing market prices on behalf of its members. This can be illustrated as follows. The average interest on savings is normally lower than on the professional money markets and capital markets. More than 60% of Rabobank's lending operations in guilders is funded from the enormous resource of Dutch savings of which Rabobank has a market share of 40 percent. Thanks to this strong position Rabobank's funding costs are lower than those of its competitors in the

Netherlands, who have considerably smaller market shares. Lower funding costs are obligatory to be able to live up to our co-operative principle. It means being able to charge borrowers lower interest rates and pay a fair price to savers. It means also that its overall interest margin is better. Thanks to that Rabobank can operate as a price setter for the whole market in the Netherlands. All customers will profit from that. As a matter of fact, the positive influence of co-operative banks on interest rates is not only felt in the Netherlands; Rabobank discovered that the average interest margin of banks in countries with a sound co-operative banking system is much lower than in countries who do not have one.

In propagating the co-operative credit philosophy, Rabobank does not restrict itself to the use of words only. The bank takes for instance action by providing know-how to help economic development in developing countries as well. Therefore, Rabobank has created, amongst others, the Rabobank Foundation. With voluntary donations of local Rabobanks and equal donations of Rabobank Nederland this foundation helps locally based small scale co-operatives to get started. The Rabobank Foundation supports these initiatives financially as well as by providing experts assistance.

The pioneering spirit and the future

In 1995 a discussion within the Rabobank Group was launched about its orientation. The question basically was: will we remain a credit co-operative? The alternative would be to transform ourselves to an equity-driven company. However, it was not a question of choosing between two rigid organisation concepts; i.e. the emphasis has been put on remaining a credit co-operative or transforming ourselves to a broader customer orientated co-operative. The discussion lasted for three years. In a completely democratic process the members of the Rabobank Group have decided to keep to its roots, i.e. a co-operative bank,[4] but to broaden our services to all customers. To facilitate this change voluntary membership has been introduced.

In short, the Rabobank has evolved from an (agricultural) credit institution to a (general) 'All Finanz' institution. The pioneering spirit is still an intrinsic element of the culture of especially the local banks. Also the present corporate philosophy is still in line with the pioneering spirit from the past, as the outcome of the so-called 'co-operation discussion' in 1998 pointed out. At an abstract level the corporate philosophy can be defined as a co-operation of people with different backgrounds in a specific member-organisation to support the self-sufficiency of some of the members, which will come to the good of the (local) society as a whole. This is still the case. Only the basis of organising has shifted: one hundred years ago this member-organisation started out to support the rural population in self-sufficiency and economic development; at the beginning of the 21st century this organisation stands for the self-sufficiency and economic self-reliance of all population groups and not only in the Netherlands, but also abroad (mainly in developing countries through activities of the Rabobank Foundation).

The culture and structure of the Rabobank is one where there is space for innovative ideas and bottom up processes. Moreover, decision processes and renovation have an organic character. This makes the Rabobank Group very flexible and interesting to work at. But it also means decision processes take time, mainly because of the space for discussion. However, a major advantage is that once a decision has been taken, it gets a lot of support and commitment.

A second discussion within Rabobank is about innovation and responsible business. It is clear that local banks in the Netherlands are better equipped to service the local community commercially and co-operatively. The professionalisation and internationalisation of the Rabobank Group raises questions whether this can be extrapolated to our international activities as well. At the moment this seems to be very difficult. Especially in our international activities a dilemma exists in keeping up with our pioneering spirit. The shift from a (agricultural) credit co-operative to a co-operative aiming at fostering (all) customer value, raises the question how to fill in our co-operative ambition on an international scale. Contrary to the Netherlands the Rabobank internationally is a price-follower. The question will be how we internationally can distinguish ourselves from equity driven commercial banks. This (second) discussion is still going on.

Within the Rabobank a third discussion has been initiated about the question whether or not the emphasis on the social and economic aspects of life is still sufficient. Do the ecological aspects of life also have to be taken into account? That is, will the Rabobank evolve from a socio-economic orientation to an orientation driven by the concept of sustainability in which apart from a social and economic orientation, the concept of ecology comes into the picture? Within Rabobank this idea has been called the 'triple-P concept', which stands for – in arbitrary order – people (society), planet (ecology) and profit (economics).[5] As far as banking is concerned, we are talking about sustainable banking.[6] The new ambition-statement of 1999 points this out: 'The Rabobank Group believes that sustainable growth of prosperity and well-being must never be at the expense of nature or the environment. The Rabobank Group aims to keep this objective in mind in its activities and contributions to sustainable development.' This also means helping customers becoming more sustainable. All kinds of products and services will be developed to facilitate this, like investment funds, insurances, environmental loans, advisory services et cetera.

This is a real major change. Firstly, because sustainable development is not a familiar subject in the banking community. Secondly, because of the sometimes conflicting interest of members in the short run. It is in this context that the Rabobank Group is elaborating on its pioneering spirit: self-sufficiency of all its customers, in the short run as well as in the long run. Or better, the very long run:

the concept of sustainability also takes the (expected) interests of future generations in its decisions. To accommodate this, Rabobank has consciously chosen for
being sustainable, also in an ecological sense. It will be a good thing to explore
this new heading of banking. As a large commercial and co-operative bank, the
challenge for the 21st century will be to make 'sustainable banking' the renewed
pioneering spirit.

ENDNOTES

1   For further reading see for example Lavelle, A. (1998), *The Art of Co-operation – The
    Netherlands and its Rabobank*, Wormer.
2   See for example Rabobank Group, *Annual Report 1998*, Utrecht.
3   See for example Dierick, A.M. (1996), *Het coöperatieve bankwezen in Nederland,* Serie
    Bank- en Effectenbedrijf 26, Amsterdam.
4   Implicitly this also meant that the Rabobank Group wouldn't transform itself to an
    equity company.
5   This concept originates from Elkington, J. (1998), *Cannibals with Forks: The Triple
    Bottom Line of 21st Century Business*, London.
6   In 1998 the Rabobank published a book titled *Sustainable Banking*. At this time it is
    only available in Dutch (with a short English summary): Jeucken, M.H.A. (1998),
    Duurzaam bankieren – Een visie op bankieren en duurzame ontwikkeling, Rabobank,
    Utrecht.

The growth of credit unions and credit co-operatives: is the past still present?

Paul A. Jones
(Liverpool John Moores University, UK)

Financial exclusion and the co-operative revival

Toxteth is an inner-city area of Liverpool. Over 38% of the population are unemployed and most people struggle to make ends meet either on welfare benefits or on low incomes. Like 4.4 million other people in Britain,[1] most people in Toxteth live on the margins of financial services provision. Yet, as in many other similar places, most banks no longer find it profitable to preserve an effective local service. Three banks have closed their Toxteth branches over the last ten years. The one remaining bank is, in 1999, reducing its service from five to just three days a week. Whilst people elsewhere take for granted the use of cash machines, credit cards and a range of banking facilities, people in Toxteth find themselves increasingly excluded from any form of affordable financial service. Banks, they believe, are neither interested in them nor appropriate to their needs. Indeed, many people do not have a bank account. Not a small number are forced into the hands of extortionate finance companies.

In the mid-eighties, a group of people came together in Toxteth. Like the Rochdale pioneers of the nineteenth century, they shared a common belief in the ability of their community to respond collectively to its own social and economic needs. They were convinced that the only way that Toxteth would have a decent financial service was if the people of Toxteth created it for themselves. Inspired by a renewed spirit of co-operation, this group of about 25 volunteers, most of whom were women, trained together and worked to mobilise the support of a network of local community organisations. In February 1989, the group opened their own financial co-operative and the Park Road Community Credit Union was born. In 1999, this credit union has 1,700 adult and 500 junior members. It has assets of £304,000, members' savings of £254,000 and, in the financial year 1997-98, made loans to its members of £270,000. The credit union is still run by a team of 60 local volunteers. It operates from a tiny two-bedroomed terraced house in a typical Liverpudlian street. Yet it has gone some way to achieve what many of the banks in the area could not do. It has enabled its members, all local residents, 68% of which live on welfare benefits, to access an affordable financial service able to respond to their own needs and circumstances. Park Road is just one of a growing number of British credit unions that are proving to be part of the answer to present-day social and financial exclusion.

Credit unions – a modern movement founded on nineteenth-century principles

Credit unions are not-for-profit, financial co-operatives that offer low-cost financial services to their members. They are based on international co-operative and democratic principles which have remained essentially unchanged since the days of the co-operative pioneers of the nineteenth century. The first known credit union was set up in Heddesdorf, Germany in 1869. Since then, they have developed in two distinct but related directions. In most European countries, they became the European co-operative banks. These are now dominant consumer financial providers that serve the general public. In North America, a different model of financial co-operative enterprise took hold. Using, for the most part, the name 'credit union', these member co-operatives have a much more local and autonomous structure than their European cousins. They are based on a strong notion of a common bond, understood as a relationship that defines a certain unity between the members. Membership of a credit union is, in fact, restricted to people who share the common bond. This is, determined, usually, as either living or working in a particular locality, being employed by a particular employer, following a particular occupation or being a member of an association or society. Credit unions, as known in Britain, Ireland and Eastern Europe, developed out of this North American model.

Credit unions are found in 87 countries throughout the world. Between them, these credit unions have some 85 million members. In Europe, they are strongest in Ireland, where around 44 per cent of the population are members of more than 550 credit unions. Collectively, these credit unions have more than IR£2.6 billion in assets. In Central and Eastern Europe, the credit union movement is growing fast. In Poland, for example, in just four years, 220 credit unions have been established, serving almost 260,000 members and having assets amounting to $158 million (US). Already credit unions are the fourth largest financial service provider network in the country. Similarly in the Czech Republic, in March 1999, there were 77 credit unions with over 70,880 members. Credit union movements have also been established in Russia, Romania, the Ukraine, Latvia and Lithuania and are emerging in Albania, Slovakia, Macedonia and Georgia. In fact, the largest credit unions in Europe are the US-based credit unions serving the US military and United Nations organisations. The US Navy Federal Credit Union, for example, has 1.8 million members world-wide and operates from bases in Italy, Spain, Greece and the United Kingdom.

There have been credit unions in Britain since 1964. However, the greatest rise in the number of credit unions has been over the last ten to fifteen years. In 1985, there were just 64 credit unions in Britain, in 1999 there are over 600 with over £118 million in assets and around 216,000 members. Overall, there has been two main strands to British credit union development. First, as in Toxteth, groups of local people have come together, in predominantly low-income areas, to set up their own community credit unions. The second strand of development has been amongst groups of workers in a particular profession, company or organisation. Some of the largest credit unions in Britain are organised by employees in local government or working for the police force, for bus companies, as taxi drivers or for British Airways. The largest work-based credit union in Britain is, for example, Glasgow Council Credit Union in Scotland serving employees working for the municipal authority. It has over 10,000 members and over £11 million in assets.

Co-operation – the best approach to tackling local social and economic needs?

Wherever they occur, co-operative credit unions arise in response to both social and economic needs. In nineteenth century Europe, the first credit unions were created to alleviate the hardships associated with the growth of modern capitalist economies. In the early twentieth century, credit unions in the United States, as described by Hannon, West and Barron,[2] were pioneered very much as a grass-roots social movement aimed at enabling working people to obtain credit at reasonable rates. The ideology and rhetoric of the early US movement was often a crusade against loan sharks and moneylenders. Similarly, Ferguson and McKillop[3] explain the development of Irish credit union movement as a direct response to the high unemployment, the high interest rates, and the growth of illegal money-lenders that were symptomatic of the economic depression suffered in Ireland in the early 1950s.

In Britain, it was the social inequality and deprivation, faced by many communities through the eighties and nineties, that encouraged many local groups to set up credit unions. As Oppenheim and Harker point out,[4] in 1992 33% of the British population were living in or on the margins of poverty. People in this situation inevitably faced increasing financial exclusion from mainstream banks and financial institutions. Banks were just not keen to attract people in poverty as customers. It was no coincidence that it was at this time that the registration of community credit unions expanded significantly. Similarly, the rising costs of mainstream banking services led groups of workers to set up credit unions that would offer them both easier access to low-cost loans and possible higher dividends on savings. Similar developments were replicated in Central and Eastern Europe where the social and economic situation since the collapse of communism, and the resultant lack of confidence in banking services, has stimulated the opening of credit unions.

Credit unions offer an important opportunity for people to work closely together for their own mutual benefit. There is no evidence that the profit-maximising and investor-owned banking sector has either the interest or capability to respond to the needs of financially excluded and low-income groups within society. In certain circumstances, co-operative enterprise may offer the best approach to meeting the social and economic needs of particular communities. According to Fischer,[5] in accessing those segments of the market which are unattractive to mainstream banking institutions, credit unions have a competitive edge insofar as the presence of a common bond generates a certain trust between the members of the organisation. This trust offers credit unions real benefits in limiting the problems of gathering information, of transaction costs and of risk. It means that, in certain circumstances, credit unions have the potential to offer a much more efficient and cost-effective service to low income groups than either banks or other financial institutions. Clearly, a significant factor here is ownership. Credit unions are often able to access people and communities in ways inaccessible to banks as they are owned and controlled by those people and communities themselves. Hargreaves[6] stresses this point when he writes, '*The issue of ownership lies at the very heart of social exclusion*'. Capitalist enterprises have no problem in recognising the value of promoting employee share ownership schemes in order to generate a sense of ownership among their workers. Credit unions are able to generate a similar sense of ownership among the financially excluded and thus enable them to avail themselves of financial services appropriate to their needs. In Britain, the potential of credit unions is increasingly recognised by the Government, by municipal authorities and by other major agencies. Credit unions are regarded by them as being best placed, within the financial services industry, to provide low-cost financial services to those on low incomes or to those who have no access to affordable banking services. In fact, the British Government has proposed that credit unions play a key role in tackling financial exclusion. Equally, many municipal authorities see credit unions as essential contributors to the social and economic regeneration of their areas.

The British experience – the challenge of providing a professional service

Faced with the challenge of adopting a much more high-profile role in financial service provision, the British credit union movement has had to face up to a concern that has been troubling many credit union activists for some time. This concern is that many, particularly community, credit unions are not growing as significantly as they are, for example, in Ireland or in Poland. Consequently, their potential to make a difference within their communities is not being fully realised. With some exceptions, the average membership of British community credit unions does not exceed 200 members even after many years of development. Many of these credit unions are also financially very weak. Yet, at the same time, many work-based and some community credit unions are sustaining substantial growth and making a real impact among groups of workers or within communities. Undoubtedly, the highest growth rates are found in work-based credit unions. These make up just 15% of the total number of credit unions in Britain, but account for 50% of all credit union members and hold 70% of all credit union assets. Nevertheless, among community credit unions, there are examples of medium and high growth enterprises. Among these are Park Road Credit Union, in Toxteth, mentioned above, and Dalmuir Credit Union in Clydebank, Scotland. This latter credit union has, in 1998, around 5500 members, 50% of which are identified as unemployed or unwaged, and over £3 million in assets.

In endeavouring to create a financial co-operative movement that is able to respond to the needs of a much wider population, the Association of British Credit Unions (ABCUL), Britain's major credit union trade association, has taken the lead in trying to understand why many community credit unions attract only a few hundred members and how they can be supported to achieve greater growth. Among the factors that ABCUL has identified as restricting credit union growth rates in Britain are poor national legislation and inappropriate models of development.

It is commonly understood that current legislation in Britain is excessively restrictive and has been one of the main factors limiting the expansion of credit unions. An unpublished 1996 report from the World Council of Credit Unions stated, '*The current credit union legislation in Great Britain is amongst the most restrictive in the world*'. The Credit Union Act 1979 not only severely restricts the ability of credit unions to attract savings and to make loans but also limits the size, viability and scope of their common bonds. Over the last two years, ABCUL has been leading a campaign to modernise the legislation and the Government is now responding. Forthcoming changes in legislation will allow credit unions to offer a broader array of services and provide greater security for member savings, thereby significantly increasing the ability of credit unions to meet the needs of those who would most benefit from their services.

However, poor legislation alone does not explain why many credit unions have remained so small. For, despite the legislation, there are examples of both work-based and community credit unions that have grown significantly. A 1998 national research project,[7] undertaken by Liverpool John Moores University in association with ABCUL, The Co-operative Bank plc and the English Community Enterprise Partnership, identified yet another factor that has held back the British credit union movement. The research found that many credit unions had been developed according to a particular organisational model which assumed that credit unions were very small (maybe only a few hundred members), entirely operationally organised by volunteers and aimed solely at very low income-base populations. In many ways, this model stressed the social objectives of credit unions to the exclusion of the economic objectives required for long term sustainable development. Instead of fostering the growth of a volunteer-led, professional co-operative financial service, able to meet the financial needs of large numbers of people, this model helped promote the image of credit unions as marginal poor people's banks. Undoubtedly this has restricted the growth of credit unions, even within the low income communities to whose needs the credit unions had aimed to respond.

Research conducted by Kempson and Whyley of the Personal Finance Research Centre identified *'that people on the margins of financial services want to deal with organisations which are financially secure, trustworthy and understand their needs'*.[8] Credit unions are, for the most part, successful in communicating trust and understanding the needs of their members. They grow out of existing social bonds either in work places, in organisations or within local communities. In fact, Fischer[9] has stressed the fundamental importance of pre-existing social bonds in the organisational development of credit unions. He has pointed to the fact that a credit union's success often depends on the strength of the social bonds on which the organisation is founded. However, it is clear that if they are to fulfil their potential, credit unions have to adopt models of organisational development that target long-term economic viability and ensure the financial security spoken about by Kempson and Whyley. As co-operative financial institutions, credit unions must operate to appropriate commercial standards and be able to offer a fully professional financial service to a large number of members. This involves using rigorous business development programmes to establish a wide and diverse membership base, to attract savers as well as borrowers and to ensure the quality of their service and financial products. In Britain, this will entail credit unions becoming less reliant on volunteers for the day-to-day operation of the organisation. The Liverpool John Moores University research revealed that 86% of community credit unions recognised that volunteer burn-out was restricting their growth. The increasing introduction of paid staff to run credit unions, whilst volunteers develop their role as policy makers and directors, seems intimately linked to long term security and quality of service. Significantly, Dalmuir Credit Union, in Scotland, with its 5,500 members, employs two full-time administrators and several part-time staff.

Credit unions necessarily compete in the financial market place. Hargreaves[10] writes that *'the strong, clear message to co-operators is that there is no hiding place from the demands of competition. It is a case of compete or die. Organisations which provide goods or services which do not compete well in terms of price and quality will fail, whether they are owned by co-operators or tycoons chewing fat cigars'.* Where credit unions succeed, they are not regarded as old-fashioned nor decaying nineteenth century societies, but rather as modern financial institutions, particularly suited to responding the needs of middle and low-income groups. Wherever they are seen as a professional financial service, offering quality financial products, credit unions and credit co-operatives world wide are sustaining substantial growth. In Colombia, for example, between 1990 and 1994, the growth of assets in credit co-operatives exceeded the growth or assets in the investor-owned banks by a ratio of 3 to 1. At the end of 1993, credit unions had achieved penetration rates of 100% in Dominica, ranged from 30% to 49% in five other countries and from 10% to 29% in another 16 countries.[11] Growth rates in some countries, as in the United States and Ireland, have resulted in some strong reactions from the banks. In these countries, banks regard credit unions as increasingly strong competitors and have, perhaps somewhat inevitably, tried to instigate actions against credit unions in order to reduce their influence. In Britain, where credit unions are still, for the most part, in their infancy, the priority is to ensure that credit unions grow into economically secure financial institutions able to offer a quality, professional service to a much larger proportion of the population.

Important lessons from the US community development credit union movement

ABCUL has learnt some important lessons from the experience of the National Federation of Community Development Credit Unions (NFCDCU) based in New York. US community development credit unions serve predominantly low-income communities and tend, by US standards, to be smaller than mainstream credit unions. They have, on average, 1,300 members and around $2.4 million in assets per credit union. Yet, from the outset, these credit unions are established as professional financial institutions, most having secure premises and paid staff and with the capability of offering their members a range of financial services. They operate often with the support of a strong, credible sponsoring organisation and all have a business plan aimed at establishing economic viability within a short space of time. To this end, community development credit unions recruit 500–1,000 potential members, all of whom sign pledges of membership, before they ever open for business. Many of these credit unions are economically and socially very successful. Since 1980, for example, Self-Help, a community development credit union in Durham, North Carolina, has loaned $325 million (US) to low-income members – particularly Black people, women and rural residents – in order to buy homes, build businesses and strengthen community resources. Rosenthal and Levy, of the NFCDC, write that *'the best reason – and perhaps the only compelling reason – to organise a new credit union is to provide reasonably priced financial services to those who would otherwise not have access'.*[12] The Liverpool John Moores University research found that this clarity of focus was often lacking within smaller British community credit unions whose volunteers gave a range of reasons, often more social than economic, for organising credit unions. However, research findings confirm that more successful British work-based and community credit unions, like their US counterparts, have a much clearer vision of themselves as co-operative businesses aiming to offer a fully professional service within the financial services sector.

In order to assist credit unions to develop into financial institutions that are able to serve a large membership and to offer a wider range of services, ABCUL has drawn up a set of pre-requisites that any new credit union needs to have in place before it begins operation. At the same time, it has developed a series of national training seminars designed to ensure that any existing credit union, lacking these elements, is enabled to achieve them as soon as possible. Based on the experience of the US community development credit unions, ABCUL now considers that for any credit union to succeed, it must have all, or nearly all, the following elements in place:

- a solid business plan, which targets growth and success.
- the effective leadership of a volunteer board and committees, consisting of individuals who are well regarded in the community and have the skills and vision to develop the credit union and make it grow.
- support and sponsorship from respected local institutions, to promote the credit union and give it credibility.
- initial funding or in-kind support to provide the credit union with:
  - attractive premises, conveniently located to people in its community, and
  - trained professional staff to operate the credit union .
- an effective marketing and promotion programme capable of attracting at least 500 to 1000 members during the first few months of operation for new credit unions and at least 1000 to 2000 members for existing credit unions.

These elements, in one way or another, are found in successful credit union movements throughout the world. None of them compromise the basic commitment of credit unions to co-operative, mutual and social goals. However, wherever credit unions have grown significantly, they have all been established as professional financial institutions able to operate effectively within an increasingly competitive market place. This can be seen clearly within the Irish credit union movement as well as within the 365 credit and savings co-operatives that hold 32% of all domestic deposits in Cyprus. In Britain, the challenge is to consolidate progress so far and to ensure the sustainable development of the co-operative credit union financial sector.

Future support for the credit unions as unique financial organisations?

The British credit union movement is, in many ways, at a watershed. It can accept the Government's challenge to become a major provider of financial services, particularly for those on low incomes or facing financial exclusion. Or it can remain a movement, for the most part, marginal to the needs of mainstream British society. The Liverpool John Moores University research indicated that 76% of British credit unions are aiming to become, as their Irish and Cypriot cousins, a much more professional financial service. They already operate within established social bonds and networks. It is this that distinguishes them from banks and gives them a competitive edge within segments of the market inaccessible to, or avoided by, banks. They already have developed, in many cases, market niches through which those facing financial exclusion have access to low-cost financial services. What is needed currently is the investment, the support and organisational management expertise to ensure that all credit unions grow into the sustainable co-operative organisations that are found in other more mature credit union movements throughout the world.

Credit unions in Britain have currently two unusual, but powerful, sources of support; the municipal authorities and the banks. These are unusual in the sense that, in no other country in the world, have municipal authorities taken such a direct interest in the development of credit unions and, certainly, in most countries, credit unions are not so much supported by banks but regarded by them as serious competitors. In Britain, many municipal authorities see credit unions as key partners in the social and economic regeneration of communities. They regard the opportunities afforded by the co-operative ownership of credit unions as a real benefit in dealing with the particular problems of social and financial exclusion. Recently, the Local Government Association has drawn up new guidelines[13] for municipal authorities which aim, following ABCUL recommendations, to ensure that credit unions grow into large and economically viable organisations.

In a number of localities, credit unions have already developed profitable local relationships with banks. As Eileen Halligan, the administrator of Toxteth's Park Road Community Credit Union, points out, '*Park Road reaches the people that banks cannot or do not want to access. We're not in competition with them at all, we are in touch with the people they wouldn't touch at all*'. Park Road is, in fact, in negotiation with its local bank about opening the credit union in the bank premises on the two days when the bank itself will be closed. Clearly, banks have a responsibility to the communities from which they are withdrawing. There is a lot of suspicion in Britain that banks and building societies effectively black-list entire communities and make it incredibly difficult for anyone from those communities to access their services and facilities. A number of writers, for example Conaty and Mayo,[14] consider that credit unions would benefit significantly if the Government were to introduce legislation similar to the US Community Reinvestment Act 1977 (CRA). This forces US banks and mainstream financial institutions to reinvest in the disadvantaged areas from where they take deposits. This re-investment has often been directed by banks through credit unions. However, in Britain, a more collaborative approach has been adopted. In the summer of 1998, the Government set a up a Treasury Task Force with the remit to explore ways in which banks and building societies could work more closely with credit unions to increase their effectiveness and widen their range of services. This Task Force consists of senior representatives from banks, building societies and the credit union movement and will publish its findings later in 1999. Indications are that its recommendation will be to establish a national central service organisation for all credit unions, equipped with the resources and personnel to provide the necessary organisational development support that credit unions in Britain currently need.

In Britain, as is proved throughout the world, credit unions have enormous potential to make an impact on the wider social economy and to deal with the social and financial exclusion of communities in ways banks never could, nor would, contemplate. In Britain, credit unions have a significant window of opportunity, insofar as both central and local government, together with the banks on the Government Task Force, are committed to supporting their growth and development as sustainable, modern financial organisations. That commitment of government, in the longer term, will need to be reflected at a European level. Credit unions in Britain and Ireland are currently exempt from European Banking Directives.[15] Any change in that exemption would seriously hinder the development of the credit union movement. Even within the last year, the Irish Bankers Federation lodged two formal complaints with the European Commission claiming that the corporation tax exemption for credit unions amounted to unfair state aid and that credit unions should not be exempted from Banking Directives. Currently, the Irish credit unions are confident that, with Irish government support, this current challenge to the distinct and unique status of credit unions and credit co-operatives will be rebutted. Yet, this is a serious issue for European credit union movement, including those movements in countries envisaging joining the European Union in the future. Credit unions are unique. As co-operative, democratic and mutual organisations, they make a real difference to the lives of ordinary people and, in particular, to excluded and marginalised groups in society. Credit unions grow out of human and social values, but they only become really effective when, supported by appropriate legislation, regulation and taxation, they are enabled to grow large and strong enough to be able to deliver a range of low-cost financial services to people who need them the most.

ENDNOTES

1   Figures taken from Kempson E. and Whyley C., *Kept out or opted out? Understanding and combating financial exclusion.* The Polity Press in association with the Joseph Rowntree Foundation, 1999.

2   Hannan M.E., West E., and Baron D., *Dynamics of Populations of Credit Unions.* Filene Research Institute, Madison, 1994.

3   Ferguson C. and McKillop D., *The Strategic Development of Credit Unions.* John Wiley, England, 1997, p. 33.

4   Oppenheim C. and Harker L., *Poverty: the Facts.* Child Poverty Action Group, London, 1992.

5   Fischer K.P. *Financial Co-operatives: A 'market solution' to SME and rural financing.* Working Paper No 98-03, Centre de recherche en économie et finance appliquées (CRÉFA), Université Laval, Québec, Canada, 1998.

6   Hargreaves I., *New mutualism in from the cold.* The Co-operative Party, London, 1999.

7   Jones P.A. *'Towards Sustainable Credit Union Development'.* Report of a national research project carried out by Liverpool John Moores University, the Association of British Credit Unions, the English Community Enterprise Partnership and The Co-operative Bank p.l.c. and supported by the Local Government Association and the Local Government Management Board. Association of British Credit Unions Ltd., Manchester, 1999.

8   Kempson E. and Whyley C., *Kept out or opted out? Understanding and combating financial exclusion.* The Polity Press in association with the Joseph Rowntree Foundation, 1999.

9   Fischer K.P., *Financial Co-operatives: A 'market solution' to SME and rural financing.* Working Paper No 98-03, Centre de recherche en économie et finance appliquées (CRÉFA), Université Laval, Québec, Canada, 1998.

10   Hargreaves I., *New mutualism in from the cold.* The Co-operative Party, London, 1999

11   Figures quoted by Fischer (1998) *ibid.* Fischer notes that these figures only apply to World Council of Credit Unions which does not represent the totality of credit unions and credit co-operatives in the world. World-wide penetration rates are therefore in excess of these figures.

12   Rosenthal C.N. and Levy L., *Organising Credit Unions: A Manual. National Federation of Community Development Credit Unions. Version 1.1* New York, 1995.

13   Available from the Local Government Association, London.

14   Conaty P and Mayo E., *A Commitment to People and Place – the case for community development credit unions.* A report for the National Consumer Council, New Economics Foundation, 1997.

15   Council and European Parliament Directive. 77/780/EEC Article 2 (2).

The co-operative bank as a socially responsible problem solver by corporate mission

Heidi Muthers-Haas and Helmut Muthers
(Network for Innovative Bank Development, Austria/Germany)

Tradition as a catalyst – not as insurance

An incomprehensible megalomania has broken out among the commercial and savings banks, which obviously seek prosperity and future security in the size of their balance sheet. Such a strategy, however, is hardly compatible with the often solemnly declared customer orientation. Even co-operative banks now increasingly direct themselves towards the 'larger' rivals instead of exploiting their own opportunities and satisfying the needs and demands of their members and customers with tailor-made services in order to form their specific profile and secure their business in conformity with their social environment. Even here, shareholder value has largely pushed aside the human (Christian), social and society-reforming ideals of the pioneers of the last century. That is despite the fact that the pioneering spirit of then corresponded to an approach that we would characterise as a 'win-win' strategy today.

The legal form of a co-operative was established exclusively to foster the activities and businesses of the members through mutual and joint operation. The philosophy of a co-operative is rooted in the service to its members. Thus, its natural function is not to increase the balance sheet and its profits, to expand on investment banking, to deepen market penetration with so-called modern standardised bank products etc., but to satisfy human needs and solve specific problems.

The co-operative idea of Friedrich Wilhelm Raiffeisen was a visionary concept to solve dire problems of a society in change – a characterisation that also fits into our turbulent times. Supporting the change from a materialistic society towards a humanisation also of economic activities – despite increasing anonymity and mass-markets – is as important today as it was at the end of the 19th century; if not even more urgent.

Today, the motivations of the founders should again offer orientation and be the drive behind the co-operative credit organisations in Europe:

- *Motivation for survival*, i.e. the absolute will to secure a livelihood. Mergers are contrary to this as mergers always imply deleting at least one business.
- *Motivation for help*, i.e. the awareness to depend on mutual support in a positive sense, practising solidarity and providing help for self-help. Today, science confirms that the capacity to co-operate is the most important ability of networked systems. However, it is a ruinous competition that is practised nowadays, which does not benefit any customer but will eventually damage the banks' own business.
- *Motivation for reforming society*, i.e. the willingness to enter new ground, to change society, make it a more humane place and to base all actions on ethical and environmental values. However, the majority of the current co-operative banks is seeking conformity with other credit institutions. The result is a deceptive security lacking courage for uniqueness in the devotion to solidarity.

"Those who fight for profit only, earn nothing worth living for."
(Antoine de Saint-Exupéry)

To resuscitate the energy of the pioneer spirit and to promote a comeback of the credit co-operatives

In the competition with commercial and savings banks, a co-operative bank is more likely to succeed if it emphasises – in combination with the specific values of the legal form – its own identity and exploits its peculiarities and strengths of its staff for the benefit of its members and customers.

Following this objective, it is the small size and, resulting from it, the local knowledge and inclusion, the proximity to the market and the closeness to the people of the region that make innovation possible necessary for a secure subsistence. Among the various innovation opportunities, the problems and demands of the customers and members are the most reliable selection criteria for the bank, and, for the people in the region (society), the best way to eradicate bottlenecks in development.

We would like to provide the 'modern' co-operative organisations with the following ethical imperatives:

- *Do it as professionals and entrepreneurs!* i.e. Contribute creatively to progress and innovation of the economic process, discover new economic opportunities, risk them and carry them out.
- *Do it for people!* i.e. Respect and protect the untouchable dignity of human beings and let them become more of a human being in and through your work.
- *Do it for society!* i.e. Find your purpose, your duty in the common responsibility and effort for a sustainable development of society.

A bank or an economy that does not look beyond itself does not fulfil its function, which is offering service to society. It will loose its livelihood, as would a heart that only supplies itself and not the organism, which it depends upon.

"In you must be alight, what you want to enflame in others"
(Augustinus)

During our consulting activities, we accompany banks and their staff in the attempt to revive – with enthusiasm and pioneer spirit – the co-operative duty in its benefit-driven form. The aim is the co-operative bank as 'pacemaker of its region'.

Solving imperative problems of members, customers and people of the region (the co-operative bank is strongly linked with the successful development of the region in which it is rooted) takes the following steps: The first three steps clarify the competence of each employee through concentrating on the personal strengths, concentrating on suitable fields of activity and business and concentrating on a promising and 'appropriate' target group. In a fourth step, the need of the target group is defined by its most pressing problem. In the fifth step, all individual powers are concentrated on the solution of the target group's problem. Hurdles in the innovation process are eliminated through co-operation in a sixth step. The last step serves the stabilisation and securing of the position that the target group has reached. The aim is to realise inimitable top-results for a particular target group. The motivation of the bank employee does not, however, rise from an egoistic attitude: 'How do I sell, e.g., as many investment products as possible?' but from the rather altruistic attitude: 'Which bottleneck of the people in my target group must be eliminated in order to make them personally and economically more successful and independent?'

The following paragraphs describe four examples of co-operative bank practices that have been developed on the basis of strength profiles of individual employees and need profiles of particular customer groups:

(a) Specialising in securing the standard of living for the aged

The *strength profile* of one of the younger employees of a co-operative bank revealed that he had a good inclination towards 'old age services', which seemed to complement his existing tasks. His first test group were farmers. Through discussions it turned out that the difficulties linked to such services were bigger than expected, but also that the employee was emotionally not fit for this target group. A new target group was looked for: younger (aged up to 35 years), married executives who wish to buy property but whose old age provision does not match their present income. This time the 'chemistry' was right. The discussions revealed problems such as too high tax burdens, lack of time, not knowing an appropriate financial advisor and no life planning. The strongest fear turned out to be the loss of social status and the loss of quality of life in the older age.

The employee concentrated his innovative output on the 'preservation of the standard of living in old age': creation of a special appraisal concerning the amount of wealth at the presumed start of pension and alternative recommendations for safeguarding the standard of living during old age. The preparation of the contents of the service provision in interaction with the target group, including special training in financial mathematics to complement his existing knowledge, took a period of about two years and is being constantly deepened. To round it off, the employee co-operated in the course of the time with accountants, freelance insurance brokers and property companies.

What is special and inimitable in the employee's competence of today, is his reputation among his target group and the intellectual lead he has built up during the process of concentration in the last years. The service is recommended by word of mouth and requires no other form of advertising. All persons involved benefit from the employee's activities, which represent the much desired 3-winners-model: customer – employee – bank.

(b) Specialising in ecological housing

This innovation developed out of the personal life situation of one of the bank's young customer adviser, who had just built a house for his young family, respecting ecological criteria. Testing the 'young family' target group, the wish for an home ownership emerged as a priority issue.

The people in his target group actually needed information and advice that went beyond the traditional way of conceiving building and living, a need which is actually there a long time before the question of financing arises. This encouraged him, in a first step, to carry out regular events on this subject and to establish an information fair, in which he provides e.g. lists of craft businesses, specialised magazines, books, catalogues, information on location and property offers. Joint fair visits and discussion circles rounded off the information service of the first phase. Since healthy living is a priority in this target group, the employee has now various partners he can address or co-operate with, such as doctors that take a holistic and preventive approach, feng-shui specialised architects, institutes for the measurement of electrical smog and other disturbing agents; even a dowser belongs to this relations group. Thus, he gets slowly but surely more familiar with the needs of his target group and becomes the indispensable centre for their questions around this subject. Within the target group, who the partner for financing the property purchase or the building project should be is of no issue anymore thanks to the relationship that grew out of the preceding services.

(c) Specialising in the optimal financing of business investments

An astonishing and very effective innovation was achieved by a senior customer adviser with, among other things, an outstanding knowledge of various financing models. He not only knew the usual products of his bank but also, due to personal interest, creative financing instruments from the non-banking sector. Based on this, he developed an appealing service for his target group: successful self-employed people, who are too busy to take proper care of their business finances. Together with his target group, this employee worked out a service which was soon to be known beyond the region. This was because he, as an expert, dealt with everything from access to credit to all paper formalities that saved his customers time and trouble.

His selection criteria regarding the right financing is based on strict product neutrality in the sense that he exclusively represents the personal interests of the entrepreneur. The comparison between different credits (bank, public funds, leasing, insurance etc.), including tax aspects, is his speciality. Using direct access to large data banks he finds out about the amount and kind of public funding that can be applied for. He combines different credit forms to different financing models in a way that distinguishes the combination with the least expenditure. The payment plans for each model show in a clear and understandable way the total expenditure, monthly payments and the remaining debt. For the model that is favoured by the customer, he searches the offers of many different finance institutions in order to find the best conditions on the market. His customer receives full support for all negotiations with the potential lender up to the signing of the contract. And: the customers pay the bank employee a fee for his service as only freelance financial advisers would be paid.

(d) Specialising in a good start into self-employment

This example disproves reservations some boards have in regard to the promotion of female employees. This well trained customer adviser who had grown up in a family of entrepreneurs, saw her life situation change when she became pregnant. As an activist in a women network she had already advised many female start-up entrepreneurs. Having experienced the transmitting of the carpentry family business from her parents to her brother she had also grown sensitive and knowledgeable about problems related to enterprise succession. This experience determined her target group: 'young female business starters in handicraft and small and medium-sized enterprises'.

The first target group discussions which she led during her pregnancy, revealed difficulties that she knew all too well: problems of co-ordination with the family or the partner, the inhibitions about taking up a loan and a critical need for self-confidence, which explains the wish for expert information as a solid planning base. The strongest concern was about having a good certainty in the planning in order to balance private life and business commitment.

Her innovation was at first based on setting-up an information pool: obtaining, evaluating and providing reliable information on the establishment or transfer of a medium-sized or crafts enterprise by or to a woman and a database on businesses that are looking for a 'successor'. The employee works today part-time from her home, to the benefit of all involved. She already supports the female business starters in the decision and planning phase and offers financing and insurance alternatives. She co-operates with several networks, associations, experienced practitioners, course services, lawyers and accountants.

All these service innovations have the characteristics of internal business creations, well described by the concept of 'intra-preneurship'. They are based on concentrating each employee on his/her strengths, which are the greatest productivity and output reserves in a bank. Development process as described above are realised with approximately ten people at the same time in order to achieve a reasonably broad effect. Only those innovations are developed that are tailor-made for actual target group problems and that can be realised from within the bank or through co-operation partners. The employee, who goes through this entrepreneurial step in the bank, needs an environment in which individual working and 'learning at the pulse of the customer' is possible. The rewards for letting the employee mature for two or three years – with very low investment risks and development costs – are a new image and business fields with maximum added value, which through the outstanding profile of the particular 'target group specialist' and his/her distinct knowledge also prevents the bank from being interchangeable with any other.

No one can be helped to succeed without discussing intensively his/her future

Taking societal responsibility seriously, the co-operative bank has to confront itself also with the following issues:

✔   What importance do we give to our societal mission?
✔   How can we support the home region of our members?
✔   Where are the bottlenecks at the level of the region, the town, the members together, each member?
✔   How well are our members prepared for future problems, challenges and opportunities?
✔   How do the enterprises in the region develop? Are jobs under threat?
✔   How can new jobs be created, which jobs would be most desirable?
✔   How do the surrounding towns and the hinterland develop?
✔   How does the population of the region and the town change (migration, immigration, commuters, age...)?
✔   What peculiarities has our town, our region?
✔   What is the quality of life, working, leisure?
✔   Which regional funds can already be utilised and which should be aimed for jointly?

✔ What alliances can we form?

✔ What values – not only cultural – exist, which of them should be developed further?

✔ How does the information exchange in the region work, about what should everybody be informed in order to build common awareness?

✔ What can we contribute, initiate?

Further benefit aspects in the context of the societal duty of a co-operative bank are at present being thought up, tested and realised in several organisations:

✔ Alternative profit distribution – part of the profit is used for objects of public interest, e.g. the preservation of a wetland.

✔ General information events.

✔ Projects to foster equal opportunities and equal rights for women in the business world.

✔ Support for community projects that serve local needs through private initiative.

✔ Funding opportunities in regard to the development of regional enterprises and jobs, quality of life and leisure.

✔ Organisation of flexible housing rights, which provide the member – according to his age – housing rights on different forms of housing on a property base to housing and nursing rights in an old peoples home

✔ Co-ordination of activities among the members themselves.

✔ Strengthening of communication in the region.

✔ Regional development through conferences on possible futures.

A co-operative bank, that innovates through solving problems in this way, develops almost naturally into an institution that helps to rid its environment of bottlenecks – it becomes a pacemaker for its region and a responsible force for society.

Chapter four

The mainstream bank's social responsibility

What should be the social responsibility of banks?

Jacques Zeegers
(Belgian Bankers' Association)

It would be difficult to have an accurate image of the social responsibility of banks without reference to the framework in which they operate, that is the framework of a social market economy. Banks are, above all, businesses whose purpose is essentially economic. Their purpose is to offer to customers, public authorities, private persons or businesses a range of financial services which ought to enable them to achieve their own objectives. The social added value of these services is not inconsiderable and is certainly much more important, generally speaking, than the 'social' functions that we would like, rightfully or not, to be undertaken by banks.

The existence of an efficient, reliable and rapid system of payment, which offers all the necessary security guarantees, represents a considerable asset for the economy, and in the future this will certainly be the case in the information society, the development of which will depend heavily on a high performance payments system on the Internet.

In their role as financial intermediaries, banks contribute to the financing of a huge number of varied projects, most of which have considerable social and economic value. In short, without a high-performance banking system many socially beneficial initiatives would not even exist.

The first duty of a public-spirited business (*entreprise citoyenne*)

The first duty of a business which likes to think of itself as public-spirited, is to conduct its main business in a proper manner, which consists in offering its customers products and services with the best possible quality-price ratio. The Banks are no exception to this rule. Indeed, according to a survey recently conducted by CRIOC (the main Belgian Consumers' Research Association), this is what the public expects first and foremost from a credit institution. Experience has clearly shown that competition is the best way to achieve this. And competition in the banking sector has been increasing enormously in recent years in the wake of technological advances, globalisation and the creation of the euro.

Furthermore, the banks have a particular responsibility towards their depositors, who entrust them with their funds. Banks must be able to meet their commitments at any time. This is important not only for the depositors, but also for the economy as a whole: history has shown that a massive withdrawal of funds, following a public loss of confidence in the banking system, can be the origin of serious economic problems.

Therefore, the banks ought to exercise particular care in the use of funds deposited with them. The credit policy of banks must be compliant with rigorous and objective criteria. In this respect the margin for error is very narrow. A single percent of additional loss on their credit portfolio can cancel out their total profit. They must also have sufficient capital available in order to be able to absorb crises and to protect their depositors' money in the event of serious loss. And in order to have sufficient capital adequacy, they must offer their shareholders an adequate profit, for otherwise, the latter will place their money elsewhere.

The economic as well as social importance of an effective system of protection for investors justifies the case for a tight control of banking activity by the public authorities.

To maintain that the primary responsibility of banks is to conduct their business in a proper manner is not just idle talk. French, American, Japanese and Scandinavian taxpayers are well aware of the costs of mistakes made by badly managed banks: think of the socially beneficial work that could have been achieved with the hundreds of millions of dollars thus squandered. And the consequences of the absence of standards or rigorous controls in the financial sector are only too evident in South-East Asia.

Nor can the role of the banks in the field of employment be ignored. The banking sector provides high added value jobs for about 80,000 people in Belgium. It has to be said that, as a result of increased competition in the sector, technological advances and mergers, the number of jobs has stopped growing in recent years, and it could even decrease slightly in the future. But if account is taken of the number of jobs created indirectly by the sector through subcontracting, the balance sheet still looks very positive.

Banks also have a 'societal' responsibility

To maintain that the social value of the economic activity of banks is by far the most important of course does not mean that they do not also have a societal responsibility.

In its recent annual reports, the Belgian Bankers' Association stressed the idea of banks having a sense of civil responsibility. First of all this implies that the banks conduct their business in a proper manner, as mentioned above, but it also implies that in the course of their economic activity, banks show a concern for the environment in which they operate. Often their own interest is at stake. This is particularly the case in relation to overindebtedness. It is not in the interests of any bank to put its customers in the position of being unable to repay their debts. Therefore, they pay particular attention to this phenomenon. But of course it is necessary, when approaching this problem, to see to it that a fair balance exists between the interests involved. Measures taken to deal with overindebtedness must not have the effect of raising credit rates or imposing selection norms such that many citizens with a legitimate right to credit find themselves excluded completely. Another example concerns the protection of the environment: it is not in the interests of any bank to lend money to a polluting industry which may run the risk of failure as a result of damages and interest payments for which it would be liable.

Social exclusion is another area where the social responsibility of banks comes into play. In today's society, having a bank account has become indispensable in terms of getting one's income or making payments for the basic necessities of life. Without one, normal life is impossible. This is why in 1998, following a request from the Minister for Economic Affairs, M. di Rupo, the Belgian Bankers' Association drew up a 'charter for basic bank services' signed by 25 banks which undertook to offer unconditionally to every citizen the opportunity of opening a bank account consisting of at least three services: withdrawals, transfers and bank statements. Of course, credit facilities are not included in this basic service. The bank must in fact always be able to estimate the repayment capacity of each borrower. The 'right to credit facilities' would only lead to worsening the debt burden problem of overindebtedness.

There is no such thing as free banking

There are those who think that the idea of a basic service should extend to requiring the banks to dispense with bank charges. Although the idea of providing a public service exists in a number of sectors such as the post office, electricity or public transport, it is very rarely coupled with free provision of that service. That a service should be available to everybody is one thing. That it should be free is quite another. There is no objective reason for requiring banks to provide free banking. Besides, it has to be noted that there are no free services. Every service has a cost. Therefore, the question is not whether the service should be free but, who should pay it. There is nothing to prevent a democratically elected government from deciding to offer certain citizens free access to certain services. But in a market economy, the cost has to be borne by the collective whole with all the necessary transparency in order to avoid creating competitive distortions. In the European context, it would not be acceptable that Belgian banks have to bear certain charges, whilst their competitors in other countries would be exempt.

Another area in which the social responsibility of banks can have a bearing is that of relationships with customers. These relationships should be proper and based on mutual trust and transparency, and should take precedence over concerns for short term profit. This is why the Belgian Bankers' Association has drawn up a code of conduct designed to govern relationships between the banks and private customers.

Equally important in the social role of banks are their obligations in fiscal matters. As with all businesses, they have a duty to pay their taxes in accordance with the current rules and with the principles of a constitutional state. They must also avoid becoming involved in possible fraud committed by their customers. But that does not mean they must adopt the role of policeman in the matter, because that would lead to a breakdown in the relationship of trust that ought to exist between a banker and his customer. In recent years, the legislature has rightly concerned itself with the protection of privacy. Of course, this also applies to bank customers for whom the banker has a duty to act discreetly. The rules relating to 'bank secrecy' aim at ensuring of a proper balance between the demands for the protection of privacy and the fair perception of tax. In no way does bank secrecy aim at protecting the bank. Furthermore, there has never been any bank secrecy with regard to taxes due by the banks themselves.

The Banking and Finance Commission keeps a scrupulous watch to ensure that banks do not engage in practices which might encourage tax fraud. At the end of 1997, it published two circulars on 'particular mechanisms' and on the prevention of tax fraud, which have been closely examined by the Belgian Bankers' Association. The Belgian Bankers' Association set out guidelines aimed at avoiding any unhealthy competition between banks in the fiscal domain and at keeping in mind the spirit rather than the letter of the recommendations of the Banking and Finance Commission.

Should banks promote specific societal options?

The preceding considerations show that the social role of the bankers as well as their ethics lie at the heart of their activity. The latter rests entirely on the notion of trust – that of the depositors in the banker to whom they entrust their money, and that of bankers in the people to whom they grant credit. And no trust can exist without a basic morality amongst all the parties involved.

However some people would like to go a step further. They wonder whether bankers should not use the (limited) means at their disposal to promote specific choices of society. An 'ethical' bank is defined as one which favours the financing of activities which have a certain 'social' interest or which refuses to finance activities considered harmful such as the production or the sale of arms, or which refuses to collaborate with businesses known to exploit child labour in the third world. There are also 'ethical' products, for banks with a more general purpose, which wish to offer their customers the opportunity to spend their savings on certain types of investment.

As it happens it seems to me that the term 'ethical' is badly chosen, because it would imply that banks which do not adopt this approach, which is their right, are not concerned about professional ethics. One could say that there are banks with a social purpose as opposed to banks with an economic purpose, but this is also an unfortunate expression in so far as it would mean that economic purposes are opposed to social purposes, which is clearly not the case.

Anyhow, it is perfectly legitimate to give citizens who wish so, the opportunity to deal with financial institutions which, along with their economic purpose, claim to have a social purpose even if this means rewarding their investors with a slightly lower rate or giving their shareholders a smaller dividend. There is nothing wrong with men and women using the freedom they have gained thanks to their savings, for investing in projects which promote an improvement in the quality of life in our society (or at least which prevent it from deteriorating).

Politicians, not bankers, should define the general interest

Such initiatives certainly deserve encouragement, but nevertheless, one must also be aware of their limitations.

The major part of monetary flows concern 'ordinary' economic activity, the social value of which cannot be denied, especially in terms of jobs and income. 'Ordinary' banks will therefore always be necessary and will continue to dominate the market.

As stated above, ethics is inherent in the banker's trade. Although the principles which underpin the ethics are often quite clear, their application requires reflection and judgement in each individual case. Over-simplistic criteria detailed in a commercial statement do not necessarily meet the needs of all situations. Take, for example, the sale of arms. Everyone is against violence and there are some who think that a total ban on the sale of arms would by its very nature limit their use. This is a perfectly respectable opinion, yet probably unrealistic in so far as each individual must be able to defend himself against unfair aggression. Arms trading is not reprehensible in itself, but it is clear that it must be strictly controlled. And it is also clear that this task should not fall to the banker but to the democratically elected powers, in other words the government or the legislature. It is their job to define the general interest and to see that it is respected. Although the banker must always ensure that his actions are in accordance with the ethical codes of his profession, one cannot respect him to play the role of arbiter for the choices of society, which are often controversial. When granting credit, for example, the banker must respect both the spirit and the letter of the law, he must obey his conscience and of course, he must also ensure that the credit risk is not unreasonable, but it is not incumbent upon him to interfere in the private affairs of his customers.

The societal responsibility of commercial and savings banks

Prof. Dr. Leo Schuster
(University of Eichstätt, Germany)

If we wanted to categorise the stakeholders of banks, we could distinguish probably between direct stakeholders – such as owners or shareholders, employees
and customers – and indirect stakeholders. The latter, which are the focus of this
article, would include society in general and institutionalised society (see chart 1).
The institutions, groups and individuals brought up for discussion here are of
immense importance for both the commercial and savings banks. Not only do
they represent potential customers or even new fields for business activities, but
they also are the source of certain external effects: from the state comes the law,
the markets bring competition, the media is the source of image-forming factors
and from people and community initiatives come counterweight and protest.

The difficulty of a society-orientated banking policy is to satisfy, if possible, all
of the stakeholders as it is they who determine the societal acceptance of a bank
and, on the base of this, its reputation. Banks need reputation as bank services are
based on trust, i.e. they are to a large extend businesses of confidence. If a bank
looses society's confidence, for any justified or even unjustified reason, it will have
severe consequences and, in extreme cases, could come to a run on this bank. A
loss of confidence that affects the bank sector in general usually leads to government intervention, be it in the form of financial or good will support measures –
as recently in Japan – or through new and tighter regulations, as in the case of the
European Union's banking directives.

The reason why banks are so exposed to society is due to their specific functions vis-à-vis businesses and the economy as a whole. Their commercial
instruments are cash, credit and capital, whose distribution to the economy and
society gives to the banks a determining control over goods and services. This puts
banks into a privileged position, which makes them to be considered sometimes
as quasi-public institutions.

Beyond that, banks (specifically in Germany) have further power potentials in
the form of delegated voting rights, holdings in the capital of enterprises and the
personal relations and networks through supervisory board mandates. This potential is the more effective, the more of these factors are used combined.

Chart 1: The stakeholders of commercial and savings banks

Indirect stakeholders		Direct stakeholders	
Society in general	Institutional society	Individual society	Bank–internal society

• National and international public
• Social groups
• Politics
• Media
  • *press*
  • *radio*
  • *television*
  • *internet*
	• State(s)
	  • *government / legislator*
	  • *central bank (ECB)*
	  • *control boards*
	• International organisations
	• Markets
	  • *finance*
	  • *goods*
	  • *technology*
	  • *information*
	  • *consulting*
	  • *human resources*
	• Other institutions
	  • *municipalities*
	  • *churches*
	  • *associations*
	  • *universities, schools*
	  • *trade unions*
	• Temporary interest groups
	  • *local/community initiatives*
	  • *single interest groups*
		• Clients
		  • *investors*
		  • *borrowers*
		  • *issuers*
		• Owners
		  • *shareholders*
		  • *cooperative members*
		  • *partners*
		• Supervisory boards, advisory committees etc.
			• Management
			• Employees
			• Internal advisors
			• Works council
			• Pensioners

Additionally, there are authority functions the banks fulfil on behalf of the government, e.g. retaining taxes in order to pass it on to the treasury or, to use another example, assuming police functions in the form of reporting suspects under the directives against money laundering. In addition, the central bank carries out its interest rate and monetary policy by using the bank apparatus; i.e. it uses the financial institutions as instruments for economic and structural policy.

These mutual relations between society and its different parties as well as the banks are the subject of the 'societal contract'. It consists both of explicit rules, i.e. legal regulations, and implicit demands whose fulfilment is expected by society but cannot be enforced by taking legal actions. It seems as if the tensions between the banks and society, frequently revealed by opinion polls, are caused by the latter. Prejudices, e.g. that banks are making too big profits, are numerous. To some extend they are unjustified whilst in other cases they are due to fraud or dubious business. It cannot be denied that such accusations concerning the black sheep among the credit institutes are justified and should be condemned.

Chart 2: Functional framework of the society-oriented banking policy

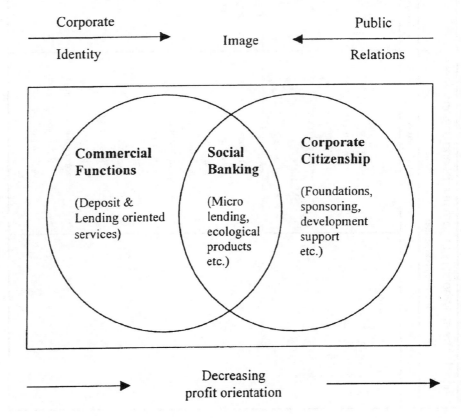

However, due to the phenomena of the banking-specific collective reputation, the public verdict does not punish this particular institute but the entire credit business. In this way, the sin of one institute becomes the problem of the whole industry.

Society-orientated banking policy

Commercial and savings banks realised a long time ago not to concentrate their policy on owner-, market- and customer-related activities only, but to include and take into account the entire societal environment (see Chart 2).

This is known as 'Corporate Citizenship' in the Anglo-Saxon world, where the concept is more developed than in German-speaking countries. It means the societal commitment of a bank beyond its actual business activity. Of course, Corporate Citizenship, if it wants to keep its credibility, must not be misused as a cover for non-serious business practices. Banks are not always very keen on it, sometimes even necessitating government intervention as happened in the United States where the Community Reinvestment Act was introduced in 1991. This law secures poorer neighbourhoods, largely Black or Latino communities in American cities, access to financial services with the support of banks. But there is also a whole range of specific schemes within the framework of 'Social Banking', which serve the fight against the 'new poverty', regional discrimination and economic decline. Thus the concept of 'microlending' is becoming widely used, to qualify small credits up to e.g. $2000 for initiative minded people to start their own micro-activity. By putting borrowers into joint liability groups the repayment rate can been kept at 98%, thus making this sector interesting even from a profit perspective.

The basic idea of 'Social Banking' results from the recognition that particularly among SMEs the boundaries between pure market-related activities and social commitment are moving towards the latter. Big banking institutes, driven today by a strong culture of shareholder value, cannot and do not want to devote themselves anymore to supporting existing or starting small and micro-businesses. Thus, it is important for them to operate in a diverse banking system where financial institutes respond to a variety of business philosophies, size and regional responsibility. In Germany, it is especially the co-operative banks and the (largely public owned) savings banks that have a strong role to keep in terms of regional and local responsibilities, a commitment they may keep provided they are not privatised or excessively concentrated through mergers.

The origins of the co-operative and savings banks are actually rooted in the provision of assistance to businesses in need of support and to the poorer parts of the population. Today, with over four million unemployed and the phenomenon of 'new poverty', similar motives are back on the agenda even in Germany. Less wealthy parts of the population should be accepted as a customer group, for whom certain bank services are no less essential. For people trying to find their way back to a job, a current account service (an 'account for everyone') is all too vital. The idea is not to favour a 'social fantasy' that would not fit with market mechanisms, but to respond sensibly to a customer segment with an adapted service and price strategy.

Although the term of 'Corporate Citizenship' is less common in Germany, there is, however, a set of activities by the commercial and savings banks that fall within this area, such as donations, sponsoring of culture, science and education, support for economic development and other projects. Virtually all groups of banks have shown their commitment, especially through their general interest oriented foundations. Among the private banks, the Alfred-Herrhausen-Foundation of the Deutsche Bank and the Jürgen-Ponto Dresdner Bank-Foundation serve as good examples. The savings banks, which similarly to the credit co-operatives were founded 150 to 200 years ago specifically for reasons of financial security and access to credit, have since made societal responsibility their first ideal. This is expressed exemplarily by the 200 foundations of the savings banks and their initiative for boosting the regional business location ('Standort: hier') in Germany (see Chart 3).

Chart 3: Services of the savings banks for the economy and society
- Extensive infrastructure: branches outside conurbations
- Regional economic and structural support: 33 own investment companies
- SME and start up support: business start-ups, innovation centres, follow-up fairs, foundations
- Stock market introductions
- Development support of new technologies: biotechnology
- Entrepreneur and innovation prizes: 'Innovations-Oscar' (since 1993)
- Network for technology advice (NTG): 350 consultants (semiconductor technology, multimedia, logistics, optics etc.)
- EU-information service (DSGV): Eurocontacts, East-asia etc.
- Special credit programmes

The savings bank's commitment in the fields of environmental protection and ecology, which are part of the most urgent problems in our society, is particularly worth mentioning. Special environmental and community banks had initiated this new banking orientation. The 'mainstream' then followed. Nowadays, they check creditworthy projects additionally on their environmental impact, carry out environmental audits and launch eco-funds, which invest in ecological (solar and wind energy) and socially sensible projects. Investment funds, based on ethical, environmental and social criteria are established, which in addition to the usual selection criteria – such as high yield on equity, healthy gearing ratio and competent management – take into account certain exclusion criteria (nuclear energy, tobacco industry, etc.). A special form of environment-friendly policy is represented by biodegradable credit cards, which have been developed by the British Co-operative Bank in co-operation with Greenpeace.

A constant problem for bank clients is to get their own way in regard to their ideas and complaints. Although the complaint management belongs nowadays to the total quality management in most of the banks, a neutral hearing is not always guaranteed. However, the German private banks have set up an arbitrator – the so-called *Ombudsmann* – who can make arbitral awards up to a value in litigation of 10,000 DM. The credit co-operatives and savings banks have created similar regional boards of arbitration. In this way disputes can be settled out of court, which positively affects the societal acceptance of the credit institutions.

From this essay it may be evident that the role of banks in our society goes far beyond mere commercial activity and that the industry increasingly thinks of itself as a societal player that has to ensure its existence through investments in society. It goes without saying that these various investments intend to positively influence both the corporate identity and the image of the commercial and savings banks and thus have a sales-promoting effect. This is because banks are primarily market economy organisations, for which profitability is a prerequisite in order to satisfy the desires and demands of customers, owners and society as a whole. Corporate Citizenship requires financial input but should also produce notional and material feedback. In this sense, I finally want to propose a 'societal balance sheet' as an additional but no less important calculation. While today the societal costs are only partly recorded and thus hardly suitable for further calculation and controlling, the costs that result from societal responsibilities should in future be converted into a specific code, e.g. for the rating of banks, for benchmarking or – in the case of co-operative banks – as a proof of the fulfilment of their specific duties. This code should emerge as 'Societal Costs Adjusted Return on Capital' (SCAROC) for example next to the 'Risk adjusted Return on Capital (RAROC).

A bank searching for its social fibre: NatWest Group

Peter Hughes and Andrew Robinson
(NatWest Group, UK)

Picture a derelict factory in the centre of Birmingham. Which social bank do you think provided the loan finance which helped create workspace for a vibrant community of people working in the arts and creative industries?

Picture a loans scheme to help low-income individuals carry out energy saving improvements to their homes. Which community finance organisation do you think partnered the local authority to establish the scheme?

Picture Working Support, a charity in the East End of London which set up two new community businesses – a café and a gardening company to help unemployed people with learning difficulties into jobs. Which charitable foundation do you think awarded the grant to Working Support?

Picture an independent petrol station in rural Cumbria. Which mainstream commercial bank provided the finance to help the station continue trading?

The answers are that it is NatWest which is behind the social bank, the community finance organisation and the charitable foundation projects. The final example was funded by a social bank.

These anecdotal examples demonstrate that mainstream loan finance providers can be innovative and exciting and operate on a commercial basis. Nevertheless, these are just stories, experience is mixed and there is a challenge for mainstream banks to capture the ideas that work and how to go about systematically replicating them.

About NatWest Group

Today NatWest Group is a portfolio of businesses providing a broad spectrum of financial services to customers ranging from individuals and small businesses to multi-national companies.

It was formed in 1968 when the National Provincial Bank, along with its subsidiary District Bank and the Westminster Bank, agreed to merge. NatWest can trace its roots back to the seventeenth century through the amalgamation of nearly 200 private and joint stock banks.

NatWest Group is one of the largest and best capitalised banking groups in the world. It has total assets of around £185 billion, operates in 33 countries, and employs approximately 70,000 staff. Loans and advances to customers as at 31 December 1998 total just under £79 billion.

The Group's objective is to have a major and profitable presence in each of its chosen markets and many of its businesses are recognised as market leaders with well established corporate brands (including NatWest, Coutts and Lombard). Our principal business activities under the NatWest brand are retail and corporate banking, card services, mortgage operations, life and investment services and general insurance. It has over 1725 branches, one of the largest ATM networks and serves around 7.5 million personal and business customers. Lombard provides asset finance to commercial customers and is an established brand in personal loan finance. The Coutts Group is a premier name in private banking, both in the UK and internationally.

Development of corporate citizenship

NatWest along with the other clearing banks was an early leader in Corporate Community Involvement. Its established a distinct community relations function at Group level in the late 1970s and was a strong proponent of the first philanthropic wave of corporate responsibility.

The philanthropic characteristics of the community relations programme remained unchanged until the early 1990s. The programme was centrally managed, diverse (over 300 sponsorship relationships and 1500 donation clients at Head office level alone) with priorities largely set either by the function management or the Group Executive team. Criteria for support were largely reactive, based on the applicants received and a perceived requirement to balance conflicting demands on the resources available. There were pockets of excellence within the programme, including the Mini Enterprise in Schools Project (MESP) which was an early example of collaboration between Government (DTI) and the private sector in an area of crucial interest to both parties; and also the Inner City task force, a £3million initiative run with Business in the Community which laid the foundations of its work in economic regeneration today. Success was measured by the size of the spend and the responsiveness of the programme to perceived community funding requirements. Indeed, the exclusion of business interest as a criterion in decision making was encouraged.

This wave ended in the early 1990s. The twin catalysts were heightened competitive pressures and that profits had reached a cyclical low. At one stage, the declared community relations spend calculated using the Per Cent Club guidelines in the UK accounted for 10% of Pre-tax profits and placed NatWest, first amongst corporate contributors in the UK.

Although the commitment to the overall scale of spend remained undiminished, economic realities spelled the need to fundamentally review its nature.

The strategy was to be pro-active, to focus spend on areas linked to the business, and ultimately to seek integration of community relations into normal commercial practice. What was also clear was that expectations were a long way from the desired goal. Externally, NatWest was seen as the 'biggest giver' and internal expectations did not link community and investment as bedfellows. Given the strategy, you would not start from the position which was the NatWest historical legacy.

The task was tackled in two phases. First, 'financial effectiveness and enterprise' was agreed by a Board level Committee as the theme to be applied across the programme. Although a genuine attempt was made to link existing commitments to the over-arching theme, in retrospect the power of the theme was in significantly managing down the number of relationships, without a reputational backlash.

Second, a range of new programmes were put in place which matched the aspirational strategy. Early developments included the financial literacy programme, independent money advice and the establishment of a Charitable Trust to bring focus and accountability into donation giving.

Delivering value required a commitment to measurement. Change triggered a series of research initiatives, most notably a benchmarking study carried out on behalf of NatWest by David Logan. This later evolved into the London Benchmarking Group and has recently further widened its membership.

Current corporate citizenship policy

Albeit refined and developed in the light of experience, the corporate community investment strategy has remained largely unchanged from the original aspirations of the early 1990s.

What has emerged is subsidiarity of community budgets to businesses coupled with an interaction between the businesses and the corporate centre over policy.

Current corporate citizenship focus areas of activity are financial literacy, developing communities and helping staff give time and money.

Broadly, external drivers for NatWest are two-fold. First, the competitive climate has intensified with new entrants such as the Supermarkets, the insurers, Marks & Spencer and Virgin establishing in the banking services part of the marketplace.

At the same time, the new Government in the UK does represent changed priorities and ways of thinking which represent both threats and opportunities to traditional banks. Just some of the key policy initiatives of relevance to the Banks (and others) are as follows:

- Social exclusion – access to financial services is on the agenda
- Community regeneration – the role of finance in building wealth
- Shareholder value – Social responsibility and economic efficiency
- Cost savings – Electronic solutions to managing Government

Social exclusion, for example, represents both a threat and direct and indirect business opportunities. For NatWest, experience of Bancorp demonstrated the case for involvement. To the industry, the US Community Reinvestment Act

(CRA) represented a costly and bureaucratic burden, reducing flexibility to act. However, NatWest Bancorp regularly scored at the highest levels for its CRA rating and used this as a reputational tool to gain competitive advantage. As the debate moves to the UK, there is a need to engage to ensure that the outcomes of policy change are beneficial to all parties and are based on firm knowledge of the problem.

Case study: Community enterprise as a business opportunity

This represents a good example of how the dynamics between a community investment team and a business unit can influence social outcomes and demonstrates how relationships have changed.

Through its community contacts and sponsorship relationships in the UK such as Charities Aid Foundation (Dimensions of the Voluntary Sector) and the National Council of Voluntary Organisations, the Community Relations team were aware that the voluntary sector was large and growing. At 4% of Gross Domestic Product, the Voluntary Sector was already larger than both Agriculture and Automotive, both with established centres of expertise within NatWest, but there was no equivalent for it.

Why? Two factors seemed to be at play. First, management information systems are constructed around nature of business, not legal form. Voluntary sector organisations did not represent a significant sample. Second, the voluntary sector has traditionally been grant-funded which has reinforced a risk averse approach to loan finance. From a business perspective, experience in the last session showed that the voluntary sector was anti-cyclical in income terms.

Links with NatWest Bancorp had already alerted Community Relations both to the different legislative structure in the US and the existence of intermediary loan finance providers, the Community Development Finance Initiative (CDFI). The concept of a CDFI did not yet exist in a sustainable way in the UK, but there was clearly community sector interest from organisations such as Birmingham Settlement and CAF in testing the idea.

Hence, there were two imperatives to action. First, the public policy imperative. Gordon Brown spoke at a Birmingham Conference to community activists back in 1995 and expressed interest in the US Community Reinvestment Act. Our knowledge, through NatWest Bancorp provided an insight into how such programmes worked and the importance of intermediaries as a distribution channel. Second, there seemed to be a *prima facie* case for developing a strategy in this field, but there was limited capacity to test the propositions using internal data.

How to bridge the impasse? Answer, a series on investments in community projects. Business in the Community approached NatWest as a funder for the Local Investment Fund. Through creating a £3 million loan pool, LIF would test the proposition that there were bankable deals for community organisations which were falling through the mainstream bankers net. Community Relations funded, provided that the business put an Executive on the LIF Council and seconded a member of staff to run the fund.

This is what happened. Knowledge of LIF, engagement with community enterprise and the choice of Andrew Robinson with a skills mix bridging the community and banking, all helped build the business case. Andrew has now returned to Small Business Services and has been given the remit of building a portfolio of projects across the Community Enterprise spectrum. The first of these is an innovative savings product for the mainstream market in the UK. As part of the subsidiarity principle, SBS now has responsibility for the key relationships with CAF and NCVO to integrate the learnings directly into strategy.

What has happened?

Broadly speaking, there are two drivers for a mainstream bank to seek to discover its social fabric. The first is that can be good for business. The second is that there is a growing expectation that all companies will become increasingly open and accountable for their actions.

The business case

An indicative, but not fully proven business case for lending to the voluntary sector exists. NatWest is the market leader in lending to the voluntary sector in the UK and knows that this leadership is worth around £50m in income to the retail part of the bank. However, the vast majority of this income is based on the supply of non-lending products. Lending does take place but this is not the norm. The reasons for this are complex. Tradition, caution by boards of Trustees or the Executive, concerns over the capacity of the organisation to sustain borrowing and lack of an asset base all may play a part.

As the case studies at the start demonstrate, there are examples of good practice, but these are patchy. A challenge for NatWest is how to build and learn from local experience. There is a self-fulfilling prophecy that if a deal is done on a commercial basis, by definition it will cease to be perceived as innovative. However, banking is a judgement business and the interpretation of what is commercial does vary depending on the individuals concerned.

A strategy to address the social economy has been established. The first step has been to set up a centre of excellence within the small business services arm of the retail business.

Paradoxically, the first product to emerge from the team is a savings product for the personal market! This is a Trojan horse to use the market to capture the understanding on the near-commercial deals. The product offers customers capital protection coupled with the opportunity to forego interest. This interest is then used to capitalise 11 charitable loan funds, based on the 9 Regional Development Agency areas in England plus Scotland & Wales. The board will comprise community figures and NatWest bankers. Together, they will make decisions on viable projects which would not get commercial loan finance at affordable rates. NatWest is also investing a proportion of its social responsibility budgets into the funds.

The social responsibility case

In management terms, there has been a recognition that strategy needs to be more sophisticated to respond to changing demands on corporate responsibility. Divisions between environmental, social and economic performance are blurring. Legitimate demands for reporting and accountability are moving out of the environmental arena and moving into the social impact of business. This phenomenon embraces both core business and traditional corporate responsibility activity.

Management of this phenomenon at Group level is being handled by integrating the previously separate functions of Community Relations and Investment, Environmental Management, Government Relations and Issue Management within a single Public Affairs Unit. This change will become fully effective by the beginning of June. Resources are being re-aligned around the three functions of issue management, stakeholder relationships and reporting/communication.

A driver for the need to integrate is the requirement to be break down silos. Centres of excellence have been established, for example, our leading position within financial services on environmental responsibility. We are building on this legacy by producing a social impact review to combine environmental, community reporting and the wider impact of business on society. Stakeholder reaction to this publication will be used to plan future action.

Conclusion

Mainstream commercial finance is part of a spectrum of the ways in which individuals, charities and businesses fund what they do. From grant to commercial loan, from own resources to borrowed, finance is the lifeblood of activity. The responsibility of a bank is to find ways in which it can satisfy commercial and viable business opportunities. At the margins, incentives from Government or other charitable funders may change the economics of provision. However, through the Community Bond and through partnerships with other players in the market, we believe that there is a need to demonstrate a practical rather than a theoretical case before we seek this type of support.

European banks' environmental and social policies and business practices survey – The Giuseppi Report

James Giuseppi
(National Provident Institution, Global Care, UK)

Acknowledgements

Guy Hughes, People & Planet (formerly operating as LAMB – the Lloyds and Midland Boycott).

Ed Mayo, New Economics Foundation.

Rob Lake, Traidcraft Exchange.

Introduction

This section examines the environmental and social performance and practises of European banks. The information is largely drawn from respondents to a survey investigating a range of environmental and social issues including environmental and sustainable banking, third world debt and human rights, community involvement and business practices.

Banks performance on issue were assessed to produce a league table of best and progressive practices amongst the banks surveyed. The chapter ends with an outline of a model bank of best practices.

Methodology

A questionnaire was the primary source of information for this survey. The banks were also encouraged to supply any written information, which they felt would give a further insight into their operations and practices. Site visits, meetings and telephone interviews were also conducted, when possible. A variety of additional sources were also used (such as press articles, publications, NGOs, previous and external research sources) and are credited accordingly.

Over 70 banks were included in the original survey list, several of which were involved in mergers. The response rate was over 50%. A summary of the respondent's reply was sent to the relevant bank, and they were asked to comment on the profile prior to publication of the report.

Internet research was useful in judging which banks consider it important to use this form of media to publicise their services and activities to the public, their customers, staff and competitors.

Questionnaire – scope and limitations

The method of using questionnaires surveys has limitations and they are currently over-employed for surveys. However, they are useful as a tool to focus the attention of those being surveyed, when followed by subsequent telephone or e-mail contact, as was used in this case.

No domestic workplace questions were included in the questionnaire as it was assumed that European banks adhere to the guidelines of the Social Charter, which covers equal opportunities and workplace practices. Banks also tend to be leaders in the area of workplace practices.

Overview

a. Environment

Sustainable banking

The definition of this term, for the purpose of this project, would be the decision by banks not to make loans to businesses that operate without any consideration of their ecological and social impact. The standards that were used to judge this criterion were whether the banks had environmental screens included in their lending policies and whether they conduct environmental checks of their customers' businesses. Such practices are described in this chapter as 'responsible lending'.

A significant proportion of the bank respondents are signatories to the United Nations Environment Programme's 'Statement by Financial Institutions on the Environment & Sustainable Development' (UNEP Statement). This statement commits signatories to support sustainable development and environmental protection, and to effectively communicate their policies in these areas. Unfortunately, the best practice guidelines in the UNEP statement is lacking application in the banking sector. However, the statement does draw benchmarks of expectations. DG Bank realistically stated that as a signatory, the Bank 'demonstrates the awareness of the existing problems'. Only HypoVereinsBank stated categorically that 'loans strictly follow the UNEP guidelines'.

Although banks themselves are not the worst offenders in terms of direct environmental pollution, they have significant indirect impacts due to where and to whom they loan money. 'Public opinion does not see business efficiency as the only value on which a bank can be judged. Social and increasingly environmental responsibilities are given an equal level of importance. Such obligations include the challenge of incorporating and applying environmental criteria to loan policies and company evaluations'.

For example, according to Swiss law 'the risk for banks to become directly liable for environmental damages caused by their borrowers is relatively low. However, such risk does exist where a bank exerts influence on the decision-making process of a polluting company and thereby actively influences a specific decision which leads to an impairment of the environment or when acting in advisory capacity and due diligence procedures are not met.'[1]

However, such laws in Switzerland are not applicable to their banks' operations beyond their national border. For example, the role of UBS in the Ilisu Dam project, Turkey: 'Funding a project (Ilisu) which violates World Bank standards on 18 accounts would send a strong signal to the public that the mega-merger with SBC has resulted in a significant weakening of the environmental policies of UBS.'[2]

A Sulzer/ABB publication on Ilisu says: 'As UBS was the leading Bank in the financing of previous projects it was awarded the task of structuring and arranging the financing for Ilisu.' UBS indeed has a long history of financing GAP[2] projects, prior to the merger, some of which go against the policies of their own Environmental report. UBS was one of the first banks to sign the UNEP Statement. In defence of UBS's role, the environmental manager stated that it was UBS that brought the Ilisu project into the realm of the public, and invited representatives from WWF and Berne Declaration to discuss the issues raised. Friends of the Earth have stated that they believe that construction of the Ilisu Dam will cause major environmental damage, further increase tensions in this Kurdish region and will probably lead to war in the region due to the disruption of water supplies from the Tigris. As Turkey is a NATO member, many other countries would be drawn into a conflict if Turkey was attacked by Syria or Iraq, which is considered likely by the UK Defence Forum in case of a disruption to the water supply. If the companies involved in the Ilisu dam project are not deterred by the prospect of being instrumental in causing military conflict, perhaps they would be concerned by the possibility of future liability claims by local stakeholders.

It is a similar case of double standards for the giant Dutch Bank ABN. Unfortunately, ABN chose not to complete the questionnaire, but instead sent its annual and environmental reports, which make no mention of the environmental damage or human rights abuses that occur due to mining activities financed through previous ABN loans. During subsequent dialogue, the Investment Relations manager stated that, in accordance with the Bank's current standards, the funding of such operations would probably be declined by ABN Amro on environmental grounds. This would indicate that the Bank is now taking steps to incorporate its environmental policy into its business practices. The environmental report states that 'the Environmental policy of ABN is designed to ensure that environmental aspects are fully integrated within 15 years as a key factor in all company decisions, in such a way that ABN makes a worthwhile contribution to a sustainable society'.

In the UK, no loans have yet been declined on environmental grounds by Lloyds TSB. Lloyds TSB believes in dialogue with customers to improve environmental performance rather than refusing banking services. The majority of banks refuse to accept the responsibility of their clients' actions, claiming that they are not the environmental regulators or enforcers and that their financial services are merely products. This means that banks are not measuring their customers' environmental performance, and until this happens, customers will not feel obliged to implement any measures beyond legislative compliance. Access to financial services is empowerment, without which the customers' operations would be severely curtailed.

The European Commission has provided guarantees, through the European Investment Fund for banks to offer loans on preferential terms to EU-based SMEs that are either operating on an environmentally beneficial basis or providing products or services that are environmentally beneficial. European banks were offered the opportunity to act as the local intermediaries and adjudicators for such loans. BCP in Portugal highlighted in the survey response that it has made use of this opportunity and now positions itself as the environmental bank in Portugal.

'Good housekeeping'

Although banks are not obvious environmental polluters, they do tend to be large consumers of energy, especially paper, and they can be major property holders. Good housekeeping refers to the steps banks take to reduce their own direct negative impact upon the environment, for example through management of their facilities and properties. Such measures would include practices like recycling waste, reducing CO_2 emissions and using renewable energy and product sources. To effectively implement such practices the norm within the sector is for the bank to issue a formal corporate environmental policy or an environmental report so that such practices could be communicated not only to customers and outside observers, but also to their own staff. The survey investigated whether employees receive environmental training and if managers' responsibilities included the implementation of the bank's environmental policies.

In Denmark strict environmental legislation exists and the Danish respondents all practise good housekeeping. Housekeeping includes reducing their direct environmental impact by recycling paper (of which banks are major consumers) and targeting reductions in energy consumption and CO_2 emissions.

In Finland, Merita 'does not consider the bank to have an environmental impact', but the newly merged MeritaNordBanken in Sweden stated they have an environmental policy but did not enclose it with their reply.

Amongst the French banks, where the rate of reply was poor and most of the information is based upon AReSE research material, Dexia came out as the clear leaders in this area whilst CCF, Paribas and SocGen are making no discernible efforts at all. AReSE stated that BNP, a respondent to our survey, is a 'socially responsible group' but they do not have an environmental policy.

The German banks all have good practices in this area, along with the Dutch and the Swiss. It is a shame that the Swiss Bank, Sarasin & Cie, did not reply, as their environmental department is well respected for their proactive stance on environmental matters and sustainable development.

In Ireland retail banks AIB and Bank of Ireland are proactive in this field, but Anglo Irish Bank could only state that the bank 'follows best industry practice'.

Spain is generally poor in terms of the environmental stance of companies, but the banking sector seems to be the leader in environmental management as it slowly develops environmental policies and applies good housekeeping practices, the leaders in the sector being BCH and BBV.

b. Overseas operations

Banks with overseas operations in developing nations have the opportunity to promote progressive standards of workplace practices globally, thereby encouraging such practices locally. The results of the survey would indicate that the majority of banks with overseas operations could improve their performance in this area.

Banks have the opportunity (and the moral responsibility according to the Rio Resolution Statement) to integrate environmental and social criteria into their investment policies and thereby practise responsible lending. The responses – particularly those concerning debt alleviation – are an indication of their attitude towards overseas responsible lending. Most banks still holding debts to developing countries are prepared to participate in international multilateral initiatives to review repayments.

'Third World debt'

During the Seventies, European banks were encouraged, by their governments to lend money to developing countries. It was seen as being beneficial to the developing countries. Unfortunately, the loans were granted on unsustainable terms. For example, sovereign debts had unrealistic terms of hard currency repayment based on commodity export prices, which, of course, may fluctuate. When such prices dropped too low, the debtors defaulted on their repayments. The levels of debt have been so high that such defaults caused debt crises. Lenders, specifically banks such as NatWest in the UK were in danger of collapse.

The nature of Third World Debt has changed during the nineties. Of the world's poorest nations, the amount of total debt to private banks is now around 10-12%,[3] whereas previously the banks held the major portion of loans to the

poorest nations. The various debt crises during the last decade prompted the trans-
ferral of the responsibility of the loans from the private to public sector. The IMF
and World Bank issued further loans to indebted countries to repay the original
debts. European governments took over portions of the debt, and banks sold some
of the debt on the secondary markets. These measures saved the relevant banks
from, if not collapse, at least serious financial losses. The lack of transparency of
the relationships between the banks, central banks and governments, means that
there is no way of establishing on what basis the bail-outs were arranged. They
also make the majority of debts virtually untraceable and created no relief from
the debt burden for the indebted countries.

It is unclear how the debt crises of the last ten years will actually affect banks'
lending activities. Concerns raised by pressure groups, such as LAMB (Lloyds
and Midland Boycott) in the UK, remain relevant. Will public money continue
to be used to bail out the banks when they make irresponsible lending decisions
which later backfire? On what terms did the European governments agree to save
those banks at risk of collapse?

In the US, all companies, including subsidiaries of foreign based companies,
are obliged to declare where they are lending or investing money abroad. There
is no such legislation for similar declarations in Europe. Certain information is
available concerning which countries are creditors, and to what levels,[4] but tracing
the debts to individual banks is almost impossible without the co-operation of the
relevant banks.

In Europe, due to the lack of transparency in the reporting of banks' results,
they are able to avoid fully disclosing to where they have lent money. The essence
of Jubilee 2000, the international campaign to reduce the developing world's debt
burden, is to motivate the general public across Europe to put pressure on their
governments to work with the banks to write-off such debts. Banks seem generally opposed to unilateral action, probably based on the assumption that
European governments will once again provide assistance.

The Initiative for Heavily Indebted Poor Countries (HIPC) is targeted at
relieving the world's poorest countries of their debt burden. However, the HIPC
Initiative is unlikely to achieve its aim of relieving debt burden, because of the
conditions imposed; for example, the very high percentages of export income that
HIPCs are expected to pay.[5] In addition, 'this initiative fell short of the needs of
debtor economies because creditors remain all powerful, judge, jury, bailiff, interested party and witness, all in one.... creditors are unwilling to relinquish their
power in favour of a fair and efficient procedure satisfying the most basic legal
principles.'[6]

The Eurodad report states that the main supporters of this initiative came from
the smaller European countries such as the Nordic states, Switzerland and the
Netherlands. Meanwhile Germany, Japan and Italy formally support the initia-

tive but practically block its implementation by insisting on strict compliance with the rules. Their stance appears due to their own current domestic economic difficulties, which are increased for Germany and Italy by the strict budgetary requirements to qualify for the single European currency. However, as noted by Jubilee 2000, Germany is forgetting that without the massive cancellation and restructuring of her debts to sustainable levels after WWII, Germany would never have achieved her 'miracle' economic and social recovery. However, the German banks, which did voluntarily disclose their positions as creditors to developing nations, highlighted that they were actively involved in programmes to alleviate the burdens of such debt. Such action primarily takes the form of debt rescheduling, e.g. by Commerzbank, Deutsche and DG banks. Only one of the German banks, a mortgage bank, admitted issuing such debt but gave no details of any programmes to alleviate debt burden.

The lack of an international insolvency law needs to be addressed in order to overcome the problems arising from earlier irresponsible lending and prevent future similar mistakes. 'Commercial banks have quite often, though not always without 'persuasion', granted debt reductions in various forms, (but) if international insolvency allowing countries to go bankrupt had existed in the 1970s, loans would certainly have been given more cautiously'.[7]

At a meeting in Tegucigalpa, Honduras, in January 1999, representatives from 16 Latin American countries gathered to formulate a continent-wide agreement, and to co-ordinate campaigning. The Tegucigalpa Declaration called for:

- Transparency in the lending/borrowing process and inclusion of all parties involved.
- Integration and co-ordination of all parties involved, applying an insolvency procedure to indebted countries along the lines of bankruptcy laws existing in countries such as the United States.
- Allow indebted countries the right to declare themselves insolvent. Debtors and creditors will appoint an equal number of judges for a Tribunal or Arbitration Jury.[8]

The establishment of an independent Debt Review Body (DRB), set up by the UN or international court of justice, to act as an arbitrator, is required, to defend the sovereignty of a debtor nation, while being fair to creditors.

'The overwhelming purpose of the concordat would be to ensure that the money released (i.e. debt service remitted) goes into the service of the poor.'[9]

Such proposals would appear to offer a realistic, humanitarian and sustainable solution to the debt crisis. Now the active participation of the creditor governments and banks is required.

Human rights

The growing trend of globalisation of banks means that their influence stretches far beyond the borders of the countries in which they operate. As banks become multinational organs, their indirect government support through syndicate loans or financing of infrastructure projects, may make a difference to whether an oppressive government gains or remains in power. If the banks issue and apply a code of conduct for their operations in countries with oppressive regimes, investors may then be able to make a judgement on the social responsibility of such banks.

The rights of individuals also need to be upheld in such countries, if banks wish to avoid being seen in a negative light. A template for such codes is Amnesty's publication 'Human Rights Principles for Companies' published in January 1998. Encouragingly HypoVereinsBank and Anglo Irish Bank support the proposals 'in principle' but 'not formally', and Bank of Ireland, Erste Bank, Banco Central Hispanoamericano, Christiania and Banco Comercial Portugues also confirmed support for the document. BNP allows staff to host Amnesty activities on the Bank's premises on a voluntary basis, whilst Credit Suisse claimed they were 'not actually supporting Amnesty's principles, however, we have taken due notice of the document'.

Burma

Burma is treated as a special topic because, although while similar to China in being governed by an oppressive regime, the democratically elected leader is under house arrest and has called for international dis-investment.

In the US, the Federal Government issued a law banning new investment in Burma. In the state of Massachusetts, and many US cities including New York, Los Angeles and San Francisco, there are 'selective purchasing laws'. Such laws effectively create a boycott of companies that have business interests in Burma. Although there is no specific legislation in Europe that forbids companies from operations in Burma, the EU has revoked tariff privileges for Burmese imports due to Burma's forced labour record[9] There has certainly been sufficient publicity for companies and individuals to be aware of this issue.

BNP has a representative office in Burma, which has contact with local banks 'sporadically' for documentary credits. However, these credits can be used by the Burmese authorities to purchase products or services, which may help to prolong the oppressive regime. BNP stated that they have 'very limited business to date'. BNP prefers to 'consider our representative office as an observer in the hope of better days'. HSBC has a single staff representative office to internally monitor developments within the country. Deutsche Bank also has dealings with Burma, but failed to specify details. The other respondents stated that they have no operations in Burma.

c. Community involvement

Access to banking

The commercial banking sector has a key role and responsibility in overcoming the problems arising from social exclusion, as recently stated by the UK Government. Access to banking has become an indispensable necessity for people of all classes, in order to receive payments, to finance consumption and to provide for retirement.[11] The 'strategic economic position (of banks) coupled with their State charters and guaranteed deposit insurance renders them *quasi*-public institutions or at least positioned to be more socially responsible than ordinary private undertakings'.[12] Although in some EU states there is legislation to ensure access to banking for all individuals, the actual services offered by banks are often inappropriately priced for lower income sections of society. 'Less financially sophisticated and low-income consumers may be generally time-consuming for banks. The expense of time, coupled with the lack of opportunity to cross-sell other bank products to customers who do not have very much money illustrates the way banks actually seek to make money from their customers'.[13] In the present era of high competition and 'lean-banking', devoting resources to this area of business can be overlooked due to the overriding profit concerns.

The banks' products are often priced out of proportion to the service offered, for example the very high penalty charges of going overdrawn without prior permission from the bank. In France such action can actually lead to the exclusion of that individual from the right to hold a bank account and therefore become an '*interdit bancaire*', which can lead to further exclusion from the workforce because salaries are paid directly into bank accounts.

The majority of banks responding to the survey were aware of the issue of access to banking. However, only a few of the retail banks had formalised specific policies and products to address this issue. Of those, efforts were directed more towards supporting small and low-income businesses, rather than individuals. For example, banks such as Deutsche, Den Danske, Banco Popular Espanol and Banco Central Hispanoamericano stated that small and low-income businesses are part of their retail banking focus. A proactive stance is taken by Allied Irish banks which are working with the Irish Government to automate state Benefit payments through the electronic banking infrastructure. Whilst Anglo Irish Bank is not a retail bank, it has extensive relationships with the Credit Union movement, which often provide financial services to individuals otherwise excluded from using banks.

Social inclusion has specifically become a focus of attention for the major U.K. banks, who are all, to varying degrees, investigating or introducing services in the areas of community banking and micro-credit. Such projects have previously been addressed by the smaller banks in the non-listed sector, such as the pioneering

Triodos Bank. Triodos only lends to 'value-led projects' with social and environmental objectives and operates in The Netherlands, Belgium and the UK. It has a combined balance sheet of £250 million across the 3 countries. Although this figure is relatively small, Triodos Bank has a very low loss rate because they insist on being knowledgeable about their markets.[19]

Also in the UK, NatWest states that social exclusion is in the bank's top five priorities to address and has established a Social Exclusion Unit to explore how the bank can improve access to banking for disadvantaged individuals and communities. Meanwhile, LloydsTSB invested £9 million into community programmes in 1998 mainly to support regeneration in socially deprived areas and the bank is also supporting initiatives to provide community-based financial services to such areas.

In Germany, Commerzbank addresses, cultural and social issues through the 'Commerzbank Foundation', because 'the quality of a society can also be gauged by how it treats its disadvantaged members'. However it is evident, that throughout Europe, if banks are really to address the issue of access to banking then more attention is needed to develop appropriately priced services for lower income sections of society.

Charitable giving and community involvement programmes

In the United States, the Community Re-investment Act (CRA) ensures that financial institutions, whose annual turnover is above a certain level, re-invest into registered community programmes. 'CRA has been a key tool in the redevelopment of lower-income and minority communities since its passage in 1977. In recent years, the regulations which implement CRA have undergone substantial revisions, in part, so that the law would reward institutions based more on performance and outcomes (loans to lower-income communities, bank branch locations, etc.) rather than on promise and process (e.g., marketing, documenting contacts, etc.). CRA places an affirmative obligation on banks and thrifts to meet the credit needs of their community. Historically, CRA has been a critical tool in improving access to credit and promoting development in lower-income communities'.[15]

Such legislation does not yet exist in Europe and it is the prerogative of each bank how, or indeed if, they wish to address the issue of community re-investment and charitable giving.

Jyske Bank in Denmark considered that payment of the high level of Danish corporation tax was equivalent to community re-investment, where the government decides where the money is spent. Bankinter in Spain appears to hold a similar view. Banco Pastor concentrates all its operations in the area of Galicia, where the Bank was founded and a local charitable foundation, 'Foundation Barrie de la Maza', owns a 42% share of the Bank, due to the generosity and lack of heirs of the Bank's founder. Argentaria supports community initiatives through Fundacion Argentaria.

Certain banks did not wish to disclose where and how much was spent or donated to the community, and others stated that their programmes were either ad hoc or changed annually.

An example of best practice again seems to be the approach of Allied Irish Bank, which has a strong programme of charitable giving and community initiatives. Each year approximately 2% of pre-tax profits is allocated for community based initiatives. In 1997, £5 million was donated in Ireland and the UK through its 'Corporate Giving Programme', addressing issues ranging from poverty and business start-up support to youth, environmental and arts projects. Anglo Irish Bank also annually allocates a similar percentage of pre-tax profits.

In the U.K. in 1998, LloydsTSB donated £26.5 million, 1% of its pre-tax profits, Barclays – £19 million and NatWest – £15.9 million. Such donations are primarily focused on education, the arts and sport, as well as varying degrees of community support. Barclays highlighted that they offer secondment placing for staff, mainly in the charitable organisation or social banking sectors. Such advice and mentoring can be of immense value to the recipient organisations and individuals. A lack of knowledge of financial processes and management are often the biggest barriers to access financial services

Commerzbank, through its Foundation, is another leader in this sector, allocating 3% of pre-tax profits. The Foundation is primarily focused on improving both the living and working conditions of people in the vicinity of Commerzbank's Head Office, whilst also taking into account environmental considerations.

d. Business practices

This section in the survey referred to how the banks treat suspicious deposits and whether the banks invested into 'negative criteria' types of business. These issues provide information about the level of disclosure by the banks.

Disclosure

The rate of replies to the survey is an indication of how much further the banking sector has to go before it can be considered to be genuinely promoting transparency. Of the banks that did reply to the questionnaire the majority declined to provide any details of their interests in military suppliers, tobacco companies and the nuclear industry.

The European banks, which are based within the E.U., are obliged by directives to prevent money laundering (Money Laundering Directive 91/308). However, non-E.U. European banks are not obliged to comply, for example the Swiss banks. Switzerland has its own legislation and regulations.

The principle of the Swiss Banking Secrecy Law protects the financial privacy of clients to the degree that bank employees are criminally liable if such confidentiality is broken. Similar laws exist in Austria and Luxembourg. Approximately 99% of all Swiss banks are members of the Swiss Bankers Association and the sector is strongly self-regulated. It was such self-regulation in conjunction with the supervisory body that decided to allow details of pre-1945 dormant accounts to be made public recently. Federal regulation concerning all dormant accounts is currently being considered, and the banking sector is urging that the time lapse for release of details to the state authorities is 20 – 30 years. This comparatively long period, compared to the 5 years in the U.S., is due to the banks' wish to maintain a long relationship between the banks and clients and their families.[16]

Exceptions to the Swiss Secrecy Law do exist in other regulations, such as in the case where the client is under criminal investigation in Switzerland, or in case of bankruptcy. The Swiss banks are not obliged to report any suspicious deposits in accordance with the EU Money Laundering directive, because Switzerland is, of course, not a member of the EU. In Switzerland, since 1990, there have been regulations stating that deposits, which are suspected of being connected to money laundering activities, must be reported to the authorities. However, primarily due to the Secrecy Law, Swiss Bank accounts remain one of the preferred destinations for money transferred from dubious sources. Allegations of deposits, such as 'Marcos' Millions', continue to abound. The two Swiss banks responding to the survey, Credit Suisse and UBS, refused to disclose any details of the banks' investments or lending, stating that those details were 'proprietary business information'.

There was a poor reply rate from Italian and French banks, with only one reply from each country, Banca Fideuram and BNP respectively. The Spanish banks responded well. They appear in a favourable light due to their generally good levels of disclosure and the fact that most appear to be making some efforts to improve their environmental stance in a country that is not traditionally a leader in this field.

The results of the survey for the Danish banks were surprising for a country which is generally considered to be proactive in the area of environmental protection. Both BG Bank and Jyske Bank would only respond to the questionnaire over the telephone. Den Danske Bank did not return the questionnaire, but instead chose to send a standard reply letter. Although this might indicate a willingness to disclose and publicise Den Danske's positive environmental and social practices, they thereby avoided replying to some of the more difficult questions.

German DG Bank and Commerzbank did disclose that they have business interests in the listed negative industries. However, such openness can be seen as a positive aspect, especially as the former stated that the negative industries amount to only a minute portion of their loan portfolio and Commerzbank named to whom they make such loans. Such transparency may encourage investors that the bank is less likely to be hiding potentially damaging information.

The example set by The Co-operative Bank in the UK of providing an independently verified Social Report can be regarded as best practice within the sector. The Bank's 'Partnership Report' includes the views of seven interdependent stakeholder groups: shareholders, customers, staff and their families, suppliers, local communities, national and international society, past and future generations of co-operators. Such a balanced approach to reporting provides clear information as to the operations and attitudes of the bank, and gives the potential investor the confidence that there is less likelihood of any damaging information appearing in the future.

Disclosure case study: The role of European banks in their dealings with the Nazis

Although this subject was not part of the survey it is relevant, as a case study, to the issue of business practices and disclosure as a social issue that gives rise to financial liability.

It has taken more than half a century for dealings with the Nazis to be acknowledged by German, Swiss, Austrian and other European banks. The findings of Independent Committee of Eminent Persons (ICEP, or Volcker Committee), which will be published by the middle of 1999, and the results of the Bergier Commission, are likely to prompt further claims. The French banks, SocGen and Paribas, and the British Bank, Barclays, have also been in negotiations relating to settlement of claims against them relating to the banks' actions during the war.

The German banks

It has been revealed only very recently that both Deutsche and Dresdner banks bought gold from the Nazi-controlled ReichsBank, whilst being aware such gold was stolen from Jewish companies, homes and individuals. Dresdner Bank was known as the SS Bank, whilst Deutsche Bank helped to finance the construction of concentration camps. Such revelations appeared in the wake of the US class actions made against the Swiss banks. Deutsche Bank's planned merger with America Bankers Trust has also forced such issues into the open as the US regulators' probe Deutsche's past.

German companies originally stated that they are not liable to any claims because these were dealt with by the terms of settlements after the end of the war. However, Deutsche and Dresdner have now agreed, together with other German corporations, to contribute to an umbrella fund to make reparations.[19]

The Swiss Banks

Revelations appearing from this scandal certainly tarnish the image of the Swiss as a neutral entity during the War. The Swiss banks, acting in concert, were far more biased towards the Nazis and, indeed, assisted in the financing of the Nazi military effort.

In 1998, UBS and Credit Suisse reached agreement with lawyers and representatives of the class action plaintiffs and certain Jewish organisations to settle claims of Holocaust victims and survivors. The two Swiss banks agreed to pay a total of USD1.25 billion.

It was the need for US regulators' approval for the UBS merger with SBC that finally forced the Swiss banks to address the issue of dormant accounts. It was not from a moral desire to make amends for the banks' actions during the war, otherwise they could have acted much earlier, rather than waiting decades before releasing details of the dormant accounts. Nevertheless, the Swiss are now acting positively, with the establishment of the Holocaust Fund by the major Swiss banks, the Swiss National Bank and private Swiss enterprises.

The Austrian banks

Like others of their European counterparts, the Austrian banks have avoided addressing the issue of compensation to depositors, or their relatives, whose accounts were seized under the instruction of the Nazis. However, Bank Austria has been more forthcoming than PSK, the Post Office Savings Bank. PSK does not admit their active role during the period of Nazi 'occupation' and therefore does not acknowledge the claims for repayment.

Summary of case study

The process of settlement is likely to drag on for several years during which time yet more claimants will die. Without even considering the moral issues involved, due to their lack of previous disclosure, the banks have to deal now with these embarrassing and damaging claims. However, there is no likelihood that this episode will stimulate any change in the Swiss Banking Secrecy Laws. Improved disclosure will only be possible through action by the banks themselves. By highlighting the potential financial losses caused by their lack of disclosure, it is hoped the banks will learn from their mistakes and avoid such scandals in the future.

CONCLUSION

The publicly listed commercial banks are traditionally conservative. Although certain banks are taking steps to become more progressive in their attitudes towards sustainable development, examples of which are listed in the Best in Class and Progressive tables below. The sector as a whole is only slowly beginning to address the issues involved.

Best in Class (Table 1)

Company Name	Country	Strengths*	Concerns
Den Danske Bank, A/S	Denmark	1. 2. 3.	1) Limited disclosure: issued standard reply.
Commerzbank AG	Germany	1. 2. 3. 5. 7. 8.	1) Loans/Invests in military and nuclear (balanced by disclosing details).
DG Bank	Germany	1. 3. 7. 8.	1) Loans/Invests in military and nuclear (balanced by disclosing details).
HypoVereinsBank	Germany	1. 5. 6. 7. 8.	
Allied Irish Bank	Ireland	1. 3. 5. 7. 8. 9.	
Argentaria	Spain	1. 2. 3. 5. 6.	1) 3rd world debt.
Banco Central Hispanoamericano	Spain	1. 2. 3. 4. 7. 6.	1) Unknown effect on BCH's proactive stance by merger with Santander.
Banco Bilbao Vizcaya	Spain	4. 5. 7. 9.	
Bankinter SA	Spain	2. 8.	1) Environment. 2) <5% of loan book in military, nuclear or tobacco.
Banco Pastor SA	Spain	4. 5. 8.	1) Environment.
LloydsTSB	UK	1. 2. 3. 5. 6. 7. 9.	1) No loans declined on environmental grounds.
National Westminster	UK	1. 3. 5. 7. 8.	
Royal Bank of Scotland	UK	1. 2. 3. 4. 5. 6. 7. 8.	

Progressive Banks (Table 2)

Company Name	Country	Strengths*	Concerns
Erste Bank der oesterreichischen Sparkassen AG	Austria	4. 5. 8.	1) No environmental audits. 2) 3rd World debt and no debt burden initiatives
Banque Nationale de Paris	France	2. 3. 5. 8.	1) Burma office. 2) Lack of external environmental consideration.
Dexia (Credit Local de France)	France	7.	1) No reply.
Bank of Ireland Group	Ireland	1. 3. 5.	1) Investments/loans in tobacco. 2) Minimal reply
ABN Amro Holdings	Netherlands	7. 2.	1) Lack of disclosure. 2) Loans to finance controversial mining projects.
Christiana Bank	Norway	1. 3. 7.	1) Loans to finance mining and oil extraction (reflects Norwegian economy).
BCP Banco Comercial Portugues	Portugal	5. 7. 8.	1) Invests/lends to tobacco industry.
Credit Suisse	Switzerland	1. 2. 5. 7.	1) Lack of disclosure of business investments.
UBS (merged with Swiss Bank Corporation)	Switzerland	3. 7.	1) Lack of disclosure of business interests. 2) Funding of Ilisu Dam project.
Barclays	UK	1. 3. 5. 7.	1) Slow to develop env policy, compared to country sector. 2) Lack of social exclusion measures.

*Key to 'Strengths', which were categorised on the following basis for simplicity:
1. Responsible lending
2. Workplace practices
3. Good housekeeping
4. Ethical business policy
5. Community initiatives
6. Overseas operations workplace practices
7. Environmental stance
8. Disclosure
9. Responsible financing of trade to developing countries and/or debt relief.

From the results of the survey, the prime areas of concern are the banks' attitude towards transparency and accountability and their lending policies. Transparency at every level is necessary to instil stakeholder confidence. European banks generally remain particularly conservative in their attitude towards transparency, but accountability and liability will ultimately decide how they progress in the future.

The majority of the banks wish to avoid the role of moral arbiter and do not consider themselves as regulators. Banks hold a 'quasi-public' role in society, but generally seem unwilling to accept that fact and adopt the linked responsibility. Too many banks still consider that what they provide is merely a retail product, with responsibility ending at point of sale. But financial services empower the banks' customers and therefore control how companies operate. A change of attitude by the banks has been shown over the last few years, reflected by the increase of environmental reporting within the sector. The banks now have the opportunity to anticipate further change and take a progressive stance.

Although many banks are taking steps to improve their own operational ecology, the development of product ecology – the incorporation of environmental aspects into the banks' product and services – is made primarily on the basis of their own risk reduction. In order to promote best practice, the banks need to start measuring their customers' environmental performance. Until this occurs on a widespread basis, the majority will do nothing more than adopt minimum compliance to existing regulations.

However, if small banks, like those in the co-operative, mutual and social sectors are able to impose environmental and ethical conditions in their loan portfolio and, not only survive, but also make a profit, then surely the bigger commercial banks can be more proactive in this area.

As communication concerning the issue of sustainable development improves, governments, companies and individuals increase the attention they pay towards this matter. Companies, by necessity, are becoming more accountable to a broader range of stakeholders.

We commend all respondents for their disclosure, and encourage commitments to regular social and environmental reporting, which necessarily indicate social responsibility. Europe can learn by the experiences of U.S. steps to address social exclusion. This may require statutory legislation, but is possible through self-regulation.

The Jubilee 2000 Coalition has proposed a variety of possible methods to overcome the developing world's debt burden and avoid repetition of previous lending mistakes. It provides the banks with the chance to be rid of an embarrassment that continues to be a nuisance, at least in terms of public relations. Proactive support of such proposals, or constructive dialogue to create universally acceptable measures, will be required make use of this opportunity.

The model bank of best practices

Drawing on best practice in the sector, combined with proposals for improvements, a model bank has been described below. Such a bank would include within their operations the following:

- Application of the guidelines of the UNEP Statement, as practised by HypoVereinsBank.
- Accountability can be achieved through independently verified Social Reporting on a regular basis, along the lines of the Co-operative Bank in the UK. Such reporting requires communication to all stakeholder groups and transparency of all actions. As a step towards that goal, banks can encourage and support customers to conduct better environmental practices and regular environmental reporting. BCH in Spain supported such practices by sponsoring seminars and conferences. Larger companies could implement independently verified Environmental Management System (EMS), to ensure that resource usage is monitored and efficiency savings can be targeted.
- Supporting such initiatives as the European Investment Fund, as done by BCP in Portugal, to provide SMEs which are providing environmentally beneficial products or services with favourable lending terms.
- Environmental screening of customers' operations, that includes measuring of customers' environmental performance. The latter part is an area that banks are generally avoiding, claiming that they should not act as the environmental policemen. However, unless performance is measured, companies will tend to operate only to minimum compliance.
- Supporting Community Finance Initiatives. These tend to require adaptation to local requirements, as well as innovative lending and knowledge of the market and borrowers, as practised by Triodos Bank. Support may also include premise use, staff secondment, knowledge transfer, training and mentoring, which is currently conducted by a number of the surveyed banks.
- Implementing fully transparent overseas lending policies, which use lessons

from previous debt crises to reduce risk to the Bank and the debtors. Transparency, as recommended by Jubilee 2000 coalition and similar organisations, is a fundamental criterion to ensure that sustainable lending terms may be agreed by all stakeholders.

- Publishing an ethical policy that clearly states any areas to which the banks would refuse to lend, and also highlights the standards by which customers and suppliers would be required to operate, along the lines of the ethical policy of the Co-operative Bank in the UK.

- Adapting social inclusion policies to improve access to banking services for those sections of society that are being increasingly excluded. This would include for example providing simple, easy-to-use accounts, access to branches or at least ATMs which also accept deposits placed in convenient locations.

- Best practice in the workplace including an equal opportunities policy, comprehensive training programmes, thorough maternity and paternity benefits.

Such features in a bank do not preclude making a profit, as has been proven by those companies incorporating some of the above practices. In addition to providing a financial return, such a bank would provide social and environmental benefits. Self-regulation of the European Banking sector, or E.U. regulation, may be required to create minimum standards for banks to apply. Alternatively an extension of the UNEP Initiative guidelines could provide global standards, incorporating the above benchmarks. Banks have always been keen to consider their position as a cornerstone to society. By adopting the above measures and a proactive attitude towards sustainable development, the banks can maintain such a position in our society of rapidly evolving expectations.

ENDNOTES

1   Peter Bosshard, Bern Declaration.
2   GAP is the Turkish acronym for South-East Anatolia Project – the vast program of dams built on the Euphrates and Tigris.
3   *Taking stock of debt*, Eurodad publication.
4   Ibid.
5   Philipp Hersel 'The London Debt Agreement of 1953 on German External Debt: Lessons for the HIPC-Initiative' in EURODAD (1998) 'Taking Stock of Debt'.
6   K. Raffer, Introductory Statement, Panel Discussion, London 18 March 1999.
7   Kunibert Raffer 'The Necessity of International Chapter 9 Insolvency Procedures' in EURODAD (1998) 'Taking Stock of Debt'.
8   Ann Pettifor, Director, Jubilee 2000 Coalition UK, 'Concordats for debt cancellation'. 18 March 1999.
9   As above.
10   Simon Billenness, Franklin Research & Development, 711 Atlantic Avenue, Boston MA 02111, USA.
11   *A European Regulation for Social Responsibility of banks? Learning the lessons from the US*

American Community Reinvestment Act. Jan Evers.

12   *The Social Responsibility of Credit Institutions in the EU*, Institut Für Finanzdienstleistungen e.V. (IFF), Hamburg, Benoit Granger, Malcolm Lynch, Leo Haidar, Udo Reifner and Jan Evers.

13   *The Social Responsibility of Credit Institutions in the EU*, Institut Für Finanzdienstleistungen e.V. (IFF), Hamburg, Benoit Granger, Malcolm Lynch, Leo Haidar, Udo Reifner and Jan Evers.

14   *Small is Bankable: Community reinvestment in the UK*, Ed Mayo, Thomas Fisher, Pat Conaty, John Doling and Andy Mullineux, November 1998.

15   *The Community Reinvestment Act and Community Development Financial Institutions. Qualified Investments, Community Development Lending, and Lessons from the New CRA Performance Evaluations*, Daniel Immergluck, Woodstock Institute, September, 1998

16   Swiss Bankers Association, Silvia Matile.

17   *International Monitor* March 1999, produced by the office of New York City Comptroller Alan G. Hevesi. www.financenet.gov/nycnet.htm

Competitiveness and creation of social added value in the private banks

Patrick Ochs (HEC Montreal, Ochs Conseil, G.R.I.S.E.)

Introduction

A new spirit of co-operation is developing between public authorities, institutions, non-governmental organisations and private sector businesses with the aim of promoting the economic and social reintegration of disadvantaged groups. The fact is that large-scale aid and assistance programmes are no longer sufficient in the fight against poverty and social exclusion. The current national and international context provides a favourable moment for the development of other approaches to banking proposals, and for the development of concrete actions to address exclusion and poverty. The social responsibility of private banks lies at the heart of these debates. Can we consider that these private players will commit their resources in a market which, according to the forecasts of UNCTAD, will involve 500 million people world wide by 2005?

In the developing countries, private operators and the public institutions are working together in partnerships which result in investment and credit opportunities, the effects of which are particularly significant, as much on a social level as on an economic one.

In the industrialised countries, the social, economic and cultural challenges of the third millennium raise fundamental issues about how today's society will evolve. Certain inevitable transformations will result in the emergence of other, new poverty, new excluded groups, for whom few formal answers can be found in the private sector.

Is it possible to call into question, once again, the traditional view on transaction costs and to create in the private banking sector a new social added value? A vision clear enough to be considered strategic?

The answers are not clear, since it is, a priori, a matter for these organisations to reconsider the conditions for growth and the allocation of resources in a highly competitive banking environment. Several investigations, interviews with experts and comments from private banks[1] allow at present however to formulate the following hypothesis: *the creation of social added value can create new conditions for growth.*

This article has a two-part structure illustrated by examples. First it will consider the definition of social added value and try to offer a better under-standing of its contribution to the development of private banks. The second part will deal with the bringing together of the necessary skills for competitiveness and the creation of social added value.

1. The creation of social added value

1.1 A seedbed for initiatives

The curbing of quantitative controls in matters of exchange and credit, the opening-up of borders and the international agreements on free trade shed light on inadequate systems of control and de facto, different levels of risk. These new challenges are important because it is unquestionable that there is banking over-capacity in the world. Most banking organisations are wondering about the rapid changes in their sector, on the profound developments and the newly emerging markets.

At present several countries[2] are recognised as seedbeds for initiatives for groups which are incapable of providing for their own needs. In fact it is possible for these individuals excluded from the social system to regain their autonomy thanks to the tripartite intervention of political authorities, private and public banks,[3] and the informal sector. These initiatives can be defined as *accessible finan-cial engineering which promotes the social reintegration of people who have partially or totally lost their economic autonomy.*

It is a question of *financial engineering* because the methods of operation are conditioned by the climate in which these services can get underway and evolve. Other management balances are necessary for re-thinking proposals, added value and management tools which promote the reintegration of excluded groups in a social and economic system.

The services offered are *accessible*. More precisely the means of access to credit or investment are not tied into the traditional framework of financial distribution: proximity networks are indispensable.

Social reintegration is required by the fact that the forms of aid and assistance in a good number of countries no longer meet the needs of excluded people. They must have at their disposal complementary means to recover their financial autonomy by their own efforts. For these groups it is a question of achieving rein-tegration by action and not by assistance.

The groups concerned are *those who have partially or totally lost their financial autonomy*. At the end of an initial period of assistance for these individuals they must find solutions to recreate their own conditions for reintegration and indi-vidual financial autonomy. Established in Bolivia, one of the poorest countries in Latin America, the BANCOSOL bank, created in 1992, is developing programmes aimed at micro enterprises. According to Michael CHU, Chairman and Managing Director of BANCOSOL this bank... 'is today the largest bank in the world specialising in services for micro enterprises and at the same time the bank showing the highest profits despite an average loan size of $828'. Today BANCOSOL reports a rate of risk of less than 1%, that is to say that 99% of credit repayments are assured by the micro enterprises.

1.2 The creative forces of the future

In the industrialised countries the initiatives are not strictly identical. They exist, but rarely explicitly. Certain banks and financial organisations are engaged in both thinking and activity directed at these markets which up till now did not seem to interest them.

Today in Europe plenty of examples show[4] that sponsors, banks and financial companies are attempting to do something by offering credit or investment opportunities to poor or excluded groups. Current research on microfinance, exclusion, poverty and the loss of financial autonomy reinforces the idea that these groups, excluded from the social system, do not have access to traditional means of credit or investment. The responses from social institutions, charities or non-governmental organisations correspond to a need for assistance. Significant experiments[5] of *reintegration by interdependent action* confirm the hypothesis that these individuals without income are capable of generating new wealth themselves, if alternatives[6] to the traditional forms of credit and investment were made available to them. This situation deserves further consideration. Is it possible to combine financial systems with job creation? How can financial operators be mobilised in the fight against social exclusion? Are private banks called to enter into a new social contract which is only one of the responses to the limitations of global competitiveness? Certain bankers are actually asking whether it is possible to offer financial resources to socially excluded groups and thus to create a new dynamic in the creation of wealth. For them it involves offering rehabilitation and a proactive role to those who are in a situation of dependence. Essentially, it is a question of helping these groups to move from a situation in which they are victims paralysed by a feeling of fault, to one in which they become the *creative forces of the future*. This dynamic is both social and economic. It fits into a tripartite process in which political institutions, private operators and non-governmental organisations simultaneously play a part. In this process the current initiatives of the private operators seem to confirm the idea that these pioneer bankers in Europe are trying to create *accessible services, which are value creating, by the micro financing of productive activities for social and economic self-integration.*

- *To make available* to groups from disadvantaged areas loan terms more preferential than those on similar sized loan normally granted elsewhere
- *Value creating services*, because in the last analysis what is important to the bank is to break into a new market, but at the same time to reassure and maintain the loyalty of its current customers in the light of these societal activities

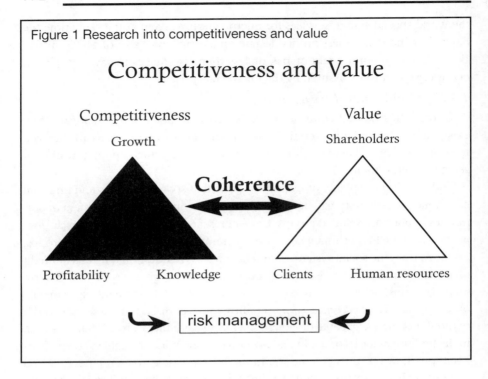

Figure 1 Research into competitiveness and value

Competitiveness and Value

Competitiveness

Value

- *The micro financing of productive activities* corresponds to credit and investment services for the poor and those excluded from traditional banking systems, with the aim of allowing them to create their own conditions for the creation of individual wealth.
- *Social and economic self-integration* which corresponds to the capacity of each self interest agent to build its own future using finance instruments, skills networks and an attendant technical and moral framework.

Of course there are important constraints for certain private banks. Several experts from private banks are discussing the same subject 'how is it possible to maintain an optimum level of net banking product when the time spent processing a micro credit of 5,000FF is usually more than that spent processing the documentation for 500,000FF...'. The current procedures of some of these private banks seem to have a strategic character.[7] This leads these players to go down a route which in the end allows them to create at one and the same time competitiveness and another form of added value (see Figure 1). This creation of social added value could be defined in the following way. *Social added value results from the combination of intangible investments which create value for the shareholders, the employees and the bank's customers.*

For the shareholders the creation of value will have a financial significance,[8] for the employees it will reflect a social cohesion and for the bank's customers it will signify the societal character of the bank. These groups, which up till then had not been included in the market research undertaken by these institutions, seem to offer new growth prospects at a time of strong competition amongst banks. In fact, in the industrial countries, *enlightened self interests* seem to represent a potential market.

2. Another combination of skills

2.1 Invisible assets

Social upheaval and economic turbulence register in the different global money markets. For all the banks the imperatives seem to be the same: an exceptional level of competitiveness in transaction costs and effective risk management. But awareness and knowledge of these socially excluded groups is not built into the financial institutions, despite the potential these markets can represent. What is more, other combinations of resources seem therefore to be necessary to create different conditions for development in a highly competitive banking environment.

In the case of private banks the strategies based on past thinking are giving way to emerging ideas. For the bankers of this new global village the knowledge combinations are different because they allow the creation of real intangible capital. Clearly these organisations are on a learning curve (see Figure 2).

For some, this change of course is a sign for others. It also flags up important risks for others less well-prepared for the integration of new undeniable knowledge to create specific services intended for the 'left-outs of competition'. In 1987, Hiroyuki Itami wrote in one of his articles that through an effective accumulation of invisible assets such as expertise combined with the loyalty of customers an

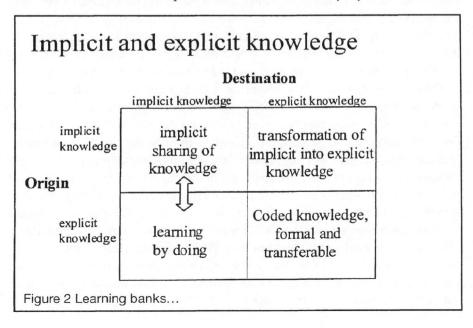

Figure 2 Learning banks...

enterprise could reach a dynamic strategic agreement.[9] These invisible assets which result from a coherent combination of intangible investments probably represent significant beginnings and commitments for generating new sources for the creation of added value.

The Triodos Bank established in Holland, Belgium and the UK took a conscious decision to draw up new banking practices. This bank stated clearly in its objectives its willingness to work together with and to finance projects and businesses whose activities incorporated social, cultural or environmental concerns. During an interview one of its chief directors confirmed that ' this factor of social added value was even recognised in other financial institutions'. This voluntaristic step is a strong argument for a structure endowed with specific knowledge capable of meeting the needs of intangible investment finance. There is no alternative but to think that within the framework of its development this bank has endowed itself with added skills which allow it while it is learning to lay claim to a particular area and as a result acquire a real competitive advantage.

This added knowledge allows response to unusual requests but it also has a positive effect on the more traditional customers according to Frans de Clerck, one of the directors of the Triodos bank. 'Some of our customers, aware of the efforts we are making for projects of this type, forego part of their interest rates'.

Clearly the stakes for the next decade for these global financial operators lie in a subtle combination of different skills in order to achieve a social added value banking position in one of these activities or for the whole organisation. Although the banks observed are capable a priori of generating proposals and overcoming the risks, they all seem to confirm that it will be necessary to rethink the structure of management and the style of their relationships. Private sector operators and organisations who subscribe to this train of thought are emerging. Today the private banks seem to endorse a philosophy of the implicit sharing of knowledge. Some of them humbly admit to learning as they go along. (Figure 2).

On the other hand, they try to contribute to the fight against exclusion while conforming to the balances of management. Several experts agree that 'The attempts at the measurement of profitability have not been satisfactory...'. The only evaluation indicators currently emerging from banks concern volumetric measures pertaining to specific microfinance portfolios, measures of the positive effects on regular customers and global profit including these new activities. On the other hand this direction must not obscure the financial profitability research into the private players in microfinance. Although the relationship with groups excluded from economic systems is different, it is no less true that the transaction costs cannot be analysed in the same way. 'The initiatives are rare but the port-folios are profitable....'. On close inspection, it becomes clear that the values conveyed by the bankers who go down this route are always shared by the human capital which makes up their structures.

In these banks staff participation is strong and the initiatives enriching on an individual and collective basis. Thus M. Coudray, President of the Credit Mutuel Bank of Brittany confirmed that '…collaboration cannot be avoided at an operational level, which implies commitment from everyone, … but in a situation of this nature the administrators also recognise their original values… This is certainly a strategic angle which differentiates it from the classical banking system'.

In France, the history of the Savings Banks, and in Quebec the Desjardins Movement indicate that fundamental values can at the same time become essential reference points for staff and customers. For these banks, to be capable of developing a strategic positioning means accepting that they must endorse values shared by the entire staff.

2.2 Intangible capital

It is difficult to forget history, the driving forces behind the values and direction, which have brought the co-operative banking movement to life. Yet in this permanently changing environment, the bulimia of acquisitions and the anorexia of structures seems to have the effect of modifying the competitors' game plan. The most powerful bankers find themselves together and very often with the same strategy at the crossroads of the most profitable markets. That *all* should compete against *all* is the imperative to which *all* the operators in the world of finance subscribe. Certain banks break with the classic organisation of the private competitors but they are probably consistent with the vectors of today and tomorrow (Figure 3). This form of social citizenship, this integration of all groups in the process of acquisition and redistribution of wealth seems to represent one of the axes of restructuring within the co-operative movement. These concepts in the fight against exclusion, against poverty, are accumulating, to the point at which they represent a real intangible capital composed of dominant social values.

Thus the Desjardins Co-operative Movement established in Quebec seems to start out by combining skills in local banks situated in geographical zones which contain the largest proportion of disadvantaged groups. According to Bruno Montour, vice president of development at the Desjardins Confederation: 'In 1996 in the context of increasing poverty (more than 1,000,000 victims of social exclusion in Quebec) the Desjardins movement, concerned about these social changes, engaged in a process to satisfy new need not covered by the traditional area dealing with market financial services…. Today more than 300 local banks out of 1200 are taking part, that is to say more than 10,000 people in the whole network…'. The roots in the fabric of the locality and the presence of local leaders in the boards as well as the strong competitive impetus are inducing the confederation, the federations and certain local banks to commit themselves to the

Generating intangible knowledge capital

1. growth

2. profitability

3. knowledge.

Figure 3 Research into consistency of direction

development of microfinance. This approach is left to the local banks which encourage the movement to evolve whilst they move forward their initiatives. The latter can be modified by strategies, because they are instigated by operational staff but are spread across the totality of the structure.

Conclusion

Looking towards the next century confirms the idea that private and institutional investments are going to have to reckon with the socially responsible economy. Therefore responses to the market will be different: the customers of private banks who in the past did not mix with one another are, in the future going to represent collective funds which are interdependent. Clearly the cohesion between the bank and its customers will experience the birth of social values which will survive future economic crises. Customer capital will always find the direction of new market and human capital will always seek to blossom.

The implementation of this microfinance process in the private banks is a strong argument for redefining the relationships and joint actions of the public and private sectors which then would promote a local base, direct public accessibility and adapted financial intervention.

Financial intervention is developed as a function of the specific characteristics of groups and their respective economic performance. Experience proves that this type of intervention works better if the instruments of management are well adapted. It is probably a question of reinventing everything: from the relationship with customers to the structure of management.

Direct public accessibility seems unavoidable given the current drawbacks facing traditional banking organisations. Basically, proximity and ease of access to the public sector and the forms of private sector micro finance probably represent unavoidable criteria in order to reach groups who are excluded from the everyday forms of relationship.

A local base seems necessary or even indispensable. National and international experience proves that relationships are established when players are playing the same game and a real local meshing takes place.

NOTES

1   This research has been undertaken to try to understand better whether private sector players, like the banks, can through micro finance proposals contribute to the social and economic reintegration of the poor and the excluded. The methodology used is exploratory in view of the innovative nature of this qualitative study. A first stage was devoted to bibliographical research. A second stage consisted of conducting interviews, based on an in-depth semi-managerial interview guide, with fifteen French and foreign experts directly concerned with the analyses and the current happenings in micro finance in the field of banking.

2   For example Bolivia, Peru, Bangladesh.

3   In 1980 Mohammad Yunus started a trend in Bangladesh with the creation of the Bank for the poor. This model was then copied by other banks, such as Bancosol in Bolivia.

4   This statement results from in-depth semi-managerial interviews conducted by the author with the directors of private banks, co-operative banks and financial organisations established in Europe, for example Bance Etica in Italy, Triodos Bank in Holland and Belgium, the Brittany Credit Mutuel Bank in France...

5   For example in France with the ADIE network

6   In 1989 some of those involved in associated trends took an interest in the problem, namely Patrick Boulte, Jean Baptiste de Foucauld and Maurice Pagat, who created the European Business Network for Social Cohesion (EBNSC).

7   This statement results from in-depth semi-managerial interviews conducted by the author with the directors of private banks, co-operative banks and financial organisations established in Europe and North America.

8   Like the goodwill which results from the valuation of the intangible assets of the bank.

9   Itami, H and Roehl T.W. *Mobilising Invisible Assets*, Cambridge, MA, Harvard University Press, 1987.

Social banking: products for community development

Udo Reifner
(Institute for Financial Services, Hamburg, Germany)

Social banking

What is social banking?

Social banking is a socially responsible form of banking in which suppliers of financial services have a vested interest in the social outcome and effects of the distribution of their products.

It is therefore, on the one hand a form of private banking in a competitive environment, necessitating profit orientation and cost cutting as major goals of its economic activity. On the other hand it implies a reference to social standards. These can be introduced either by:

*   internal moral standards of social responsibility from the corporate identity and market image of the bank, or:
*   through legal obligations for community reinvestment and equal treatment of citizens, or:
*   merely by the pressure of institutional investors and other customers who are willing to act as agents for public goals.

In its basic form, social banking requires only that bankers become conscious about their business. Marketing, control, as well as the reporting systems can become tools of social research and data collection that can detect developments that leading towards social discrimination.

In its more advanced form it requires experienced, knowledgeable and especially creative bankers that develop new products and procedures for the distribution and administration of financial services which promise better social effects for users and society, without creating losses and disadvantages for the general business of its provider.

Who is in charge?

The challenge of this marriage between the two traditionally contradictory principles of profit and social responsibility is a tempting one. Bankers and the social sector seem to be in contradiction. The traditional education of bankers furthers a formal attitude towards profit maximisation through training which excludes social and political issues from the business of money. On the other hand, a money averse attitude is the typical tradition of socially minded people who care for and work against social exclusion and poverty.

Social banking is a challenge to both. It is already present if two investments promise the same return and the bank chooses the one that has more social benefits. Thus social issues are rendered crucial for the execution of the marginal choice. If then a bank eager to achieve a greater social success with their products uses the special experience, products and methods it has designed for banking in poor areas, with people who have generally less chances of access to banking services, in order to bring such investments to the profit level of competing investments, social banking becomes a part not only of the decision and evaluation process but of the process design itself.

The main difference between ordinary and social banking lies in the perception and knowledge of its social outcome. Recognising the social effects in ordinary banking business is the indispensable beginning and promising start for a new attitude in economics. As the money system is just the heart of market economy and its tool for distribution, social influence in this area may change the whole attitude in market economics.

Social banking is therefore part of general mainstream banking exercised with a social attitude and moral commitment. It addresses firstly the traditional banking community and tries to provide them with ideas, creativity and new products. It will create bankers who are willing to contribute to a better world incorporating the economic goals of a market society in which 'future wealth' (James Robertson) is seen as dependent of the 'outcome of the lowest class' (Rawls) and where the 'moral dimensions' (Etzioni) of market mechanism will be taken more consciously into account in order to introduce 'need orientation' (Armatya Sen) into the exchange of commodities and services to further the general welfare.

Social banking has therefore two procedural qualities:

- a bank product or service adapted to a situation where financial services are required but not normally available, because of a lack of economic opportunity for conventional financial institutions such as banks and insurance companies.
- an institutionalised evaluation mechanism of (1) the real financial needs of communities or disadvantaged groups of people, (2) the economic potential for social banking products as well as (3) the effects of existing banking products.

While the first element is a task that can only be fulfilled by banks using their skills and experience, the second task cannot only be taken on by marketing departments of banks, but also by public authorities, community groups and social research organisations.

What hinders social banking?

Research and analysis describing the tendency of banks in competitive markets to discriminate against poorer people are legion. David Caplovitz's research, on how the 'Poor pay more'[1] analysing the use of financial services in a New York low income area is already a classic in consumer credit research. The research on 'red-lining'[2] which preceded the American Home Mortgage Disclosure Act and later on the Community Reinvestment Act[3] has shown another facet of the same theme in mortgage loans: the denial of access to financial services. The lack of access to a necessary bank account for poor people ('life-line account') has led to regulations in many European states.[4] German and English studies have shown that over-indebted people have usually been forced to pay higher prices and especially higher fees.[5] The same has been revealed for small businesses who were either denied access to financial services, or supplied with badly advised, risky, un-adapted and costly financial services.[6] This phenomenon has raised concern with nearly all governments who would like a more active role of the banks to further job creation in this sector of the economy.

The focus of banking has also shifted away from low income customers through a new concept of 'client orientation'. The word 'private banking' in contrast to 'retail banking' describes a modern tendency to concentrate on wealthier clients and either exclude even average consumers and small businesses or offer them stan-dardised mass products that are handled through electronic banking facilities with little advice under quite rigid conditions. In the USA where nearly all discrimina-tion is linked to race and consequently to the geographical location where ethnic minorities live together, banking discrimination manifests itself in a discrimination against certain areas and communities. In Europe as well as for example Canada, where the state plays an active role to keep city districts mixed by public invest-ment, rent control or 'bussing,' discrimination is less open because it is aimed at groups that are identified individually through direct targeting methods.

Poor clients create less banking opportunities for cross selling, use smaller amounts of each product which increases the relative weight of fixed cost. They carry a higher risk and need more time from the banking staff to handle their affairs.

The strategy to cope with these deficits is a system that finally leads to exclusion:
- First poorer clients are charged higher prices. However, this method is not only limited by usury legislation but also difficult to communicate on the market where people who perceive themselves as 'good clients' may find it difficult to understand why they are being charged where others are not.
- A second step is the acquisition and administration of financial services for poorer clients by outsourcing to brokers at the clients' expense. This leads to a hidden rise in prices. Again, this has been limited by European legislation which in consumer credit regulations forces banks to include such fees into

their price disclosure.

- As the price mechanism (charging poorer clients more for the same service) seems difficult to use, banks consequently slim-line their services through extreme standardisation and computerisation. Poorer clients are offered standardised short term products that do not provide advice, flexibility and risk management for them.
- Banks may also force poorer clients to carry their own risk collectively through additional insurance products in credit contracts or selling them risk investments (such as endowment policies) which punish early withdrawal.
- Finally, banks can completely stop serving groups of clients where they know that allocating the actual cost of the service directly to those from whom the costs originate will cause a negative public response for such obvious discrimination. Exclusion seems to be more acceptable than servicing such groups at higher prices or with a lower service quality.

Bankers may argue that they have simply specialised in private banking leaving the other business (which they may call 'social banking') to whom it may concern. Involuntarily such tendencies in mainstream banking may be made politically and morally more acceptable by its main critiques in the alternative and social sector. They also claim that social banking is something special requiring specialised services and specialised suppliers. With this quest, they create the idea of a new banking sector for 'public banking' which requires state subsidies (despite the abdication of state banks in modern societies). Ideologies which claim that capitalism and its core agents the banks are the born enemies of the poor underline this separation. They may claim that social banking has to be done by socially minded people which have to stem from the social business side. Sometimes people unskilled in banking start to provide financial services to the poor using subsidies and non-profit support to make their businesses at least seem viable. Although their overall economic effect is minimal some of them claim that their business represent the future of banking.

Traditional banks may see this as a good opportunity to excuse themselves firstly because they can refer to such institutions when they are confronted with the need for more social banking and secondly they can show by the sometimes unprofessionally high losses of these institutions that social banking is simply impossible in the realm of private banking.

A coalition between socially minded 'social welfare bankers' and hard core profit margin seekers in Wall Street is not necessarily negative in its effect. Alternative banks can develop the traditional banking skills by learning or hiring the respective staff and adding new skills and ideas to the banking business. They can then serve as 'laboratories of democracy' as David Osborne[7] called the South Shore Bank's example in Chicago. On the other hand banks like, for example, Citibank or finance companies in the USA driven by the profit mechanism may find methodologies that enable them to serve even low income communities at a reasonable profit rates, not by returning to forced exploitation, but also by new and less costly products.

To ascertain whether the label 'social banking' is being used as a business goal or as an excuse for not doing anything needs a thorough evaluation of the banking business itself. Neither the actors, nor the sponsors, nor their ideology or belief qualify any kind of financial services as 'social' but only the products and services and their effects on clients. That is why social banking activities should concentrate more on this aspect of banking.

Social banking products

A banking product is a service that makes money available at a time and in a form the customers needs for his or her special purposes. Such 'financial services' comprise credit, investment, payment services and insurance products.

Money as a means and not an end in itself

In the money profession making money is an end in itself. Consumption, housing, education, working on one's own premises or creating opportunities for living and working are therefore secondary goals which fall into the clients private sphere.

This is different from social banking products where the money business is a service of allocation to pursue social goals. It is not profit as such which drives the business but profit only as a means to measure effectiveness, success and ability to continue and to grow for the purpose underlying the transaction. But the means is as important as the end. The old equation of the bible, that a person can either be good or rich and where poverty was seen as a gateway to the true virtues of life, strongly related to pre-monetary agrarian societies and does not have the same applicability today. Money and its derivatives: profit and interest – are neither good nor bad; only the 'good' things should create profit and steer the direction of investment.

Areas for social banking

As it has been sufficiently argued in welfare economics, money and its forms of valuation of the wealth of nations through GNP and balance sheet figures cast a veil over the true differences in value of goods and services. While the GNP may rise and the Pareto optimum may be achieved when people in the upper classes of society exercise more demand for luxury goods, the rise of sales figures for Mercedes and Porsche do not exactly match with what welfare economists have in mind when they measure the real progress of a society.

A needs orientation in economics reveals that there are some goods and services that are more necessary than others.[8] The pyramid of needs sets basic needs of eating, housing and education above less important needs (although much more demand may be exercised for luxury goods due to the uneven distribution of assets). If it is true, what Rawls and Sen have argued, that the prosperity of a society in the long run depends on the outcome of its lowest classes, just like a chain gets its strength from its weakest member, then social banking products are not indifferent to this target.

The first rule then, is that credit is more likely to form a social banking product than savings. As those people who have problems coping with the basic necessities of life lack sufficient capital, the use of capital in the form of bank credit is more likely to be used in social banking than asset management would be. This does not exclude savings. Savings that are necessary for retirement or to regain creditworthiness may have a direct effect on the ability of people to participate in the economic life of society. On the other hand, much of what has been labelled 'social investment' especially in ecology funds, is only the provision of a useful resource for social banking but not yet social banking in itself. Social investors often claim that they have enough money for financing but not enough opportunities to invest them. Therefore the credit and investment side remains the core of social banking.

The basic necessities of life are: basic consumption, housing, (labour) income and communication. For the satisfaction of these basic needs, banking products have become a major factor. The needs pyramid therefore also implies a pyramid in financial service products where a bank account is the entrance to the system and credit is its most important output for meeting basic needs.

(1) **Consumer credit** gives access to transportation, especially through making it possible to buy a car. It is also the key for the purchase of household appliances and furniture that are necessary as the backbone of living standards and a foundation for a family's economic outcome. Finally, consumer credit mobilises future income and helps to overcome the liquidity problems in human life cycles.

(2) **Mortgage loans** are the precondition for access to housing in those countries like the US, the UK, Ireland and France where individual home ownership provides the core of housing facilities. In other countries like Germany with its enormous market of rented homes protected and heavily subsidised by the state the need for housing finance for all citizens is less obvious. But also the traditional tenants societies start to value the merits of individual home ownership not only for housing but for other purposes. Individual home ownership offers an opportunity for unemployed people to invest their labour productively by improving their own houses, it educates the residents in administering assets and in participating in economic life with decisions and responsibilities in their own hands. Individual home ownership also provides opportunities for small businesses and craftsmen in the neighbourhood. Access to housing finance through social banking products designed for people that have been traditionally looked upon as typical dependant tenants has become a crucial condition for urban development in metropolitan areas of continental Europe too.

(3) **Bank loans for start-ups, micro-enterprises and small businesses** are a condition for job creation especially for those people and areas where economic problems are most visible. Firstly, it is only in this part of economy where new jobs have been created during the last 10 years at all, especially in economically weak areas and secondly in spite of all other quests for risk capital and capital participation, the core of these businesses will never have any other choice than to recourse to bank loans. Therefore bank loans have to be tailored for this task of social banking.

(4) For all these loans a regular connection with the world of money transfers through a **bank account** is crucial. Without a bank account people are excluded from the most important forms of economic exchange. That is why so-called minimum or 'life-line' bank accounts play an important role in social banking.

While these four areas have a visible tradition of social banking products the number of areas which will need special social products in the future will increase at the same pace as financial services will be the intermediary of all economic development in society while discrimination in financial services will increase.

Opportunities for small savings in order to create creditworthiness and a credit history as well as for a productive use of temporary liquidity in the future will necessitate new products in investment of small amounts of money. Insurance will become increasingly important in order to insure the risks of other financial services extended to low income groups make them more accessible (linked insurance products). Insurance will also become important where insurance companies withdraw risk insurance at all from certain groups because the risks have become too high like for example car theft in Miami or fire insurance in some slum areas.

Requirements for social banking

Social banking products are **more costly, riskier and too small in size to be as profitable** as the average banking product, while targeting people who can often not even afford *average* cost.

- They are more costly because economical weakness correlate with lower education, less experience and more complex investment situations where unpredictable personal risks like unemployment, illness, divorce and accidents have to be taken into account. These products have to be tailored more flexibly to the needs of these people. More personal services and advice is required and the administration of the services cannot be automated without taking into account the lack of technical access of such people to automated procedures. Therefore social banking products have to incorporate a methodology of **lowering the transaction cost**.
- Social banking products are riskier because the main resource for the repayment of the loan, as well as fees and interest, is the labour of the individual client. Under conditions of economic weakness these people operate from, they are exposed to higher failure rates, less stable income conditions and a

lack of compensatory mechanisms or assets. In addition, they typically lack security. That is why such products have to look for **personal security** and orientate their lending towards the **cash flow expectation** of the future. **Flexibility** in repayment schedules have to be developed without putting people at risk. Procedures to check the creditworthiness of the clients have to be completely changed, from the traditional lending on security towards cheaper methods of building up **trust** as the major security.

- Social banking products lack the economies of scale in each single bank customer relationship. Fixed cost are relatively higher in such transactions than in private banking or investment banking. To make such products afford-able, fixed costs have to be lowered through **co-operation** with non-for-profit or state agencies. **Outsourcing** acquisition, advice and monitoring of the services or lending methods have to be developed to address such groups in a more **collective form** where individual services are pooled together so that bigger amounts can be handled.

- All these measures will not suffice to keep the price for such products suffi-ciently low. And groups whose use of financial services is not adequate to meet the average profit expectations of financial institutions are those groups who are least able to afford higher charges for them. Thus, social banking products also have to incorporate mechanisms of **solidarity** and **the use of transfer income**. The most common way will be the socialisation of costs through the integration of low income customers into the general customer portfolio. The additional cost of these groups are then born by the whole of the customers. But competition will counteract such behaviour so that state regulation may be necessary to force banks not to exclude those clients (as has been regulated through the US Community Reinvestment Act). Other means are the use of **state programmes** for urban development like housing subsi-dies, small business guarantees etc. Major efforts are also made by provision of more favourable refinancing facilities for creditors that extend social banking products. **Social investment** products may be designed to serve the financement of special social purposes like investment funds or refinancing contingents of state administered agencies e.g. the public housing banks in Germany or the Federal Home Mortgage Association (Fannie Mae) in the USA.

- Social banking requires the provision of **distinct basic services** extracted from package deals in order to make these basic services accessible at the lowest price. The tendency to integrate more and more financial services into one packaged product in private banking leads to a lowering of the cost of each item included in the package which favours those who would anyhow want the additional services. But the whole product is certainly more costly to purchase than one or two items separately, so that each item alone become less accessible. Basic bank accounts which are not necessarily combined with overdraft facilities, credit and plastic card or other services unnecessary for basic use of the payment system are an answer to basic needs in banking.

Forms of social banking

Little empirical research has been conducted to extract examples of social banking products from banking practice.[9] The focus of marketing activities of mainstream banking is on the wealthier clients. If any research on the effects of banking low income communities is done, this is mostly with the intention to single out more costly products and stop their distribution.

This negative attitude towards social banking in mainstream banking works as an aggravating self-fulfilling prophecy. Because social banking is solely analysed as part of such unprofitable retail banking activities, no efforts are made to design special products for these groups which would cost less and have lower risks. When private banking necessitates a more complex add-on cross selling approach low income customers are negatively affected. It is therefore not surprising that major private banks who have the most important research potential and who are the trend setters for the new client orientation, in the use of electronic banking and cross selling activities have least contributed to social banking in the past. Their ignorance about business start-up financing below EUR 50.000, about credit for self-employment and minimum accounts for unemployed people or small savings is visible at most larger German banks. On the other hand, Citibank is quite active in low income banking. But one would have problems to call this social banking. Its forms of banking with low income customers are characterised by fewer and more automated services, higher hidden fees and interest rates, costly roll-over forms of credit and obligatory insurance by-products (which in the eyes of some consumer organisations in Germany do more harm than good to many of their clients).[10] Access is not always a key to economic recovery if it only aggravates the situation in the long term.

More promising seems the experience of smaller banks like savings banks and coop banks in Germany or community banks in America who are not so advanced in their client focused approach and are still targeting their clients very globally. They have created an enormous experience with low income banking. But this experience is until now like a sunken treasure which nobody really wants to lift. The small banks are hunting after the profit margins of the big ones using the same paths to 'success'[11] while their more or less open experience remains unstructured and without thorough analysis, part of the individual skills of bank employees which may soon die out.

This is why most of social banking experience today stems from some socially oriented banks that, with very small to insignificant market shares, expressively focus on social banking. Among those models only such banks that work in competitive markets where subsidies do not hide risks and cost but leave them open for research and special treatment can serve as mines from which the necessary raw material for understanding can be extracted. Other models without special approaches hide traditional subsidies for the poor through semi-banking products and consequently are often more discouraging than helpful.

The collective approach

All given experience shows that much cost can be saved in social banking if the clients are approached more collectively. The increasing individualisation in private banking and business banking with specially tailored products that show equally a high standard in all elements of good banking products like safety, accessibility and convenience, liquidity and suitable interest rates have made such products inaccessible for social banking. But social banking is confronted with a large number of individual claims that show much more coherence than demand in private banking. If banking products could make use of this coherence and turn it into an economic value new social banking products could be created. Social banking distinct from individualised banking uses collective links between customers themselves as well as between banks and their clients belonging to the same community.

Trust and Risk

The main problem of low income banking is the higher risk linked to such investments. If traditional forms of screening are used to single out more exactly where those risks lie which later on will lead to failure the transaction cost rise exponentially. In addition such methods used in individual banking will mostly be done in vain because as the following table of the world leading credit scoring agency Dun & Bradstreet in comparison to South Shore Banks scoring system reveals business start-ups may not even be able to contribute to one single question. South Shore Bank's criteria instead target the collective environment of such start-ups.

The key experience of social banking lies in the fact that the main problem of business banking, which stems from asymmetric information about the clients ability and willingness to pay, can be circumvented by collective approaches. As Mishkin[12] has argued the main problem of credit risks lies in the problem of adverse selection and moral hazard when banks extend risky credit in a situation of asymmetric information favouring involuntarily those who misuse their offer (adverse selection) and spoil the borrowed money afterwards with promising but risky investments (moral hazard). Adverse selection and moral hazard only occur if the contracting parties have no other lien than the mutual desire to maximise their profits.

If instead credit is extended within closed and socially connected groups of people related to each other in communities, their 'community moral' and social experience of solidarity may help as an important tool to prevent people from

DUN & BRADSTREET	SOUTH SHORE BANK
• Index of Recent Payment Experience	• Development Impact
	• Healthy Edges
• Years in Business	• Visible Change
• Net Worth	• Range of Incomes
• D&B Credit Rating	• Potential Development Partners
• Legal Structure	• Community Commitment
• Suits, Liens, Judgements	• Community Identity
• Industry Risk	• Economic Centres
• Regional Economy	• Locational Amenities

playing the odds to the detriment of the creditor. Social banking products address such social forces by using three important elements on their products:

- Social banking products focus primarily on the social effects of financial services for a community, or even pursue a public goal. This attitude puts profit second and gives way for a referral to moral and ethical values including mutual **trust**.
- Social banking connects the general effects of banking with the community. If a user of such services cheats or misuses the offer, he or she does not just profit from the other selfishly acting party, but **harms the community** as a whole.
- Each member of a defined public group will **control** the behaviour of all others if the general outcome of the action is decisive for their common good.

Such effects are well known in small villages where credit unions extended credit to farmers who are at the same time members of the credit co-operative. The failure rates are extremely low. Such effects have been used in Israel among immigrants from eastern Europe in the late eighties, by asking each applicant for a mortgage loan to present at least 7 guarantors although none of these people offered additional security. The closed target group did not provide any more security because guarantees were mutual and crosswise. In Micro-lending the Polish Fundusz Mikro favours group borrowing by offering more advantageous interest rates to groups than to single borrowers. Their failure rate (for group loans) is significantly lower compared with single loans. Grameen Bank in Bangladesh has used this method by addressing farmers as family members and members of savings circles while South Shore Bank has used it successfully by addressing and identifying only with people from one city area: Chicago South Shore.[13]

The rise of credit unions and coop banks in the early 20th century testifies about the importance of trust as an economic asset. Its fall was not due to the absence of trust but to a historically outdated form of personal co-operative banking that excludes non-members and has limited access to bigger capital markets. Some of its merits can be regained through specially designed social banking products without committing its errors.

Cash flow and life cycle approach

One of the major problems in social banking lies in the fact that the liquidity necessary for a stable partnership with a bank is too thin and seemingly unpredictable. Credit history of an individual is taken as the most important indicator for his or her future behaviour. In low income groups the individual history is often either non-existent or not promising. On the other hand social research about the conditions of such households can reveal that even low income groups have quite stable expectations for what will happen to their cash flow in their particular life-cycles.[14] Research on low income mortgage applicants in the city of Rostock (in eastern Germany) has shown that although each single applicant had not enough stable liquidity during the life span of the credit to be acceptable as a safe borrower, all together would have been able to pay back all the instalments regularly.

A thorough definition of cash flow expectations for certain target groups could lead to a credit portfolio in which different cash flow problems could be hedged against each other. The combination of young people and elderly people can for example combine high initial assets and high life risks with low initial assets and improved cash flow expectations in the future. Ten years ago the French Crédit Alsacien contracted a 12 month maximum payment delay if a consumer would loose his or her job involuntarily. As a compensation the contract with the consumer organisation provided that all borrowers should pay an additional fee to finance this through additional unemployment insurance. Unlike the very expensive unemployment insurance which is only requested from those households that are most likely to be affected leaving the risk of the poorest to the poorest, such group insurance comprised elements of local solidarity and offered cheap access in economically weak areas. Caja Laboral de Mondragon in Spain has used such mechanisms by appealing to the solidarity of Basque people whose interest rates on assets were lowered when clients in business loans had problems to repay.[15]

Collective administration and transaction cost

A collective approach can reduce transaction costs. Historically, housing coops have been formed by the future inhabitants to contract loans collectively. It is not only that the size of the loan is increased giving more bargaining power to the contractants. Advice and information provision needs can also be reduced if one single skilled person will pass this information to the other. The insurance industry has since long extended **group insurance** where employers or sports clubs and other associations or even credit card companies have been taken as representatives of a group and transaction cost has been transferred to them. Acquisition, risk assessment and administration of payments and risk coverage were farmed out so that group insurance premiums could be offered at a significantly lower rate also to members of the group. Credit life insurance in America is extended in the form of group insurance without individual health checks and or difference according to age or gender. In Europe instead all banks take advantage from the enormous profit margin offered by individualised credit life insurance leaving the opportunity of group insurance out. It is just the opposite of social banking, because existing products are not used, to the detriment of the poor.

Instead group insurance could be used to cover specific problems of low income areas like unemployment, late payments for small businesses, which cause liquidity crisis, mortgage arrears in times of high interest rates etc. But the American experience shows that poor people are less likely to be organised at workspace, at universities or in associations so that it is difficult to address them collectively. Social banking would have to find out how poorer people could find their own representative e.g. through state administration, welfare organisations or religious groups.

Collective approaches can also be used to make small savings more rewarding. In the 19th century farmers in rural communities created savers' clubs in which they collected money until sufficient amounts for investment were reached. Modern forms of such savings are investment funds where risky investments with high returns are made accessible for smaller investors. But such investment funds are merely oriented towards maximum profit. Social goals like private retirement are still absent although the first steps have been made. But small savings are punished by minimum fees which eat up the whole return. Banks could much better further private investor clubs which provide the necessary flexibility for savers and which further their specific saving purposes. Instead the most often sold investment product in economic weak areas in Germany is capital life insurance and so-called housing saving contracts. They are totally inflexible and punish early withdrawal rewarding only those who keep to their contracts sometimes for up to 60 years. More than 50% of such savers do not continue the contracts to the end and the lowest income groups in particular pay the price.

Group approaches are therefore more often used to the detriment of low income customers than to their advantage. But they have a high potential for savings in marketing, administration and risk management.

Examples of social banking products

Many financial products contain elements of social banking which have been introduced when their use for low income customers had caused problems at the time where problems were still solved by ameliorating the supply instead of excluding the demand.

1   Variable rate credit with flexible instalments were offered in response to the increasing refinancing needs of low income borrowers that could not pay their instalments regularly. Some banks offered an instalment-free December responding to the regular arrears in this month.

2   In mortgage loans the need for the acquisition of homes without the ability to make down payments normally prescribed by law for at least 20% of the house value was circumvented by some banks through a system in which planned or intended 'do it yourself' improvement work was artificially added to the house value at the time of purchase. Thus, low income households without their own assets got access to home ownership.

3   In an act to prevent lifeline legislation in Germany the German associations of banks published rules of conduct in which they promised to offer bank accounts for over-indebted people without credit and card facilities at regular prices.

4   American banks offer so-called 'secured credit cards' in which customers who have been excluded from bank services on account of bad credit histories in the files of the credit monitoring agencies can make an investment. They borrow their own money in order to get a better credit history. As these products are extremely expensive their good intention for reintegration is counteracted by the exploitative effects. In savings, a lot has been done to reach out also to small money amounts like the automatic withdrawal of the spill over in the current account for a savings account or instalment savings plans with flexible access to the assets if needed.

5   Taking out loans on a whole life insurance policy is another way of providing liquidity for those to whom a steady monthly payment may cause problems. Other means were the possibility of creating 'dormant capital life insurance' which reduced the insured amount but prevented people from costly cancellations. Some banks have linked instalment credit and credit lines in order to make them more flexible and responsive to sudden liquidity problems.

   While the number of examples in mainstream banking represents only a fraction of what has been mostly unconsciously developed for matching the needs of socially weaker customers, the number of special social banking products has been very limited.

1   Special social banking products have been developed for housing especially by administrative or refinancing bodies in Europe and America. Target group mortgages up to 80% with additional 16% covered by a special insurance against failure and 4% subsidies are favoured in the US by Fannie Mae and the housing administration in the urban zones.

2   Reverse mortgages give people of old age credit to buy their house for their life time at ordinary conditions without charging them additional and costly life insurance.

3   Savings and loan house construction have been supported and subsidised by continental European governmental bodies. With the possibility of part financing homes through shared home ownership, the state has helped to

develop mortgage loans that are located between participation in capital and a loan.

4   Other mortgage facilities for co-operatives have been combined with loans given by the housing department of the city who used interest payments for raising their equity in the house so that the inhabitants could use this additional liquidity.

5   Presently there is a lot of development around small business loans in combination with fund management participation. 'Round-tables' to prevent insolvency are developed in line with loans where interest rates are increased during lifetime of the loan leaving more liquidity in the beginning and charging it at a later time when the business has made its way. New legal forms are offered in order to facilitate all kind of financial participation in such enterprises.

6   A very sophisticated social banking product is presently being developed and applied under the name of 'micro-lending'. It targets self-employment and uses all elements of social banking in order to make small amounts of credit accessible for micro-entrepreneurs. Using intermediary organisations micro-lending can be seen as between lending and educational programmes for start-ups.

7   IFF has developed other new products like micro-bank-outlets staffed with two or three employees and which can play an important role in a future banking structure that tries to keep up bank presence in areas where normal affiliates (branches) would be too costly.

8   A shared home ownership investment fund for tenants who want to buy their flats collectively has equally been designed.

9   A collective bank account of several small businesses administered through their association using the effects of overlapping liquidity has been developed by a Hamburg managed workspace for their tenants. It comes close to a model that has been developed for ordinary people to help each by pooling their use of the payment system.

All products follow the philosophy that low income customers are not interested in profit nor in creating individual wealth but just in getting sufficient liquidity to be able to live in their own houses, to build up their own enterprise, to use their own labour and to participate in financial transactions.

ENDNOTES
1   Caplovitz, D., *The Poor Pay More – Consumer Practices of Low-Income Families*, Macmillan: New York 1963; Caplovitz, D., *Consumers in Trouble – A Study of Debtors in Default*, N.Y,. 1975.
2   Squires, G. (ed) (1992), *From Red-Lining to Reinvestment, Community Responses to Urban Disinvestment*, Philadelphia: Temple University Press, 1992.
3   For a detailed description see Evers, J. and Reifner, U. (1998), *The Social Responsibility of Credit Institutions in the EU*, pp. 397-445.

4   Laws, N. and Mansfield, M., *Debt Collection Practices Across Europe, European Consumer Debt Net*, Money Advice Trust, London, February 1999; Reifner, U., 'Access to financial services – a German view', in Mitchell, J. (ed) *Money and the Consumer*, Money Management Council, London, 1988.

5   See the country reports in Reifner, U. and Ford, J. (eds.), *Banking for People – social Banking and New Poverty – Consumer Debts and Unemployment*, de Gruyter: Berlin – New York 1992 pp. 315 -648; Ford, J. *The Indebted Society*, Routledge, London, 1988.

6   See IFF (Evers, J. and Habschick, M.): *Existenzgründungen – Zugang zu Bankkrediten und Beratungsqualität – empirische Studie im Auftrag des Stern*, Hamburg, 1998, and Reifner, U. and Evers, J., *Credit and New Entrepreneurs*, Nomos: Baden-Baden, 1998, pp. 35ff.

7   Osborne, D. *Laboratories of Democracy: A new breed of governor creates models for national growth*, Boston, Harvard Business School Press, 1988; Osborne, D. *Bootstrap Banking*, Inc Magazine, N.Y., August 1987.

8   See the Nobel Prize winner in economics, 1998, Sen, Armatya, *On Economic Inequality*, Clarendon Press, Oxford 1973 (*Ökonomische Ungleichheit*, Campus, Ffm 1975, pp 8,18, 35).

9   One attempt but in German is Reifner, U. (1997): 'Social Banking – Ansätze und Erfahrungen über die Integration sozialer Zielsetzungen in privatwirtschaftliche Finanzdienstleistungen', in: Schuster, L. (Hrsg.), *Die gesellschaftliche Verantwortung der Banken*, Erich Schmidt Verlag, Berlin, 1997.

10   See Verbraucherzentrale Düsseldorf on Citibank, press release; Reifner, U., Kocher, E. and Krüger, U., *Sozial diskriminierende Preisgestaltung bei Krediten der Citibank*, (Socially Discriminative Traification by Citibank), Expertise at Institute for Financial Services, Hamburg, February 1999.

11   A recent very good example is the article of two German saving bankers who describe how their saving bank uses new socio-geographical methods to red-line less attractive customers. See: Emmerich, N. and Knura, F. (1999): '10 Thesen zur Förderung des Geldanlagengeschäfts mit Privatkunden', *Die Sparkasse* 3/99, pp. 121-125.

12   See Mishkin, F.S., *The Economics of Money, Banking, and Financial Markets*, 4th ed HarperCollins: New York, 1995, pp. 34ff.

13   For a detailed up to date description of South Shores development and US-expansion see Shapiro, J., 'Shorebank Corporation: A Private Sector Banking Initiative to Renew Distressed Communities', in: Reifner and Evers: *Credit and New Entrepreneurs*, 1998, pp. 190-203.

14   Kessler, D. and Masson, A., *Cycles de Vie et Générations*, Economica, Paris, 1985.

15   For a description of these banks see Reifner, U. and Ford, J. *op.cit.* (Fn) Part. IV. Ethical banking – New Forms of social Market Economy, p. 155.

The Community Reinvestment Act: its impact on lending in low-income communities in the United States

Michael S. Barr, Lynda Y. de la Viña, Valerie A. Personick, Melissa A. Schroder, US

(The authors are employees of the U.S. Department of the Treasury. This paper is the sole responsibility of the authors and may not reflect the official views of the Treasury Department.)

The Community Reinvestment Act (CRA) was enacted in 1977 to encourage banks and thrifts to help meet the credit needs of their entire communities in a manner consistent with safe and financially sound banking practices. According to many financial institutions, government regulators, community groups, and academic researchers, CRA has been successful in assisting banks and thrifts to identify previously unrealized market opportunities in these communities.

CRA encourages federally insured financial institutions to meet the obligations of their bank charter by providing banking and credit services to all segments of the communities in which they operate. Under CRA, the bank regulatory agencies – the Federal Reserve Board, the Office of the Comptroller of the Currency, the Office of Thrift Supervision, and the Federal Deposit Insurance Corporation – regularly review how well each institution has provided lending, investment, and banking services to low- and moderate-income groups within their assessment areas. Home mortgage lending is also considered in the CRA review, coupled with the reporting requirements under the Home Mortgage Disclosure Act (HMDA) and the fair housing lending laws. The CRA ratings are made public and are used by the regulatory agencies in their consideration of certain applications, including those for proposed mergers and acquisitions.

Changes to HMDA and CRA regulations since the late 1980s have made these laws more effective. In 1989 HMDA was amended to require public disclosure of an institution's home mortgage loan portfolio, which includes information about the race, income and location of borrowers. This enhancement contributed to the strengthening of fair lending enforcement in the 1990s.

CRA regulations were amended in 1989 to make public each institution's rating. In 1993, at the request of President Clinton, banking regulators began reforming the regulations implementing CRA by replacing criteria that had been viewed as subjective and process oriented with objective performance measures. Revised regulations were issued in 1995 which effectively streamlined the CRA review process to assure consistency in regulatory oversight. Banking and thrift regulators began to apply the new criteria to small banks in 1996 and to large banks in 1997.

Lending to low- and moderate-income neighborhoods and minority communities has increased significantly. According to private community organizations, banks and thrifts have made $1.051 trillion in loan pledges to low-income areas since the inception of CRA in 1977, with over 95 percent of the total occurring in the past six years.[1] Other data confirm a rapid increase in lending to low- and moderate-income and minority communities in recent years. Home mortgage lending, for example, has risen faster for these groups since 1993 than for the market as a whole. The volume of small business loans under CRA has grown to sizable levels and accounts for two-thirds of all the small business loans made by federally insured banks and thrifts. A substantial share of the loans, more than one-fifth, went to businesses in low- and moderate-income neighborhoods. As Federal Reserve Governor Edward Gramlich noted, 'There seems to be little doubt that most of these outcomes would not have occurred in the absence of CRA and other fair lending laws.'[2]

This paper reviews data and research studies that demonstrate that CRA has helped to increase lending to low-income borrowers and in low-income neighborhoods, and that expanded CRA lending has been accomplished while maintaining sound lending practices and bank profitability. The paper also discusses literature that draws alternative conclusions, as well as studies that find, despite increases in lending and banking services to low- and moderate-income areas and to minority borrowers, that disparities still exist between the services afforded to these communities and those offered to the market as a whole.

Home mortgage lending

Home mortgage lending data show that since improved disclosure of HMDA data first demonstrated a lending gap in the early 1990s, minority borrowers' access to the mortgage market has improved dramatically compared to the average for the market as a whole.[3]

As demonstrated in Table 1, there has been a sizable upward shift in the share of loans obtained by low-income and minority borrowers. The total number of conventional mortgage loans increased by 33.0 percent between 1993 and 1997. In contrast, loans to census tracts where the median income is less than 80 percent of the median income of the whole metropolitan area increased much more rapidly – by 45.1 percent. Similarly, loans to African Americans and Hispanics

also increased much faster than the 33 percent average over the 1993-97 period –
by 71.6 percent and 45.4 percent, respectively.

Table 1. Number of Conventional Home Purchase Loans, 1993-1997

*Between 1993 and 1997, conventional home purchase loans to low-income and minority
borrowers grew more rapidly than to other borrowers*

	Percent change
Total U.S. Market	33.0
By race or ethnicity:	
African American	71.6
Hispanic	45.4
By income of borrower (% of MSA median):	
Less than 80	40.3
80-99	30.0
100-119	24.6
120 or more	31.7
By income of census tract:	
Low or moderate	45.1
Middle	32.0
Upper	31.5

Source: Federal Financial Institutions Examination Council, August 24, 1998.

Other factors may also have contributed to the relatively quicker expansion in
home lending to these groups. The strong economy has led to widespread employment opportunities, a reduction in unemployment rates among all demographic
groups, and a rise in real income. Very favorable mortgage interest rates have
lowered the costs of home ownership and made housing more affordable.
Nevertheless, research discussed later tends to confirm that CRA has been a
significant factor in the shift in mortgage lending towards low- and moderate-
income communities. As Governor Gramlich noted, 'it is likely that CRA played
an important role in bringing about this shift.'[4]

The strong growth in home lending to minorities is effectively demonstrated
in the more rapid rise in home ownership rates among minority households than
for the population as a whole, as seen in Table 2. Home ownership rates for
African Americans and Hispanics surpassed 46 percent in the first quarter of
1999, rising from 42.1 percent for African Americans and 40.3 percent for
Hispanics at the beginning of 1994. Home ownership rates for all households in
the United States increased from 63.8 percent in the first quarter of 1994 to 66.7
percent by the first quarter of 1999.

Table 2. Home ownership Rates, 1994-1999

Since the beginning of 1994, the home ownership rate for African Americans, Hispanics and lower income households rose much faster than the US average

	US Total	African	Hispanic American	Households with income less than or equal to the median
1994:Q1	63.8	42.1	40.3	48.1
1999:Q1	66.7	46.3	46.2	51.2
Percentage Point Increase				
94:1 to 99:1	2.9	4.2	5.9	3.1

Note: Quarterly data on home ownership by categories shown in table were first tabulated in 1994.

Although home ownership rates for both minority groups still remain well below the average of all households, both African Americans and Hispanics experienced more rapid growth in home ownership than the general population over the past five years. The home ownership rate for African Americans increased by 4.2 percentage points, almost one and a half times more than the increase in the average home ownership rate. The home ownership rate for Hispanics increased by 5.9 percentage points, over two times as much as the average. Growth in home ownership rates for low-income households also exceeded the average for all households.

Research findings of CRA-related lending

Research has identified a linkage between CRA and expanded lending in low and moderate income communities. Evanoff and Segal (1996) tested the post-1990 impact of CRA and other regulatory changes on mortgage lending to low-income individuals and areas and found that through the 1980s, growth in mortgage originations in low- and moderate-income groups lagged behind that of other groups. For four of the years in which the overall mortgage market was expanding rapidly, the low-income group showed the slowest growth and the moderate-income growth also posted below average growth. HMDA data shows significant change, however, in the 1990s. After 1991, growth was relatively faster in the two lowest-income groups, with the change 'overwhelmingly statistically significant.' The authors conclude that 'this finding suggests that banks have responded to the CRA and have made significantly more loans in the low- and moderate-income markets,' consistent with the view that banks were making a significant effort to encourage applications from those neighborhoods.

Evanoff and Segal also tested lenders' objectivity in extending mortgages to minorities. They found that the odds that a minority applicant would be rejected for a mortgage loan over the years 1990-1995 diminished relative to the denial rates for whites. These findings led them to conclude that stricter enforcement of the CRA and fair lending laws since the early 1990s, contributed to the surge in credit both to low-income neighborhoods and to minority groups.

Avery, Bostic, Calem, and Canner (1996) also found that increased lending to low- and moderate-income borrowers relative to other groups (1992 to 1994) meant that affordable home loan programs were having an effect in metropolitan areas. In 1993 the number of conventional home purchase loans to low- and moderate-income borrowers increased by 38 percent. In contrast, the increase that year to upper-income borrowers was only 8 percent. Figures for growth in 1994 showed a similar pattern, with the number of loans extended to the lower-income groups rising by 27 percent while loans to upper-income applicants increased 13 percent. The study notes a number of factors which may have contributed to the relatively rapid increase in such lending on the part of financial institutions. Among them were newly perceived profit opportunities in previously underserved markets, a desire to enhance CRA compliance, or a determination that such lending would serve the lenders' interest in community stability.

A case study by LaCour-Little, cited by Governor Gramlich, supports the conclusion that CRA has made a significant contribution to the growth in the volume of lending to low- and moderate-income individuals in recent years.[5] LaCour-Little analyzed lending data from 1993-97 for a large mortgage lender that uses credit scoring to screen applicants. He concluded that at least half of the loans made to low-income individuals living in low-income census tracts would not have been made if standard credit-scoring methods were the only screening criteria. He attributed to CRA the fact that loans which scored below the cut-off level were nonetheless made. Further, the data showed that CRA lending was reaching its intended target, as recipients of the low-scoring loans were more likely to have lower income, be members of a minority group, or live in a lower-income area.

Shlay (1998) confirmed that a strong CRA in the past few years has led to a climate of favorable lending patterns to minority and lower-income communities overall. A comparison of lending patterns in six cities showed that residential loan growth between 1990 and 1995 to low-income borrowers and in low-income census tracts was either comparable to or exceeded overall market trends. Lending patterns improved both for lenders with CRA agreements with communities and for those without, although gains were smaller among the latter group. Shlay attributes the widespread growth in lending to previously underserved communities as a general shift in institutional thinking, spurred by heightened recognition of new profit opportunities and increased attention to CRA ratings.

According to Federal Reserve economists Avery, Bostic, Calem, and Canner

(1999), the recent wave of consolidation among banking organizations has not reduced home mortgage lending to lower-income and minority borrowers and neighborhoods. The study found that while consolidated organizations reduced their home mortgage lending in counties in which they operated offices, they expanded their out-of-market lending by an even larger amount, and increased their proportion of loans going to lower-income and minority borrowers by more than institutions not involved in consolidations. These results, the study notes, are consistent with the view that CRA has been effective in encouraging financial institutions, particularly those undergoing consolidation, to better serve lower-income and minority borrowers and neighborhoods.

Small business lending

In order to help regulators evaluate a bank's CRA performance, the 1995 changes to CRA also required large commercial banks and savings associations to collect data on lending activity to small businesses and small farms within their service areas, in addition to the data already reported on home mortgages. Reporting on these markets began in 1996, and a look at the recent data shows that 'CRA appears to be a highly effective federal government program in dealing with the credit needs of low and moderate income groups.'[6]

In the small business market, according to the data collected under CRA reporting, banks and thrifts made 2.4 million small business loans in 1996, amounting to $147 billion. In 1997, 2.6 million loans were awarded with total dollar volume at $159 billion.[7] These loans represented two-thirds of all the small business loans made by commercial banks and savings associations in those years, and about 45 percent of loans from all sources.[8]

Roughly half of the loans reported under CRA were awarded to small businesses with revenues of $1 million or less, and the vast majority (about 87 percent) were for amounts under $100,000. About 485,000 loans in 1996 and 525,000 in 1997, or one-fifth of the total small business loans, went to low- and moderate-income areas.

In addition to small business loans, commercial banks made large investments in community development projects – $17.7 billion in 1996 and $18.6 billion in 1997. These funds were used for multi-family affordable housing, community services, and retail and commercial revitalization in lower-income neighborhoods. In addition, data collected by the Office of Comptroller of the Currency found that from 1993 through 1998, national banks invested seven times as much in real dollar terms in community development as they did in the previous twenty-eight years.[9]

Because comprehensive data on CRA-related lending is only available starting in 1996, statistically quantifying the impact of CRA on small business and community development lending is not possible. However, many financial institutions, government regulators, community groups, and academic researchers have concluded that CRA has helped banks and thrifts discover previously unrealized market opportunities in low- to moderate-income communities. As Governor Gramlich has noted, 'While many of these [small business] loans would presumably have been made without CRA, the size of the gross loan numbers and their distribution across geographical areas suggest the importance of CRA in the process. There is also a great deal of anecdotal evidence, contained in periodic reports of the Federal Reserve Banks, of the success of various CRA community lending programs.'[10]

According to the 1998 Federal Reserve Board's Report to the Congress on the Availability of Credit to Small Businesses, many financial institutions have aggressively expanded small business lending in connection with community reinvestment programs. Bankers have indicated that identifying new marketing opportunities and redesigning their products and services to increase lending to underserved segments of the small business community are important outcomes of the new CRA reporting requirements. For the first time, financial institutions have accurate information on the geographical distribution of small business loans, and can better tailor their products to meet the needs of the various segments of the small business market.

While CRA has been viewed as effective in encouraging banks undergoing consolidation to expand their home mortgage lending in low- and moderate-income markets, research results on the effects of bank mergers and acquisitions on small business lending are more mixed. Bank consolidation has reduced the number of small banks and consequently led small business owners increasingly to turn to large banks for credit. These banks typically rely on strictly objective lending criteria such as credit scoring in order to reduce the high transactions costs typically associated with small loans. Large banks are also less likely to make relationship or 'character' loans. As a result, some empirical evidence shows that small business credit appears to decline when smaller banks merge with larger ones. This pattern was most notable for lines-of-credit loans. At the least, the loan search and transaction costs for a small business to obtain a loan have been shown to be higher.[11]

Other studies of the effects of consolidation have reached the opposite conclusion, finding that credit scoring does not restrict the total amount of credit extended to low- and moderate-income areas overall. That result may be related to the expansion of lending by credit-scoring banks to low-income borrowers outside of their local area, as the Avery et al. paper found for the mortgage market. One study reported that within their local service area, banks that credit score have a smaller share of loans in low-income tracts than local banks that do not credit score, indicating that 'relationship banking may still be the best way to reach small businesses in low-income areas.'[12]

Lending and profitability

Available evidence suggests that CRA lending has been expanded consistent with safe and sound banking practices. Banks report strong performance of loans in the low- to moderate-income housing market. For example, Bank of America in San Francisco has profitably lent more than $10 billion as part of its Neighborhood Advantage program – a system of low- and moderate-income home loans – to borrowers throughout the western United States.[13] BankBoston lent $140 million to low- and moderate-income borrowers and found performance to be no different than in its regular mortgage portfolio.[14] From 1996 through 1998, Chase Manhattan Bank financed the development of more than 1.6 million square feet of commercial space and the development of 20,271 units of affordable housing to benefit the stability, growth and economic expansion of lower-income communities. Chase Manhattan Bank 'made these loans at market rate and found these activities to be a profitable business for Chase and the performance of these loans to be excellent.'[15] First National Bank of Chicago found that by increasing the availability of its consumer and mortgage lending products, and introducing flexible underwriting criteria, the bank's penetration in low- and moderate-income community markets grew.[16] According to Federal Reserve Chairman Alan Greenspan, 'there is little or no evidence that banks' safety and soundness have been compromised by [low- and moderate-income] lending and bankers often report sound business opportunities.'[17]

Banks have also partnered with Community Development Financial Institutions (CDFIs) as an effective way of making loans in low-income neighborhoods. CDFIs are specialized local financial institutions serving low-income communities. CDFIs may include banks, thrifts, credit unions, revolving loan funds, venture capital or micro-enterprise funds that share the mission of serving unmet credit and financial services needs in these communities. According to Marisco (1995), CDFIs have the expertise and local market knowledge necessary to meet community credit needs. They are often well positioned to evaluate the creditworthiness of low-income applicants and to provide loan counseling.[18] These partnerships may lower information costs for banks, enabling them to make profitable, sound CRA loans.[19] In addition, partnerships with Neighborhood Housing Service organizations, which have reported a significant increase in investments since the new CRA regulations have taken effect, have helped nearly 16,000 Americans own their own homes for the first time.[20]

In 1996, a survey of 600 large financial institutions active in single-family lending in metropolitan areas found that 98 percent said CRA lending was profitable and that credit risk was manageable.[21] Federal Reserve Board roundtable discussions with lenders of affordable home lending programs showed that participants viewed costs of origination and servicing of these loans as higher but delinquency and default rates no worse.[22] Statistical analysis did not find any notable relationship between bank profitability and the level of lower-income mortgage lending. The lenders noted that increased risks can be mitigated through the use of flexible underwriting guidelines, buyer education, credit counseling, and early delinquency intervention. Similarly, a study by Bear Stearns found that CRA home mortgage loans had low prepayment risk for investors, and borrower credit scores (and risk) were consistent with conventional financing guidelines.[23]

The Office of the Comptroller of the Currency found that risk management techniques can be successful in reducing delinquency rates of affordable mortgage portfolios to levels that are comparable to conventional residential mortgage portfolios.[24] Delinquencies in affordable mortgage portfolios averaged 4 percent in 1996 compared to 3 percent for residential real estate portfolios as a whole. Most of the disparity was in banks new to the affordable lending market, while banks that had been in the business for several years had developed strategies for reducing delinquencies, such as pre-purchase counseling, rapid response intervention programs, and a limit to the layering of risk factors. These techniques helped to improve loan performance to a level consistent with conventional mortgage loans.

Federal Reserve Board and other studies consistently reaffirm the OCC conclusions. One study examined the net operating income of commercial banks that vary in the extent to which they provide home-purchase loans to lower-income borrowers or in lower-income neighborhoods, and found that banks that are active lenders in these markets do not have any lower profitability than other mortgage-oriented commercial banks.[25] Lenders were compensated for the higher costs of low-income lending through the adjustment of interest rates or fees for the credit risk of the particular loan products.

Barriers to capital

As demonstrated, CRA can be an effective tool for expanding credit opportunities, and hence economic development, to its targeted communities. However, market imperfections in the supply of credit persist, highlighting the continuing importance of a CRA-type mechanism for both the business and home mortgage markets.[26] In addition to empirical evidence discussed more fully below, economic literature provides theoretical support for CRA by identifying some of the market imperfections which may impede equal access to capital for creditworthy borrowers.

The theoretical studies, such as those by Beshouri and Glennon (1996) and Calomiris et al (1994), argue that government intervention may be required in circumstances where there is concentration or imperfect competition between lenders serving a region. The presence of uncertainties or the lack of information may lead to missed opportunities for profitable lending as well. If lenders are uncertain about the profitability of lending in low-income or minority neighborhoods, but acquiring information about such opportunities involves some cost, lenders may forego or postpone such lending even if at some point in the future it may be potentially profitable. Also, since information has the properties of a public good, individual lenders may invest considerably less in researching such possibilities than they would if they could permanently retain the rights to such information. This would be particularly true for institutions that do not have prior experience in minority or low-income markets and thus may find assessing the creditworthiness of minority borrowers relatively difficult. Altering the incentives of competing lenders through regulations such as CRA, these authors argue, can effectively induce lenders to incur such costs, thereby leading to a benefit for the community as a whole as well as for similar communities elsewhere.

Barriers to Business Credit

Although data on CRA-related lending in 1996 and 1997 showed a large volume of small business loans to low- and moderate-income areas, the same data reveal that the number of loans per business and the aggregate dollar amount of loans per business were smaller in low-income areas than in upper-income neighborhoods.[27] In 1997, the loan-to-business ratio in upper-income areas was roughly 40 percent greater than the ratio in low-income areas. The disparity in the aggregate dollar amount of loans relative to the number of businesses in the area was somewhat narrower, due to a higher concentration of larger businesses (such as manufacturing plants) in low-income tracts.

Lack of financial assets and access to credit are often cited as among the primary barriers to the expansion and success of minority self-employment and minority-owned businesses. Minority enterprises represent a small share of the business community, accounting for just 11.4 percent of all firms and six percent of total business receipts in 1992 despite the fact that minorities represent one-fourth of the U.S. population. While African Americans accounted for approximately 12 percent of the population in 1992, African American-owned businesses represented 3.6 percent of all businesses that year and accounted for just 1 percent of all business receipts. A study of self-employment trends since 1910 (Fairlie and Meyer, 1997) found that white workers were three times as likely to be self-employed as were African American workers. Of 200 minority business owners responding to a 1998 survey by the Organization for a New Equality (O.N.E.), 89 percent had applied for a bank credit product, but fewer than half of the applicants (43 percent) had ever received a product.[28]

Numerous studies reveal that minority-owned small businesses face greater obstacles in obtaining credit than do other businesses. Bates (1991, 1997) found that after controlling for net worth, education, age, and other factors, African Americans get smaller bank loans than whites who possess identical traits. Further, the smaller loans made to African American-owned businesses contributed to higher failure rates. After adjusting for the smaller loan size that is associated solely with being African American, the predicted number of African American firm failures drops to a rate that is close to the failure rate for white firms with otherwise similar characteristics. According to Bates, the reason African Americans receive smaller loans is rooted in both low household wealth, and an inability to leverage equity capital and human capital because of discriminatory lending patterns. All other things being equal, African Americans were able to borrow an extra $0.92 worth of debt for every dollar of equity, while whites were able to borrow $1.17. Human capital variables such as education and managerial experience were significant determinants of loan size for whites but not for African Americans; in other words, African Americans were unable to leverage their college credentials when applying for a loan to finance a small business.

A study by the Woodstock Institute (Immergluck, 1998) using CRA data found that loan marketing and originations for small business lending is consistent with explanations of discrimination or redlining. After controlling for industrial mix, firm size, and firm population, Immergluck found that lower-income and minority areas (particularly Hispanic) suffer from lower lending rates than higher-income and white neighborhoods. Wells Fargo Bank (1997) sponsored a study that demonstrated that Hispanic business owners are far less likely than non-Hispanic owners to have the business capital they need. Moreover, Hispanics are rejected far more often for financing compared with non-Hispanics.

According to a study based on data from the 1993 National Survey of Small Business Finances (Blanchflower, Levine, and Zimmerman, 1998), African American-owned firms are more than twice as likely to have a loan application rejected than white-owned firms (66 percent versus 27 percent), while the rejection rate for Hispanic-owned firms (36 percent) is about one-third higher. Even after controlling for a large number of characteristics, including location, African American-owned firms in particular are substantially more likely to be denied credit. All other things equal, the likelihood of loan denial is 26 percent higher than for white-owned firms. For African American owners with no history of credit problems the increased likelihood is still 24 percent. In addition, African American-owned businesses pay one percentage point more in interest, even for firms with good credit histories. The authors conclude that African Americans face a significant disadvantage in the market for small business credit that does not appear to be due to differences in creditworthiness or geography.

The study also found that African American and white-owned firms with similar financial and other characteristics differed widely in only one area when asked about the major business problems they faced, and that was in access to capital. This result mirrors evidence from other surveys. For example, the Census Bureau's 1992 Characteristics of Business Owners Survey found that African American and Hispanic-owned firms reported stronger negative impacts from credit market conditions and a lack of financial capital than white-owned firms.

Blanchflower et al. note that the results of their study may be biased toward finding too small a disparity in lending rates, since minority-owned firms that actually apply for credit may represent a selected subsample of the most credit-worthy. Some existing firms did not apply for a loan, although credit was needed, for fear that their application would be rejected. African American-owned firms were 44 percentage points more likely to cite this, and Hispanic-owned firms 22 points more likely. After adjusting for credit factors, a gap of 26 and 15 points still remained.

In another study, the Greenlining Institute also found evidence that minority business owners are more likely to be discouraged about obtaining credit.[29] Their survey of minority firms in Orange and Los Angeles counties revealed that three-quarters of minority-owned firms do not even bother to apply for business loans or lines of credit because they are convinced that banks have little to offer them or will reject their application.

Barriers to mortgage credit

Although relative lending rates for low-income and minority borrowers have improved dramatically, wide disparities persist. Munnell et al. (1996) showed that even after controlling for wealth, credit histories, loan-to-value ratios, and other factors affecting the mortgage loan decision, a statistically and economically significant gap between white and minority rejection rates remained. Their results showed that African American and Hispanic mortgage applicants in the Boston area face a probability of denial that is roughly eight percentage points higher than that facing a white individual with the same economic characteristics.

A number of other studies confirmed the results from the Munnell et al. study and an earlier version.[30] Carr and Megbolugbe (1993) used adjusted data from Munnell et al., plus supplementary information on credit risk, and found clear statistical evidence of differential treatment, with minorities receiving systematically lower credit ratings. Using a model similar to Munnell et al. to evaluate the Boston and Philadelphia markets, Schill and Wachter (1993) also found that since individual risk characteristics may be highly correlated with neighborhood risk characteristics, the evidence on individual lending patterns was consistent with redlining and discrimination.

Tootell (1996) reached similar conclusions about neighborhood discrimination. His study found evidence of discrimination based on the race of the applicant, and notes that the racial composition of the neighborhood is highly correlated with the race of the applicant. His evidence further suggests the existence of redlining because there is a higher chance that private mortgage insurance (PMI) will be required in minority neighborhoods, even after controlling for the economic and personal variables of the applicant, thereby raising the cost of borrowing. An applicant rejected for PMI is usually rejected for a mortgage, while if PMI is required and approved, the cost of the loan is higher.

Another report (Canner, Gabriel, and Woolley, 1991) concludes that after controlling for default risk, minority households are less likely to obtain conventional financing than white households. Minorities with the same demographic and economic characteristics as white borrowers are approximately three-fifths as likely as their white counterparts to get a conventional loan, while white borrowers with the same characteristics as minority borrowers are 2.5 times as likely to obtain such loans.

Critiques of CRA

Many of the negative reviews of CRA in the literature seem to have their foundation in an article by Macey and Miller (1993), which, the authors acknowledge, was dependent on 'impressionistic evidence' rather than on empirical work based on thorough statistical testing. The authors' main criticisms are first, if there were profitable lending opportunities within a community, banks would seek them out on their own. Second, they argue that the CRA burden is not equally shared. CRA imposes a 'tax' on some types of financial institutions (banks and saving associations) and not others (pension funds, credit unions, mortgage banks, etc.); and banks that have few retail operations (such as wholesale and trust banks) find compliance difficult. They also contend that banks located within economically depressed areas have more responsibilities and costs than other banks, discouraging banks from expanding to these areas. Third, according to the authors banks cannot comply with CRA without sacrificing profit and safety, because CRA loans are less profitable on average than other loans, and banks are forced to adopt high loan-to-value ratios, low-cost checking, and other practices that have a higher degree of risk. Further, CRA puts up obstacles to mergers and acquisitions, impeding the efficiency of the banking system. Fourth, they assert that CRA raises costs. Direct costs of compliance are high and excessive documentation is required because the CRA ratings are inexact and subjective, they contend, and indirect costs also arise from the public relations campaigns that banks have to wage in order to convince community groups not to challenge their merger applications.

Bierman, Frasar, and Zardkoohi (1994) followed up with a paper specifically designed to test Macey and Miller's conclusions with actual data. They found that banks with high CRA ratings did have significantly lower interest income, which the authors equate to a measure of bank profitability. They argue that this conforms with Macey and Miller's contention that institutions subject to CRA are at a competitive disadvantage. However, other tests of loan performance in the Bierman et al. study, as well as those undertaken by the Federal Reserve and the

OCC, do not support the Macey and Miller contention that CRA lending is less safe. In fact, loans made by banks that have high CRA ratings were not found by the authors to be any riskier than those made by low-rated banks.

The Macey and Bierman analyses were performed before the 1995 reform of the CRA enforcement system was put into place. As explained above, those reforms transformed the somewhat vague criteria into evaluations based on actual performance. The examination process was also streamlined, particularly for small banks, to make compliance less burdensome. A recent analysis by the banking regulators estimated that small banks spend only 10 hours per year on CRA record keeping and reporting requirements.[31]

Another critique by Lacker (1995) argues that evidence of market failure in neighborhood lending or of redlining by banks is inconclusive. According to Lacker, CRA thus becomes a redistributive program, transferring resources to low-income neighborhoods by imposing a 'tax' on banks and savings associations. When the law was enacted in 1977, bank charters conveyed numerous benefits; however, Lacker argues that the banking environment and technology have changed substantially since then, eroding the advantages of banks relative to nonbank competitors. He argues that banks now compete with non-bank lenders and that the CRA is an unfair burden. However, Lacker offers no evidence that the burdens of the bank charter outweigh its benefits, including deposit insurance, access to the Federal Reserve Board's discount window, and other services, and as noted above, evidence of continued barriers to capital is well documented in numerous other studies.

A further review of the Macey and Miller arguments was conducted by Hylton and Rougeau (1996). They provide theoretical arguments refuting several of the major arguments against the CRA but supporting several others. For example, they show that there are circumstances where banks will miss profitable lending opportunities even though their lending decisions are thought to be rational and financially sound. One example is when there are positive neighborhood externalities – where renovation or construction of a few houses or stores would improve the whole neighborhood, yet the value of a loan to the bank is lower than the 'social value' of the loan. Another example is the case where credit markets are not in equilibrium (for example, a bank offers a below-market interest rate for public relations purposes) and as a result, credit-rationing leaves a number of equally qualified applicants available, making it possible for the bank to discriminate without suffering any economic costs. This can also happen when markets contain a large share of borderline applicants, as is the case in the home mortgage market.

The authors also dismiss the Macey and Miller argument that CRA forces banks to search in unpromising areas for lending prospects by noting that banks already spend a great deal of time in such activities – for example, coaching borderline mortgage loan applicants. CRA might be understood as a means of making an investment in good will. These are several examples of market failures that enforcement of fair lending laws may not resolve but that CRA could alleviate.

The problems with CRA, according to the authors of this study, are that it could create disincentives for banks to expand to distressed areas, and it singles out federally insured banks and thrifts for regulatory oversight. Their recommendation is to shift to a subsidized approach involving incentives for banks to lend in low-income areas.

With respect to the possible disincentive effect, it should be noted that under current regulations implementing CRA, a bank's assessment area 'must ... consist generally of one or more MSAs [metropolitan statistical areas], ... or one or more contiguous political subdivisions, such as counties, cities, or towns,' and if the bank chooses only a portion of such areas, the area may not 'reflect illegal discrimination' and may not 'arbitrarily exclude low- or moderate-income geographies...'[32] Given these rules for determining assessment areas, it is unlikely that a bank could, in order to avoid its obligation to serve a low-income community, simply choose not to locate a branch or serve that community at all, and the authors provide no empirical support for their view.

A last point of their article is that market forces may be moving financial institutions in ways consistent with CRA. Banks have seen their deposits fall as mutual funds and other sources of investment have grown, and may increasingly turn to under-banked inner-city communities as a source of new markets, especially with the push toward direct deposit of government transfers.

Much of the literature critical of CRA referred to early concerns about the program, which have since been rectified. Issues regarding ambiguities in processes and procedures in CRA bank ratings have been corrected by regulatory reforms. The arguments in the literature that banks will always be able to identify the most profitable and sound lending decisions, absent CRA, have been demonstrated not to hold in circumstances that give rise to externalities and social costs, circumstances which are often encountered in low-income communities. Moreover, the evidence that markets for business and mortgage credit remain imperfect appears to be fairly well documented. It has been demonstrated that CRA loans are profitable, delinquency and default rates are equivalent to conventional loans, and prepayment risk for investors is low. The literature has not yet conclusively addressed the applicability of CRA beyond federally insured banks and thrifts.

Conclusion

Academic research and available data confirm that CRA has played an important role in expanding access to credit to help rebuild housing, create jobs and restore the economic health of communities across the United States. Lending by financial institutions subject to CRA accounts for almost half of all small business loans, and has made a significant contribution to the increase in home ownership in low-income neighborhoods. The available evidence also suggests that this expansion of credit has occurred consistent with safe and sound banking practices. CRA lending is profitable to banks and performance is in line with conventional types of lending. While significant strides have been made in meeting the credit needs of all communities, academic research documents a continuing need for CRA and other mechanisms to ensure that access to capital is available in all our nation's communities.

REFERENCES

Avery, Robert B., Patricia E. Beeson, and Mark S. Sniderman, 'Accounting for Racial Differences in Housing Credit Markets', in John Goering and Ron Wienk, eds., *Mortgage Lending, Racial Discrimination, and Federal Policy*, 1996, Washington, D.C.: Urban Institute Press, pp.75-142.

Avery, Robert B., Raphael W. Bostic, Paul S. Calem, and Glenn B. Canner, 'Credit Risk, Credit Scoring, and the Performance of Home Mortgages', *Federal Reserve Bulletin*, July 1996, Vol. 82, No. 7, pp. 621-648.

Avery, Robert B., Raphael W. Bostic, Paul S. Calem, and Glenn B. Canner, 'Trends in Home Purchase Lending: Consolidation and the Community Reinvestment Act', *Federal Reserve Bulletin*, February 1999, Vol. 85, No. 2, pp. 81-102.

Bates, Timothy, 'Commercial Bank Financing of White- and Black-Owned Small Business Startups', *Quarterly Review of Economics and Business*, 1991, Vol. 31, No. 1, pp. 64-80.

Bates, Timothy, 'Unequal Access: Financial Institution Lending to Black- and White-Owned Small Business Startups', *Journal of Urban Affairs*, 1997, Vol. 19, No. 19, pp. 487-495.

Beshouri, Christopher P. and Dennis C. Glennon, 'CRA as Market Development or Tax: An Analysis of Lending Decisions and Economic Development', *Proceedings of a Conference on Bank Structure and Competition*, Federal Reserve Bank of Chicago, 1996, pp. 556-585.

Bierman, Leonard, Donald R. Frasar, and Asghar Zardkoohi, 'The Community Reinvestment Act: A Preliminary Empirical Analysis', University of California, *Hastings Law Journal*, Vol. 45, March 1994.

Blanchflower, David G., Phillip B. Levine, and David J. Zimmerman, 'Discrimination in the Small Business Credit Market', *National Bureau of Economic Research Working Paper*, No. 6840, December 1998.

Bostic, Raphael W. and Glenn B. Canner, 'New Information on Lending to Small Businesses and Small Farms: The 1996 CRA Data', *Federal Reserve Bulletin*, Vol. 84, Jan. 1998, No. 1, pp. 1-21.

Calomiris, Charles W., Charles M. Kahn, and Stanley D. Longhofer, 'Housing-Finance Intervention and Private Incentives: Helping Minorities and the Poor', *Journal of Money, Credit, and Banking*, Vol. 26, August 1994, No. 2, pp. 634-674.

Canner, Glenn B., 'Evaluation of CRA Data on Small Business Lending', paper presented at the Federal Reserve's 'Conference on Business Access to Capital and Credit', Washington, D.C., March 1999.

Canner, Glenn B., Stuart A. Gabriel, and J. Michael Woolley, 'Race, Default Risk and Mortgage Lending: A Study of the FHA and Conventional Loan Markets', *Southern Economic Journal*, Vol. 58, July 1991, No. 1, pp. 249-262.

Canner, Glen and Wayne Passmore, 'The Community Reinvestment Act and the

Profitability of Mortgage-Oriented Banks', *Federal Reserve Board Finance and Economics Discussion Series* draft 1997-7, January 1997.

Canner, Glenn B. and Wayne Passmore, 'Residential Lending to Low-Income and Minority Families: Evidence from the 1992 HMDA Data', *Federal Reserve Bulletin*, February 1994, Vol. 80, No. 2, pp. 79-108.

Carr, James H. and Isaac F. Megbolugbe, 'The Federal Reserve Bank of Boston Study on Mortgage Lending Revisited', *Journal of Housing Research*, 1993, Vol. 4, No.2, pp. 277-314.

Cole, Rebel A. and John D. Wolken, 'Financial Services Used by Small Businesses: Evidence from the 1993 National Survey of Small Business Finances', *Federal Reserve Bulletin*, July 1995, Vol. 81, No. 7, pp. 629-667.

Evanoff, Douglas D. and Lewis M. Segal, 'CRA and Fair Lending Regulations: Resulting Trends in Mortgage Lending', Federal Reserve Bank of Chicago, *Economic Perspectives*, Nov./Dec. 1996, pp. 19-43.

Fairlie, Robert W. and Bruce D. Meyer, 'Trends in Self-Employment Among White and Black Men: 1910-1990', University of California Santa Cruz Working Paper, 1997.

Goering, John and Ron Wienk, eds., *Mortgage Lending, Racial Discrimination, and Federal Policy*, 1996, Washington, D.C.: Urban Institute Press.

Haynes, George W., Charles Ou, and Robert Berney, 'Small Business Borrowing from Large and Small Banks', paper presented at the Federal Reserve's 'Conference on Business Access to Capital and Credit', Washington, D.C., March 1999.

Hylton, Keith N. and Vincent D. Rougeau, 'Lending Discrimination: Economic Theory, Econometric Evidence, and the Community Reinvestment Act', *Georgetown Law Journal*, Vol. 85, No. 2, December 1996.

Immergluck, Daniel, 'Intrametropolitan Patterns of Small Business Lending; What Do the New Community Reinvestment Act Data Reveal?', *Urban Affairs Review*, 1998, forthcoming.

Kim, S. and G. Squires, 'Lender Characteristics and Racial Disparities in Mortgage Lending', *Journal of Housing Research*, 1995, Vol. 6, pp. 99-113.

Lacker, Jeffrey M., 'Neighborhoods and Banking', Federal Reserve Bank of Richmond, *Economic Quarterly*, March 1995.

Ladd, Helen F., 'Evidence of Discrimination on Mortgage Lending', *Journal of Economic Perspectives*, Vol. 12, Spring 1998, No. 2, pp. 41-62.

Macey, Jonathan R. and Geoffrey P. Miller, 'The Community Reinvestment Act: An Economic Analysis', *Virginia Law Review*, Vol. 79, No. 2, March 1993.

Marisco, Richard D., 'Fighting Poverty Through Community Empowerment and Economic Development: The Role of the Community Reinvestment and Home Mortgage Disclosure Acts', *New York Law School Journal of Human Rights*, Spring 1995, Vol. 12, pp. 281-309.

Meeker, Larry and Forest Myers, 'Community Reinvestment Act Lending: Is it Profitable?', Federal Reserve Bank of Kansas City, *Financial Industry Perspectives*, December 1996, pp. 13-35.

Munnell, Alicia H., Geoffrey M. B. Tootell, Lynn E. Browne, and James McEneany, 'Mortgage Lending in Boston: Interpreting HMDA Data', *American Economic Review*, 1996, Vol. 86, No. 1, pp. 25-53.

Office of the Comptroller of the Currency, 'Home Mortgage Lending in 1996: An Analysis of Home Loan Growth to Minorities and Denial Rate Patterns', March 31, 1998.

Padhi, Michael, Aruna Srinivasan, and Lynn W. Woosley, 'Credit Scoring and Small Business Lending in Low- and Moderate-Income Communities', paper presented at the Federal Reserve's 'Conference on Business Access to Capital and Credit',

Washington, D.C., March 1999.

Schill, Michael H. and Susan M. Wachter, 'A Tale of Two Cities: Racial and Ethnic Geographic Disparities in Home Mortgage Lending in Boston and Philadelphia', *Journal of Housing Research*, 1993, Vol. 4, No. 2, pp. 245-276.

Scoring with Minority-Owned Businesses: Closing the Credit Gap, O.N.E. *Second Annual Report on Minority-Owned Businesses and Their Banking Relationships,* 1998, p 2.

Shlay, Anne B., 'Influencing the Agents of Urban Structure: Evaluating the Effects of Community Reinvestment Organizing on Bank Residential Lending Practices', report to the U.S. Department of Housing and Urban Development, 1998, forthcoming.

Tootell, Geoffrey M.B., 'Redlining in Boston: Do Mortgage Lenders Discriminate Against Neighborhoods?', *Quarterly Journal of Economics*, November 1996, Vol. 111, No. 4, pp. 1049-1079.

Wells Fargo Bank, 'Latino Owned Businesses: Access to Capital', October 2, 1997.

Yinger, John, 'Discrimination in Mortgage Lending: A Literature Review', in John Goering and Ron Wienk, eds., *Mortgage Lending, Racial Discrimination, and Federal Policy*, 1996, Washington, D.C.: Urban Institute Press, pp.29-74.

Yinger, John, 'Housing Discrimination is Still Worth Worrying About', *Housing Policy Debate*, 1998, Vol. 9, No. 4, pp. 893-927.

ENDNOTES

1   National Community Reinvestment Coalition, 'CRA Dollar Commitments Since 1977', December 1998.

2   Edward M. Gramlich, 'Examining Community Reinvestment,' remarks at Widener University, November 6, 1998.

3   The significant income disparity between minorities and whites is the basis for the reference to minority data as a proxy for low- and moderate-income individuals in some cases. In 1997, black households comprised 12 percent of all households in the U.S. and Hispanic households (which can be of any race) represented 8 percent of the total. Median income for black households that year was $25,050, 35.7 percent lower than the $38,972 for white households, and Hispanic median income was $26,628, 31.7 percent lower than white income.

4   Gramlich, op. cit.

5   Cited by Gramlich, op. cit.; Michael LaCour-Little, unpublished paper, May 1998.

6   Gramlich, op. cit.

7   Federal Financial Institutions Examination Council, 1998.

8   Canner, 1999.

9   Office of the Comptroller of the Currency, 1999.

10   Gramlich, op. cit.

11   Haynes, Ou, and Berney, 1999.

12   Padhi, Srinivasan, and Woosley, 1999.

13   Cited by Secretary Robert E. Rubin, at the National Community Reinvestment Coalition Annual Conference, March 19, 1998.

14   'Success in Community Development Lending: 33 Examples from around the Country', The Federal Reserve Bank of Philadelphia, 1993.

15   Chase Community Development Success Stories, 1998.

16   'Community Reinvestment Advocates', The Federal Reserve Bank of Philadelphia, 1993, p. 19.

17   Los Angeles, California, January 1998.

18   See also Calomiris et al. (1994), who argue that support for community development

banks is an effective policy response to discrimination in credit markets.

19   For example, five local banks invested equity in the Louisville Community Development Bank and donated Bank Enterprise Award funds to its non-profit arm, boosting its capabilities to provide small business technical assistance. In 1998, the Community Development Bank was recognized by the Small Business Administration for providing more loans to African Americans than any other bank in Kentucky. *Courier-Journal*, Business Section, 1998.

20   Michael Collins, 'The Many Benefits of Home Ownership', Neighborhood Reinvestment Corporation, November 1998.

21   Meeker and Myers, 1996.

22   Avery, Bostic, Calem, and Canner, 1996.

23   Bear Stearns, 'Securities Backed by CRA Loans: A New Product for Mortgage and Asset-backed Investors', October 2, 1997.

24   OCC Advisory Letter 97-7, July 23, 1997.

25   Canner and Passmore, 1997.

26   Many of the studies in this section refer to racial rather than neighborhood disparities in lending. However, the effects of the racial or ethnic composition of the neighborhood are difficult to separate from the race or ethnicity of the individual borrower since the two tend to be highly correlated, and in many instances indirect neighborhood effects can be surmised from the direct racial effects.

27   Federal Financial Institutions Examination Council, 1998.

28   *Scoring with Minority Owned Business: Closing the Credit Gap*, 1998.

29   Lee Romney, 'Survey Suggests Need for Reform in Inner-City Lending', *Los Angeles Times*, Business Section, p.1, December 17, 1998.

30   In addition to those described above, many other researchers find that housing discrimination is still a common problem for minorities. See, for example, Avery, Beeson, and Sniderman (1996); Ladd (1998); and Yinger (1996, 1998).

31   1999 Paperwork Reduction Act findings released by banking regulators, June 1999.

32   12 CFR 25.41

Chapter five

Re-socialising banks: between re-regulation and welfare banking?

Re-regulating banks: the unfinished agenda

Andy Mullineux
(University of Birmingham, UK)

(1) Why regulate banks?

Deposit taking institutions, henceforth called banks whether they are mutually owned or publicly (shareholder) owned, are special. They differ from other 'firms' in that they not only produce services (e.g. payments and other money transmission services) and products (deposit and savings account packages and loans etc.) and sell them to consumers (often their own depositors), but they also have a fiduciary responsibility to the depositors whose savings and transaction balances they are safekeeping. They differ from other financial intermediaries in that they have liabilities (demand deposits) which are widely accepted as a means of payment ('money').

The difference is starkest for non-mutual banks since there is likely to be a conflict of interest between depositors, who seek low risk repositories for their savings, and hence relatively low returns, and shareholders, who eschew the safe option of placing money in a bank and seek a higher return, and hence exposure to risk of loss of wealth, by investing in shares (equities). 'Institutional shareholders' (insurance, pension and mutual funds, and the big banks in countries such as Germany and Japan) are the most important shareholders. Members of the general public increasingly tend to hold shares vicariously through participation in the aforementioned funds. In so doing they buy into more diversified, and hence lower risk, portfolios of investments.

The managers of banks are hired by the owners (shareholders) to run the bank on their behalf. There is thus a separation of ownership and control, which creates a 'corporate governance' or 'principal (owner) – agent (manager)' problem. How can the owners ensure that the managers run the (banking) firm in their best interests, rather than pursuing their own goals (high salaries, large expense accounts etc.). This is a major concern to all publicly-owned (non-private, state-owned or 'not for profit') companies. Corporate governance is a major concern of governments at present, many of whom have commissioned reviews of their corporate governance systems. UK governments have undertaken three reviews into aspects of corporate governance in the post decade (Cadbury,

Greenbury, Hampell), and a fourth is underway. The French, German and other governments have also commissioned full-scale reviews. Further, the US Treasury has expressed concerns about 'short-termism', in the sense that financiers may not be taking a sufficiently long term strategic review when allocating capital (debt and equity); and so too has the UK Treasury.

It is, however, clear that the managers of banking firms also have a fiduciary duty to a group of stakeholders other than the shareholders, namely their depositors. It is not clear that the managers should run banks solely in the interests of shareholders, for shareholders would like the managers to invest their funds, and those of the depositors, in a more risky portfolio of assets (loans etc) than the more risk averse depositors would like. The corporate governance problem is thus more complex for a banking firm and government intervention, in the form of regulation limiting the freedom of bank managers, is deemed necessary. This is usually justified by the need to protect depositors from excessive risk taking and just plain bad, incompetent or fraudulent, behaviour on the part of bank management. The regulations aim to achieve a level playing field between depositors and shareholders, to eliminate bad practise and to encourage best practise.

We have not got the space here to deal with the complex issue of what best regulatory practice is currently believed to be. Suffice to say that the on going re-regulation (deregulation or liberalisation) of banking that started a couple of decades ago is the result of a major change of emphasis. Prior to the 1970s, regulations tended to prohibit or discourage certain types of banks from engaging in particular activities. The UK 'clearing banks' (Barclays et al, for example) were discouraged from making home loans, whilst building societies did not offer 'current accounts' and the associated payments services because they were not members of the Committees of London Clearing Banks. Now UK banks and building societies not only make both home loans, offer accounts providing payments services and issue credit cards etc, but they can also sell insurance. Indeed 'bancassurance' companies, selling both banking and insurance services, has become common across Europe. Enabling legislation is expected to be passed in the US in the near future and was passed in April 1998 in Japan. In the 1930s, the US established a highly regulated banking system. Since the early 1980s there has been a substantial regulatory reform. The UK in contrast, operated a club like regulatory system; with few statutory restrictions but lots of guidance from the Bank of England.

The aim of the restrictions was to stop banks from exposing themselves to excessive or unfamiliar risks. The re-regulation has been designed to allow banks to engage in whatever investment risks they wish to, provided they hold sufficient capital to cover the losses that could result from exposure to those risks. The focus is thus on risk-related capital adequacy. The expectation is that if risks are accurately measured, a bank that exposes itself to more risk will be required to hold more capital. Since capital is expensive and earns no return, indeed dividends have to be paid, the system essentially imposes a tax on risk taking and this should condition the behaviour of shareholders and the management they employ. The second line of defence for depositors is commonly a funded deposit insurance scheme (now required in the EU and long established, since the 1930s, in the US). All banks pay into the fund in proportion to their deposits (and with risk adjusted premia in the US, but not, lamentably, the EU). Should a bank be allowed to fail by the regulatory authorities, its depositors can expect to get all (in the US, where deposits of $100,000 or less are 100% insured) or part (in the EU where, at minimum, 90% of deposits of less than €20,000 are insured) of their money back.

Additional reasons for wanting to prevent failures of large banks or large numbers of banks (systemic failures) are well known, namely: the need to prevent disruption to the payments system, which is infrastructural to commerce; the need to prevent shrinkage in the money supply (bank laundering) and a credit crunch. In other words, the need to avoid large negative external effects on the economy which can be expected to lead to or exacerbate a recession, perhaps converting it into a deflationary depression like the 1930s.

(2) The financial revolution

The net effect of the change in the regulatory emphasis has been broadly beneficial to depositors and other consumers of financial services and products. There has been a substantial increase in competition in the provision of financial services and a significant widening of the range of products available. Communications and information technology is increasingly making banking more convenient, and even perhaps pleasurable. Banks are effectively open well beyond the traditional 9.30 a.m. to 3.00 p.m. hours that were common until the 1970s. Many branches now open on Saturday mornings and services can be accessed at leisure by telephone or computer links. Cash can be collected 24 hours a day from automated teller machines (ATMs) and there has been a 'plastic card' revolution. The general quality of the provision of financial services to the personal sector has thus improved dramatically. Productivity has also been increased through greater use of communications and information technology and charges have not increased commensurately.

Improvements in service provision to small and medium sized enterprises (SMEs) has been less marked. It should be noted that this is a market in which the UK clearing banks face much less competition. On behalf of the Treasury and the Department of Trade and Industry, the Bank of England has kept the provision of services to SMEs under review since the early 1990s recession; when there was considerable criticism of the banks treatment of SMEs. The Bank's annual reports on the financing of small firms[1] have, however, born witness to a marked improvement in service provision in this sphere too. Nevertheless, the UK government has commissioned an investigation, led by Donald Cruickshank, into the efficiency of banks service provision to sales and this has subsequently been widened to cover all retail (including payments), service provisions and charging.

Despite the undoubted successes arising from the re-regulation of banks, a number of concerns have been raised. The vast majority of depositors and consumers of financial services have benefited from the revolution in the provision of financial services, but there are important exceptions. It is to this issue that we now turn.

(3) Social and financial exclusion

The revolution in the provision of financial services is increasingly driven by data processing capabilities. This is not surprising since the very existence of banks is the result of information deficiencies ('asymmetric information'). Banks are firms that collect deposits, supply associated payments services, and gather information to facilitate the lending of the funds collected in pursuit of a return commensurate with the lending risk. The better they are at gathering and processing information on potential borrowers, the more efficient they will be at pricing the risks to assure an adequate return. The revolution in communications and information technology allows banks to gather and process much more information than previously thought possible. Increasingly they can target products on the most receptive populations, offering: loans to 18 year olds about to go to university; loans to people who seem to change their car every three years; pension products to the baby-boomers as they begin to think about providing for their retirement, etc.

The big banks increasingly try to 'cherry-pick' the best personal and SME customers, using mail shots, offer products at prices which undercut those of the target's own banks. The big banks are thus tending to get bigger and many smaller banks are seeing the quality of their asset portfolios decline as they lose their best customers to the bigger banks. The rate of consolidation has been accelerated through mergers and, in response to increased competition, banks have sought efficiency gains by closing branches. Some even wonder whether branches will disappear altogether as younger, more computer-literate, generations replace the older generations as they pass into retirement and beyond.

The discussion in the first section of this chapter narrowly viewed the stakeholders in banks to be depositors, consumers, management and shareholders. The employees were shamefully ignored, but so too were those people and enterprises which have been excluded from participating in the financial revolution. Those without a telephone or a computer or access to a bank branch. Those who do not qualify to open a bank account, perhaps because they have insufficient income or knowledge about how to go about it. And those who find it difficult to raise finance from banks because they want to borrow too little (to cover the banks costs of originating and servicing the loan), have insufficient collateral (wealth) or business experience or training, or appear to be too high a risk to qualify for a loan or an overdraft or a credit card. There is growing evidence of social exclusion and financial exclusion seems to be an associated problem that aggravates the former.

There is an old adage that banks only lend to those who are wealthy enough not to need to borrow. Behind this lies the observation that banks frequently require security or collateral to be pledged against loans. Those with insufficient wealth (e.g. shares or a house) to pledge are less likely to be able to borrow. One reason those with a secure income or wealth borrow, however, is to enable themselves to smooth their consumption over a lifetime. Young people, especially those with young children, seek to borrow heavily to buy their house, car, fridge, cooker, dishwasher, television etc. because their current income is insufficient to enable outright purchases to be made. As they move in to middle age they will tend to become net savers in preparation for retirement. Once retired they are likely to become net consumers again. Should such opportunities for financial planning only be available to the relatively rich i.e. the conventionally employed and the independently wealthy? How can 'outsiders' break into the system and get a credit rating? Is there a need for further government intervention to include the would be depositors and borrowers and users of payments services in the banking system? It is well known that it is costly to be excluded. Loans from moneylenders are much more expensive than those from regulated banks and charges for cashing cheques are much higher than charges by regulated banks for traditional payment services.

(4) Including the financially excluded

Historically, those not wealthy enough to borrow from, or have accounts with, banks have tended to set up their own banks, perhaps with the assistance of philanthropists. Throughout Europe, and subsequently beyond, (in the US etc), there are examples of mutual or co-operative banks, building societies and insurance companies being established. The common aim was to pool small savings and use the accumulated funds to provide insurance or loans to members.

Many of the surviving first wave mutuals have outgrown their roots and redefined their membership. Some are very large institutions (Rabobank in the Netherlands, Credit Agricole in France, Nationwide Building Society in the UK etc.) and many have already abandoned mutuality (e.g. Halifax and Abbey National, two of the UK's largest former building societies which 'converted' into commercial banks). The merits of the continued mutuality of large building societies and insurance companies is debatable. It remains to be seen, for example, whether Nationwide's conversion to the provision of value to its owners (depositors and borrowers) will enable it to compete successfully with commercial banks who must distribute dividends to shareholders.

The more important question is whether the time has come to encourage the creation of a new wave of mutuals. There is some evidence that this is occurring through the creation of credit unions, but does more need to be done to facilitate this tendency? Is there a role for the government here in setting a regulatory and tax environment in which mutuals can thrive? But, what of the need to maintain a level playing field? For example, with some justification, the French commercial banks frequently complain about privileges enjoyed by the old mutuals; who have been the sole distributors of special tax efficient government backed savings instruments. Favouring the creation of new mutuals to fill gaps that clearly exist in the provision of financial services by banks should be less controversial. But will not the new mutuals increasingly compete with mainstream banks as they grow?

Is the answer not, alternatively, to concentrate on inducing banks to fill the gaps in their current provision? If so, how much emphasis should be placed on carrots, as opposed to sticks? My view is that banks should be given the opportunity to participate in filling of the gaps before sticks (such as US style Community Reinvestment Act) are wielded. Anyway, within the EU, the imposition of a CRA on UK banks alone would be difficult to justify, and EU level legislation might take years to pass.

Another trend in regulation has been to require banks, and other financial and non-financial firms, to disclose more information. Increasingly, this could be cheaply done using updateable web pages and banks should probably be required to publish more information on their lending and deposit taking activities. However, because they trade on information that is costly to collect and process, there is a limit to the detail of disclosure that can be required without forcing banks to publish information that competitors can trade on without going to the cost of collecting and processing it themselves (the 'free-rider' problem). So carrots look to be the best bet, at least initially.

It should be recognised that non-mutual banks are profit seeking organisations. However, the larger banks, which are too big to be allowed to fail, do enjoy considerable implicit deposit protection at the taxpayers expense and do have some consequent public duty. They should thus be expected to ensure that, for example, basic payments services are accessible in most localities in the UK. Where the last branches are closed in rural or inner city urban areas, they should, for example, be replaced by advanced automated teller machines, the networks of which are increasingly being shared by banks anyway as a result of the Link project. The banks essentially monopolise these networks and some level of UK-wide service provision can reasonably be expected. If they can make a case, then the banks should seek some compensation from the government for costly service provision in remote and difficult areas. With a suitable level of subsidy, it should not take too much to assure access to payments services with a plastic card that has a limited range of services. A rechargeable chip card or 'electronic wallet', which would prevent holders from going overdrawn with their card issuer, might, for example, be appropriate for the facilitation of access to basic payments services.

Access to credit, overdrafts and loans is another matter. Potential borrowers will be shunned: if they want to borrow uneconomically, from the banks' perspective, small amounts; are unable to post collateral; or lack of track record (credit history or rating). For personal customers, credit unions offer a route to developing a savings, and then a borrowing, record prior to approaching banks for larger (e.g. home) loans. One suspects, however, that banks could offer savings schemes that entitle regular savers access to loans after a qualifying period or after a minimum balance had been built up. Such savings accounts could perhaps also be linked to basic transaction banking accounts providing free, if in credit, basic payments services.

As regards small enterprises, micro-finance schemes may well be appropriate. There is growing evidence of successful schemes in developing countries. There is less evidence that such schemes are directly transferable to developed countries, where it is not clear that the peer pressure that ensures low default rates in Bangladesh (Grameen Bank) and elsewhere can be brought to bear in countries such as the UK. Subsidies may be needed to induce the banks to put aside funds for disbursement in small amounts and loan guarantees by the government, to protect banks against anticipated loan defaults, may be needed; at least at the outset.

There is widespread evidence that loan guarantees have been successfully utilised as a means of stimulating bank lending to SMEs (e.g. especially in Germany and the US). The Small Business administration in the US has been experimenting with guarantees targeted on businesses run by women and members of minority ethnic groups. To qualify for the guaranteed loans, applicants are commonly expected to undertake basic business training. This in turn reduces the incidence of failure, making the lending more attractive and reducing the risk incurred by the guarantors. The outcomes of these experiments should be monitored and trials of similar schemes should be introduced in the UK; where in recent years the Small Firms Loan Guarantee Scheme has increasingly focused on larger, growth orientated, firms. The new Regional Development Agencies might, for example, be allowed to trial some locally targeted loan guarantee schemes and the associated training and advice could be provided through Tecs, Enterprise and Business Links, and Chambers of Commerce.

In conclusion, there seems to be plenty of scope for involving banks, credit unions, and other new mutuals in the elimination of financial exclusion. To the extent that banks are unable to profit from their engagement, they should be compensated for any social financial service provision above and beyond their public duty. Tax concessions, subsidies, loan guarantees and basic business training provision can all be deployed to achieve the desired outcome. If the carrots fail, then its time to consider either the stick or government provision of social banking services. There is, after all, scope for greater use of Post Office Counters' services. La Poste in France has, for example, installed ATMs at many of its branches.

ENDNOTE
1   The Sixth Report, *Finance for Small Firms*, was published by the Bank of England in January 1999.

Some thoughts on mainstreaming social finance with the help of Government: the example of the Dutch Green Funds

Koert Jansen
(Triodos Bank, Netherlands)

On 1 January 1995 the Dutch green investment scheme came into effect. The scheme exempts private investors from paying tax on their interest or dividend derived from green investment funds. These are funds which are supervised by the Dutch Central Bank and which invest at least 70% of their funds in green projects. A project is considered 'green' when it meets the criteria of the Green Projects Regulation and has received a green certificate from the Ministry of Housing, Spatial Planning and Environment. Examples of sectors which are generally considered green are organic farming, renewable energies and nature conservation.

The objective of the green investment scheme is to make low interest loans available to the green sector. It works as follows: green funds pay out net dividend or interest. The investors thus don't pay any tax on this income and, consequently, accept a relatively low return on their investment. This results in a supply of low cost funds for the green funds which for them forms the basis for providing green loans at favourable interest rates.

Since the start of the green investment scheme, 6 banks have introduced green funds. Meanwhile, their combined fund volume adds up to about EUR 1 billion. The scheme is considered a great success. It fulfils its objective by reducing the financial burden for green projects while at the same time attracting a large public to the field of green investment. This success has attracted the attention of other countries and other sectors. Could a similar tax scheme work in, for example, Italy? Or could a green investment scheme be developed for the social sector? In this article I will not try to answer these – complicated – questions. Rather, I will try to address some of the strengths, weaknesses, opportunities and threats (SWOT) of the scheme as we know it in the Netherlands. This might be helpful for those who do want to explore the possibility of similar schemes in their own country or sector.

Strengths

A key 'strength' of the green investment scheme is its *simplicity*. The introduction of the scheme required the amendment of only two articles in the Law on the Income Tax. Tax exemption is clear, easy to understand and attractive, which makes it easy to incorporate in a financial product. Also the two regulations by which the scheme has been implemented – the Green Projects Regulation and the Green Funds Regulation – are based on simple criteria for the projects and funds respectively.

Important is also that the *project criteria are clear and exhaustive*. This means that there is very little room for manoeuvre. Generally speaking, the green fund will know before hand whether a project will be awarded by a green certificate and thus whether it is worthwhile starting a certification procedure. An organic farming project, for example, will certainly qualify for a green certificate when it can show it is certified by one of the Dutch certifying institutes for organic farming (SKAL or Demeter).

Crucial to the success of the green investment scheme is the *competition* it has created between the green funds in financing green projects. Without such competition, there would be less of an incentive for green funds to translate their low costs of funds into low interest rates on green loans. Hence, it would probably lead green funds to charge higher interest rates, creating higher margins. Obviously, a government scheme cannot 'create' competition. However, by being strict on the project criteria and at the same time allowing for an interesting enough tax incentive for private investors – a situation is created whereby the availability of funds is higher than that of eligible green projects.

An element of strength is finally also the *market orientation* of the scheme. Different from subsidy schemes, the allocation of funds is (within the green criteria) market driven. This means that the risk that funds are made available to projects which are not viable is relatively low.

Weaknesses

There is one exemption to the clear and exhaustive project criteria, stated above as being a 'strength' of the scheme. The Green Project Regulation includes a category of 'other projects which are to the benefit of environment and nature'. This category was introduced to create some flexibility for the government to award green certificates for projects which do not fall within one of the fixed categories. This *'open end'* in the regulation has lead to lengthy and cumbersome trail and error efforts by projects and funds. It has also lead a number of less ambitious projects to receive a green certificate. Some of these projects, such as district heating, are relatively sizeable and thus absorb substantial part of the government budget available for the scheme.

Although the scheme is simple and project criteria are generally simple and exhaustive, the procedure to receive a green certificate can be lengthy. Although this is not only to blame to government – green funds sometimes prepare incomplete applications – the various (semi-) governmental bodies involved in the certification procedure make *red tape* unnecessarily long.

Some critics of the green investment scheme say that most investors in green funds are *tax driven* and lack any 'higher' ideals of supporting the green sector. Although to some extent this will certainly be the case, it is questionable whether this element constitutes a weakness of the scheme. The tax benefit has made people invest in sectors which they would normally have left aside. By investing in such things as wind energy and organic farming, they experience that these sectors are good for their money. In the long run, these people might be willing to make these investments without a tax benefit.

Opportunities

An opportunity for the green investment scheme is to define *new, pioneering green (sub-) sectors* that need access to affordable finance. For example, ecological construction has been introduced as a green category in 1996. The maximum loan amount a green fund is allowed to make to the (would-be) owner of an eco-house has been limited to EUR 30,000. This type of limitations could be instrumental in further fine-tuning the scheme.

An opportunity is also to *upgrade project criteria* for some existing categories to new standards. For example, what was considered 'innovative' in terms of ecological construction in 1996, is nowadays sometimes considered mainstream.

Threats

As with any government supported scheme, the green investment scheme may at any time be modified or even brought to an end. The green funds, and their clients, are therefore highly *dependent* on the development of *governmental policies* and the *political composition* of the government. It is important, therefore, that there is frequent consultation between government and green funds as part of the government's monitoring and policy making activities.

The green investment scheme might well be threatened by its own success. Since its start in 1995, its success has created pressure to include projects less green than those for which the scheme was originally intended. This pressure is sometimes successful. In some cases, this may even lead to the creation of complete new categories of less green projects. Cycle tracks are an example. The *dilution* of the green ambition of the scheme is therefore a real threat.

Concluding remarks

Introducing a scheme like the green investment scheme, although simple and market oriented, has always the potential danger of failure or, even worse, of market disruption. It should therefore not only be well designed and prepared before introduction, it also needs after care: maintaining its strengths and decreasing its weaknesses. Even important is to develop a long term vision on how threats can be avoided and opportunities can be exploited, without allowing opportunistic behaviour.

Social credit in a welfare state: lessons from ADIE

Maria Nowak
(President of ADIE, the Association for the Right to Economic Initiative, France)

Micro-credit emerged in the informal sector in the third world where self employment is the predominant feature of the economic structure. The example of ADIE, which for ten years has been trying to establish micro-credit in France, illustrates the problems encountered with this approach in an industrial country with a social welfare system. In a developing country, micro-credit finances revenue-generating activities undertaken by a poor peasant population or by micro-entrepreneurs in the informal sector, for whom the main stumbling-block is lack of access to capital. In France, where informal economic activity is suppressed and where business development is the province of a very elaborate banking network, micro-lending finances the creation of businesses by the unemployed or those on social welfare, who do not necessarily have any prior experience in this field and who are working in a particularly complex regulatory framework.

I. An obstacle course

The predominance of salaried employment

Creating one's own job is a question of mentality more than anything else. One hundred years of salaried employment and its attendant advantages, fiercely defended by the unions, a public opinion in favour of big business, even if it is in the minority (93% of businesses in France employ less than 10 people), have made self-employment seem a last resort activity with little status and much more risk than salaried employment. The reality that job security has become more and more precarious is gradually eroding this perception. However it remains predominant in a country where work is highly regulated, where ideology plays an important role in political life and that of the unions, and where education does not embrace the culture of enterprise.

Integration with social security

Focusing on the mass production model, which by its very nature offers little scope for initiative from workers, has led the unions to centre all their efforts on protecting salaried employees, and to neglect the claims of initiative and creativity. Such social welfare was possible during the 'glorious thirties'.

In the past 20 years the growth in unemployment has had two detrimental effects: on the one hand, unemployment benefit or income support as well as free social security cover do not encourage beneficiaries back into work. On the other hand, social security costs are a heavy burden on all businesses, but more particularly on those just starting up. The maintenance of benefit for a period of 6 months and the exemption from social security costs for a year (which assumes a selective agreement in workplace administration) are not sufficient to ease the transition from social security to self employment, and actually promote work in the black market economy.

The complexity of the regulatory framework for self-employment

Welfare states generally have a strongly developed administrative structure. This is the case in France, where the public sector in the widest sense employs 27% of the workforce, as against 17% in Germany and the United States. This structure constantly interferes with market forces both in terms of supply and demand:

The regulatory framework of business has an elitist character. It does not meet the needs of simplicity, coherence and stability which allow the growth of self employment. One of ADIE's concerns is to adapt each year to the changes in the welfare system affecting the creation of business, including government measures such as support in the form of equity or quasi equity, and different types of training and advice made available to entrepreneurs in forms more or less suited to their real needs. Such instability is made still worse in France by the phenomenon of regional and departmental decentralisation which makes the rules, particularly in matters of assistance for jobs and businesses, inconsistent throughout the country.

For more than 20 years in France, assistance in the form of equity had existed for unemployed entrepreneurs. The forms which this assistance took changed almost every year and when finally, it was extended to all the unemployed and those in receipt of income support, the government decided to withdraw it at the end of 1996. Since then, certain regions and departments have tried to reinstate it in a small way by linking it, in certain cases, to financial and mentoring support from ADIE. Others have preferred to create trust loan funds at zero interest rates, easily absorbed into quasi equity. Yet others have pursued the two routes simultaneously, creating an abundance of funds in certain regions and none in others.

Obstacles to the use of micro-credit

Quite apart from the obstacles to creating self-employment, France (and probably the rest of Europe also) has no suitable legal framework for the use of micro-credit. Banking law permits *associations* to extend credit only to its members and on their equity. The minimum capital necessary to create a *financial company* is high (15 million FF), and the system of control (supervision, free reserve ratios) does not correspond with the specific characteristics of micro-finance. Finally, the interest rates are fixed very low (currently an APR of 11.23% for personal loans) and do not allow a sufficient margin to cover the risks, especially as, in the case of the partnership with the banks described later, it is they (the banks) who receive the interest.

As a result the financing of micro-credit is very complex. For ADIE, loans are financed up the limit of 25% on its equity (direct loans) and up to the limit of 75% by the banks, which delegate to the Association the social and intermediary financing, but package the loans to conform with banking law. The risk is shared (30% – the banks, and 70% – ADIE, plus a counter-guarantee from different guarantee funds). The cost of mentoring the entrepreneur and business follow-up are taken by local authorities, the state and the European Social Fund.

II. Results in spite of everything

A growing demand

Despite the obstacles, micro-lending is growing. Since 1990, ADIE has been able to finance and mentor 5,600 businesses created by the unemployed and recipients of minimum income support (RMI). Current demand is estimated at 20,000 per year, but could rise to 200,000 if the institutional climate was more favourable. It is worth noting, in general terms, that it is supply that is creating demand and that the spirit of enterprise does not depend on the level of training of entrepreneurs: nearly 10% of ADIE's clients are almost illiterate and 40% have had no professional / vocational training.

Rates of survival and repayment higher than the national average

The survival rate of micro enterprises is slightly higher than the national average for all businesses: 75% at the end of two years and 55% at the end of five years. About 20% of businesses grow and create other jobs. The rate of repayment is of the order of 90%, compared with 75-80% for the average of state-guaranteed loans made to Very Small Enterprises.

Growing participation by the banking sector

Constraints in banking law forced ADIE to find partnership solutions with the banks. This partnership now covers a large group of institutions, for the most part mutualist in character: Crédit Mutuel, Municipal Credit Banks, Savings Banks, Popular Banks, Crédit Agricole, Crédit Coopératif. With its history of credit to micro-entrepreneurs, ADIE allows the socially excluded to access the traditional banking system progressively. By externalising part of the risk and the extra charges of management and mentoring, its work has dispelled the myth amongst the banks that lending to disadvantaged customers involves too much risk.

National coverage envisaged in the year 2000

At present ADIE has 18 regional subsidiaries. Its three year plan envisages the intensification and extension of the network to cover the whole country until the year 2001. In addition the Association is active in Réunion Island and Mayotte Island and is busy extending its work into other overseas departments and territories.

Lower job creation costs in relation to the costs of unemployment

In contrast to developing countries, it is impossible to target, within the current institutional framework, any financial autonomy of the system. However, if you consider social and economic profitability, it has largely been achieved. In relation to the cost of (supporting) an unemployed person, estimated by the Ministry of Employment to be 120,000FF per year, the cost of creating self-employment by means of micro-lending seems derisory: 10,000FF in accompanying costs per year plus 2,000FF to cover risk. Even when you add in the additional costs such as state-subsidised advice (4,000FF) granted to certain entrepreneurs or subsidies given by certain regions and linked to financing by ADIE (15,000FF on average), the total cost is no more than a quarter of the annual cost of an unemployed person.

The social bond re-established

The main problem in a welfare state is that, the responsibility for social problems having been delegated to the state, the bonds between citizens become loose. People think that having paid their obligatory tax and social security contributions, they no longer have to be concerned about the problems of their neighbours. Even the unemployed become simply the objects of aid and assistance policies and cease to attract concern with regard to getting back into the job market. Such behaviour has serious consequences, to the extent that unemployment is not uniquely the result of government policies but also that of individual behaviour. The initiative of the unemployed people themselves, and the mutual support of those around them, play an important role in reintegration. By trusting the excluded, micro-lending allows them to regain confidence in themselves whilst at the same time restoring the social bond ('credit' comes from 'credere', to believe).

III. Perspectives

The extension of ADIE's network and its partnership with the banks lends an increasing credibility to micro-lending in the eyes of the public authorities. The Association's three year (1999-2001) plan has three objectives:

- To increase the number of financed projects from 2,000 to 6,000 per year and to include even more disadvantaged groups, such as young people living in problem areas, travellers, those newly released from prison, etc.
- To formulate proposals to the public authorities in order to develop further

the regulatory framework for micro-enterprises and for micro-credit.

- To develop exchanges with other European countries so that micro-credit becomes one of the main instruments of active policies to combat unemployment and in the fight against social exclusion. The study on the conditions for the development of micro-enterprises and micro-credit undertaken by ADIE, at the request of the European Commission and in which German, English and Italian partners took part, is a first step in this direction. It will be followed by other work in the field of training, in advice and to put pressure on the politicians of the EU member countries and the European Union.

The ultimate objective of micro-lending in an industrial country with a social welfare system is to invent, at the dawn of the twenty-first century, a new form of popular capitalism, which places together work and capital in the same pair of hands, and to build, beyond rampant liberalism and state socialism, a new social contract combining initiative and mutual support.

Community Reinvestment Partnerships: financial intermediation and local economy regeneration

Patrick Conaty
(Director, Rebuilding Society Network, UK)

The Community Reinvestment Acts (1977 and 1993) in the USA have begun to attract interest recently from both British and European policy makers – especially following the growing success since the 1993 amendments which have resulted in the escalation year on year of private capital earmarked for investment in the regeneration of low to moderate income neighbourhoods right across America. Arguably more important than the raising of community reinvestment dollars has been the encouragement the legislation has had in fostering creative partnerships between both bank and non-bank financial intermediaries – the so-called Community Development Financial Institutions. The catalytic role of these bodies which include Community Development Banks, Community Development Loan Funds, Community Development Credit Unions, Neighbourhood Equity Funds, Micro-Loan Funds, and Revolving Loan Funds for Housing Improvement has been recognised by President Clinton in a separate enabling law – the Community Development Financial Institutions Act (1993). Indeed the CRA and the CDFI laws are now working well in complementary ways.

While the passage of a European CRA would take many years to achieve and be widely resisted by the mainstream financial institutions, the fostering of community reinvestment partnerships between bank and non-bank local financial intermediaries should be proactively encouraged by both politicians and regulators in different EU member states in the way that the British Government is already doing in respect to an emerging community reinvestment partnership between banks, building societies and community credit unions. However while British credit unions are recognised as an exempt body under the EU Banking Directives, this is not the case for other non-bank financial intermediaries in Europe that are pioneering creative ways and novel financing instruments to reduce poverty, widen access to employment, and to stimulate regeneration. The wide range of CDFIs operating in the USA is also identifiable in a less developed way among the European members of INAISE. Indeed it stands to reason that like in America, a diverse range of non-bank financial intermediaries with different areas of specialisation will be necessary to reduce financial services exclusion in Europe as well. To put the issue in context, financial services exclusion and effective ways to reduce it needs to be seen against the evolving background of the globalisation of the financial services industry.

Background: banking and local economy needs

The globalisation of financial services has its origins in the 1979-83 period which was marked by both the abolition of international exchange controls and the initial phase of the deregulation of financial services in the USA and Europe. Deregulation instigated the cross-selling of financial services which today makes it hard to distinguish a British bank from a building society in respect to retail services (e.g. savings accounts, personal loans, mortgages, and money transmission) or a bank from an insurance company in respect to investment products and services. Indeed the new French word, bancassurance, which rapidly was adopted into the English language, signifies clearly that a bank is no longer just a bank. Thus Blair's passing of the regulatory responsibility for both lending and investing activity from the Bank of England to the new British super-regulator, the Financial Services Authority, was no mere coincidence but a landmark event that highlighted the relative decline of banking (especially nationally and regionally) against the growing ascendancy of a much more powerful and global financial services industry.

Prior to deregulation, cross subsidy within banking institutions was the norm in respect to service provision. Therefore less remunerative services like the provision of bank facilities in small towns or in low income urban neighbourhoods were paid for by greater revenue generating activity from funds on the money markets, from credit cards or from commercial mortgage lending. As British building societies with significantly less historic investment in operational overheads (i.e. large staffing levels and a large branch network) challenged successfully the banks in several product areas, unit delivery costs became the fierce competitive edge. With the rapid deployment of labour saving technology, the onslaught of unrelenting competition in the UK over a decade ago simultaneously sounded the death knell of traditional banking provision. As a result, the standard conception of a bank as a single institution began to be undermined by the revolution and integration in financial services that was occurring. Banking was becoming less and less a static noun and more and more a dynamic verb. Consequently, the bank branch is today surplus to requirements. It simply cannot compete in unit cost delivery comparisons with other supply routes and partner agencies such as the telephone, the supermarket, the post office, or the internet.

Thus from a restricted and sole provider in the high street, banking as a service has disintegrated beyond all recognition with the past. Indeed there is a growing sense (but not yet among politicians and regulators) that we can all do our own banking at both the corporate and the community level. Indeed the 'do it ourselves' practitioners range right across the class divide from unpaid and unemployed volunteers among over 500 community credit unions in Britain to the top corporations on the London Stock Exchange that execute their own banking in house or amongst their peers.

However while major corporations do their own banking to save on costs and fees, low income communities start community credit unions because they have no other banking choice or options apart from self-help and mutual aid. Indeed the socio-economic impact of the financial services revolution has been to widen choice and access for the rich and to reduce and restrict it for the poor. There is much evidence in Britain to indicate that as a consequence an American pattern of geographically identifiable patterns of community disinvestment is now appearing. If allowed to develop, this trend in financial services exclusion will like in the USA accelerate the growth of underlying patterns of social disadvantage including housing disrepair, the demise of local employment and declining public services. In such circumstances, even the perception of high risk can easily become self-fulfilling prophecy with at first the retreat and then the complete withdrawal of banking and insurance services from a community. The decision in London to close the last bank branch in an inner city neighbourhood in Liverpool can effectively pull the plug on the local economy. With local small traders (and shoppers) no longer able to get cash – they either quickly go out of business or are forced to take their commercial activity elsewhere with the jobs migrating with them.

While the new technology clearly makes redundant bank branches, it also makes redundant the ancient tradition of relationship banking. Lending decisions, especially for small loans, rely less and less in Britain today on personal contact with the borrower and are made now normally at regional or national level on the basis of credit scoring. Lack of property, periods of unemployment, and lack of an established credit history all contribute to low credit scores and underlie the difficulty that low income households face in qualifying for loans from a conventional financial institution. The shifting of credit decisions for small business lending to credit scoring by UK banks in recent years has further excluded from enterprise opportunities many individuals in low income neighbourhoods who would in the past been given the benefit of the doubt on the strength of the local knowledge of the local bank manager.

The preference by British banks for larger, small business loans (i.e. particularly above £250K) has been described as the 'Flight to Quality'. While in unit cost terms large loans are clearly less expensive to manage and therefore ostensibly more profitable for the supplier, from the borrower's position, larger loans require larger repayments and thus potentially represent a decline in business profitability and a threat to the sustainability of the enterprise – particularly in periods of recession. Thus in general terms large loans may be less costly but they are inherently more risky; conversely, small loans by their nature are more costly to supply, but normally less risky. There is a balance to be struck between these to extremes. Indeed this is the historic skill and art of relationship banking – the objective being to lend not too little or too much, but the sufficient sum of working capital or development credit to increase the productivity, performance, and healthy expansion of the enterprise being backed. By comparison, credit scoring is an inexact science that simply cannot deliver such a highly skilled and face to face banking service which is crucial to the financial health and achievement of local economies. While the importance of recruiting and retaining skilled teachers in areas of high unemployment is widely recognised to ensure equality of opportunity for low income children, unfortunately the similar requirement to retain the skilled bankers in disadvantaged neighbourhoods to back tomorrow's entrepreneurs is not equally recognised. As a result of such short-sightedness, the real tragic skill loss in the 1990's with the massive redundancy of thousands of relationship bankers with thirty or more years of small business lending experience has yet to be realised.

The growing preference by banks to make larger loans has the unrecognised overall effect of actually raising local levels of market risk. Indeed it is rarely observed that small loans have been historically associated with a virtuous circle of local economic well being as illustrated below.

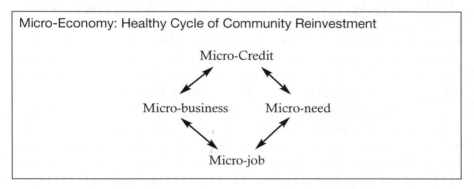

Micro-Economy: Healthy Cycle of Community Reinvestment

Micro-Credit

Micro-business   Micro-need

Micro-job

The arrows in the illustration reflect the ways that small personal loans in a sound local economy feed into the income streams of micro-service entrepreneurs – each local economic actor achieving thereby a balanced equilibrium outcome through the local match up of supply and demand effects.

Removing the supply of small loans is metaphorically equivalent to puncturing a tyre. The deflationary impact is obvious from the illustration as like the loss of air in a tyre the loss of micro-credit to a local economy leads quickly to the slow-down and in due course stopping of healthy local economic cycles. The virtuous cycle of reinvestment is thus transformed into its opposite – a vicious cycle of disinvestment. This adverse phenomenon is the case irrespective of the type of business or need (i.e. enterprise, personal or housing) denied by the withdrawal of micro-credit from a particular neighbourhood or specific locality.

Just as agricultural regions require for their survival seasonal rainfall, cities, towns and neighbourhoods require cyclical reinvestment for their sustenance and renewal. As the illustration shows, the health of the local economy relies upon local purchasing by local households and businesses, the recycling of local savings through localised investment, access to credit for local improvements to housing and business infrastructure, and access to finance for both commercial and personal needs.

Historically and unceremoniously local banks and building societies have utilised local market knowledge and relationships to play this local investment role since the Industrial Revolution. Moreover since 1945 this private sector reinvestment has been complemented and evened out by regional reinvestment and social security policies of Government. While the latter category of transfer payments are essential and the former can be corrective if well designed and targeted, working in isolation without the bedrock of cyclical community reinvestment, such Government policies are bound to fail.

As a rule, the bigger the banking institution, the bigger the average loan size. With merger activity continuing to be encouraged by pension and other fund managers, micro-loans in the emerging single European consumer and small business markets are fated on present trends to lose out. In general terms, unless they are advanced at credit card rates of interest, the micro-loans most needed by those on low income (e.g. under £3,000) are too costly and unprofitable for commercial institutions to set up and administer. Hence the fundamental need for non-bank financial intermediaries to address this non-commercial market in creative ways. The practice of CDFIs in the USA and many INAISE members in Europe indicates in abundant fashion how such intermediaries can operate effectively to provide most of the financial services needed by low to moderate customers not able to meet the criteria of conventional institutions. In some situations financial intermediaries can provide services because they are willing to take a lower return or to assume a higher level of risk. In other circumstances, they deploy effectively techniques that allow for costs to be transferred to borrowers (e.g. group loan assessment and group loan repayment) or for risks to be borne by a community of borrowers (i.e. mutual guarantees). CDFIs and social finance organisations by the nature of their social mission can attract resources to help achieve their goals (e.g. low cost investment funds, volunteer labour, unpaid Directors, and grant assistance for particular purposes) that conventional commercial institutions cannot call upon.

Scaling up social finance in the European Union

Against a rising tide of social and financial services exclusion in Europe, the fundamental need to revitalise local cyclical reinvestment is crucial. The weakening in most countries of local banking services as the traditional provider of this function needs to be recognised. If this trend is not acknowledged and addressed, patterns of large scale community disinvestment will emerge over the next decade in Europe similar to the no-go investment localities in the USA. This investor retreat which the Americans refer to as 'redlining' poses a massive balance sheet threat to those with long term investment in such potentially blighted markets. Those at risk of a property market collapse include local homeowners, business owners, landlords, mortgage lenders and property insurers. In the past few years evidence of property market failure and local housing abandonment has begun occurring right across the North of England (e.g. Liverpool, Salford, Manchester, and Newcastle upon Tyne).

In parts of Salford, house prices have plummeted by 80 percent from £25,000 five years ago to £5,000 for the same house in the exact same street.

While the outward migration of people and capital from many of these local-ities is far too severe to be arrested by community reinvestment, there are a number of areas where an effective reinvestment partnership strategy between local residents and businesses, banks, non-bank social finance organisations and local/regional Government bodies can arrest the decline and regenerate local communities. While the US market segmentation of community finance institu-tions is not directly applicable to Europe, the unique history of Government encouraged community reinvestment practice in America dating back to 1977 has fostered a pattern of niche market specialisation that in broad terms is also likely to emerge on this side of the Atlantic over the next ten years – especially if finan-cial intermediation between banks and non-banks is enabled by EU member states. The illustration below indicates the markets targeted by CDFIs in the USA.

The New Economics Foundation report, *Small is Bankable* (1998), indicated a somewhat similar grouping of British social finance organisations in three main overlapping categories – community credit unions, community loan funds, and micro-loan funds. However in terms of scale of activity, balance sheet size, age of organisation, and customer base, there is no comparison between the recently formed community loan funds in the UK and their counterparts in the USA which are generally 10-15 years older. Similarly while Community Development Credit Unions in the USA have on average 2,500 co-operative members each and an asset base approaching $3 million, British community credit unions are on average only one tenth this size. Like in France with ADIE, Britain has only one major provider of micro-loans for the self-employed, the Prince's Youth Business Trust (PYBT), which is targeted at young entrepreneurs (i.e. under 30). While PYBT has had a larger loan loss rate than the larger micro-loan providers in the USA (i.e. ACCION and Working Capital), nonetheless it has demonstrated the scope for scaling up social finance in Europe. Through its several regional offices, PYBT has financed over the past ten years the formation of over 40,000 new enterprises unable to qualify for a bank loan. Over the next five years, PYBT intends to almost double the current volume of its lending and to establish a sepa-

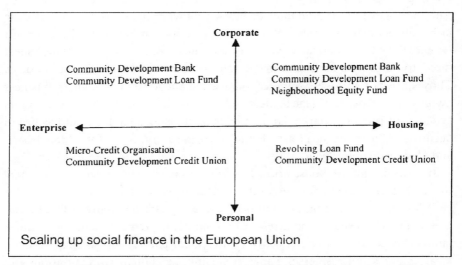

Scaling up social finance in the European Union

rate new programme to assist the older unemployed set up in business. There are as yet no Community Development Banks or Revolving Loan Funds for housing repairs and improvements in Britain.

A coherent and effective strategy for developing bank and non-bank community reinvestment partnerships in Europe needs essentially to be two fold as the approach and collaboration is totally different in the corporate and personal lending markets, as is the level of regulation that the non-bank lender must comply with; personal lending entails both high standard operational costs and additional regulatory overheads.

The Community Development Loan Funds (CDLFs) in the USA, like their counterparts in the UK and Europe, are principally small corporate lenders in the fields of enterprise and property lending. Some CDLFs specialise only in small business lending and others in the financing of affordable housing projects. A few focus entirely on lending to non-profits and Third Sector organisations. The American history of CDLFs indicates that as they develop beyond their first five years of lending most tend to develop a mixed pattern of both enterprise and property investment activity with in-house lending teams specialising in each respective field. This dual strategy assists in diversifying the CDLF's lending portfolio and helps spread the risk between larger and more secure property loans and shorter term and more insecure enterprise credit.

On bigger loans, CDLFs will frequently co-finance a project with a bank and normally secure the latter's participation by assuming a subordinate lender's position. This partnership enables many near bankable small business deals to go forward that would not otherwise have proceeded. Additionally on housing projects in the USA, CDLFs specialise in early stage project financing – working with often new and inexperienced non-profit housing developers. Assistance provided may include pre-finance development funds in some cases, but most commonly, site acquisition finance and construction credit. Once the building project is completed and the developed units rented, permanent financing is usually provided by one of the CDLFs banking partners. This longer term housing financing accounts for the tremendous leveraging effects of CDLF operations with approximately nine private or public sector dollars attracted by each dollar of CDLF investment. Given the amounts of capital required, CDLFs will normally refinance or securitise their housing finance loans during the first 1-3 years of a project. This recycles their limited funds to do more financing projects but additionally provides their banking partners sound investment opportunities with a verifiable credit history.

In the UK there are only a few Community Loan Funds – virtually all of which are less than five years old. Nonetheless future development prospects on the lending experience to date looks as promising as it has been proven to be in the USA. For example, Aston Reinvestment Trust (ART) in Birmingham in its first two years of trading has already achieved a leverage ratio of 2.5 on its small business and Third Sector lending portfolio. ART is working with six major British banks and indeed is getting its best referrals from the private sector. As ART develops its planned housing fund over the next year, its community reinvestment multiplier effect on each pound it invests should rise year on year. Like ART, the Delaware Valley Community Reinvestment Fund started out as only a small revolving loan fund for Philadelphia about 15 years ago. Today it is almost a $30 million fund that is making several large investments in inner city projects every week.

In respect to personal lending, the strategy here for scaling up by social finance organisations needs to be based on product specialisation, high volume turnover and wherever possible by off-loading costs on to either groups of borrowers (e.g. in respect to micro-credit for enterprise) or to third parties funded by grants to provide technical assistance to prospective borrowers. Fundusz Mikro in Poland is an outstanding example of how unit costs in a micro-credit operation can be kept to a minimum and high volumes generated (e.g. over 15,000 loans in the first four years of operation) with nonetheless low loan loss rates (i.e. well under 2 percent). Incentivising group loans with lower interest rates (e.g. 7-9 per cent below individual loans) has been a key Fundusz Mikro innovation along with the implementation of an ambitious business plan for rapid growth from the commencement of operations; this plan necessitated heavy up front investment in a centralised back office facility in Warsaw to service a systematic roll out of 30 small branch offices nation-wide.

In respect to the British Government's intervention to assist community credit unions go for growth over the next few years, the emerging strategy focuses on the development of a co-operatively owned central back office facility. ACCION in the USA is also developing a new strategy and methodology for its micro-credit expansion plans nationally that are almost identical to the practice of Fundusz Mikro. In respect to an appropriate legal structure for micro-lending organisations (e.g. for enterprise, consumer, or housing repairs and improvements), credit unions are attractive because of the added potential of generating low cost sources of operating funds from members savings. However to date, few credit unions have specialised in niche market and product areas – normally preferring to advance general purpose, consumer loans. Those Community Development Credit Unions like Self-Help Credit Union in North Carolina that have focused on a niche, like personal housing finance, have achieved outstanding rates of growth over the past decade. Not surprisingly therefore, ACCION (USA) sees the credit union legal structure as potentially attractive for its future growth plans.

Micro-Loan organisations and community credit unions succeed impressively in advancing personal credit for business or household needs that banks and main-stream financial institutions simply cannot replicate. Thus there is a sound basis for collaborative and strategic partnerships – particularly as there are a number of commercial opportunities open to the banks through a creative relationship. For example, while banks are not willing to provide commercial credit to new entre-preneurs in areas of high unemployment, they can, through partnership with micro-credit organisations, offer other needed banking services such as bill payment facilities, cheque accounts, and deposit accounts. Through the bank and non-bank partnership, full banking services can thus be jointly provided. Such a co-operative approach in Birmingham is presently being jointly developed between the city's 25 community credit unions and NatWest Bank with the bank willing to assist the credit unions develop shop front premises and city-wide bill payment services over the next five years. More such joint ventures are vital to demonstrate by action the wide scope of what can now be done by building upon the sound foundations estab-lished by many European social finance organisations over the past ten years.

In respect to the ways and means, advancing personal credit and very small loans (i.e. from £300 – £3,000) represents a particularly difficult challenge – espe-cially if the vast needs for micro-loans for consumer, housing repair, and enterprise purposes among the unbanked are to be addressed. The methodology for making small corporate loans is well proven and replicable by adopting the good practice of many INAISE members in this area. However for loans below £5,000, espe-cially for business needs, to achieve impact micro-credit practitioners have to set their sights on a large scale operation. The high volume and centralised back office methodology pioneered in Europe successfully by Fundusz Mikro is the way forward here and it is not coincidental that other social finance organisations are reaching this conclusion at present (i.e. ACCION and the British credit union movement – the latter for consumer loan expansion and national outreach and impact). To implement such a strategy will require in each EU member state signif-icant assistance from the banks, the public sector, foundations and social investors.

For scaling up existing operations or establishing new ventures, resourcing needs for robust micro-lending business plans will entail time limited subsidies for staffing and operating budgets, risk capital, access to low cost money transmission facilities, state of the art information technology, significant sums of below market rate, loan capital, and low cost branch office premises. For example, Fundusz Mikro required up front funding of $24 million to achieve its impressive roll out of a nation-wide branch network over four years. The Street UK initiative which is presently raising capital to attempt to replicate Fundusz Mikro's achievement in Britain and Northern Ireland needs to secure £49 million to fund a five year drive to achieve operational sustainability and freedom from ongoing subsidy. About 90 per cent of the Street UK requirement is for low cost loan capital to deliver over 60,000 loans to at least 16,000 micro-enterprises through a 40 office branch network by 2005. It is radical and ambitious thinking like this that is necessary by social finance ventures across Europe if effective plans for reducing financial services exclusion are to really begin to get on with the huge task.

In respective to legislation, the European social finance organisations and members of INAISE cannot wait on the unlikely prospect of a EU Community Reinvestment Directive over the next five years – desirable as such an objective would be. However given the 'win-win' opportunities for creative partnership between banks and non-bank intermediaries to pursue a voluntary community reinvestment agenda. There is a real need for such a possibility to be actively encouraged and supported appropriately like the Blair Government has begun doing in the UK – not just for community credit unions but for community loan funds and for micro-credit organisations as well. In brief, the list of public sector measures required to aid community reinvestment ventures in this way are similar to those legislated for by Clinton under the Community Development Financial Institutions Act. In Europe similar legislation initiated at Member State level would be especially enabling; most importantly it would acknowledge and legitimise the indispensable role required of social finance organisations in reducing both social and financial services exclusion. Unfortunately in many EU countries, non-bank financial intermediaries cannot even operate without a banking licence. This social entrepreneurial exclusion needs to be urgently addressed by the European Union. A simple remedy would be to allow other EU Member states to operate the same exemption from the First European Banking Directive that Britain holds for credit unions and to extend this exemption to the full range of social finance organisations required to target the diverse range of credit needs in close partnership with the banking sector. Indeed when credit unions that were invented by the German social finance pioneer, Raiffeisen, in the middle of the last century can no longer be established in Germany by low income citizens to reduce their own poverty and disadvantage in a self-help and mutual aid way, there is something legally amiss in the heart of modern Europe.

The regulation of social economy banking

Malcolm Lynch
(Senior partner of Malcolm Lynch Solicitors, UK)

Regulation of social economy Banking

The publication of the consultative paper 'A new capital adequacy framework, by the Basel Committee on Banking Supervision' is a useful reminder that there are shortcomings in the current capital adequacy framework for banks and it is appropriate to develop more sophisticated tools in order to strengthen the supervision of credit institutions. As the world's social economy banking sector grows, the thrust of that paper provides an opportunity and a hope that some of the special characteristics of social economy banking can be recognised by supervision authorities within the capital adequacy framework.

Social economy banking took on its formal status with the establishment of the International Association of Investors in the Social Economy (INAISE) in 1989. A small group of European credit institutions came together because of their common purpose of social economy banking; that is banking policy, procedure and practice, in particular investment, where the social outcome is a relevant criteria for the banking decision.

Whilst the Basel Committee on Banking Supervision is primarily concerned with systemic problems arising out of the internationalisation of banking groups and the development of bancassurance, social economy banks are concerned about the gaps in financial service provision which appears to go hand-in-hand with this trend. Gaps which are manifested in part in the absence of credit for the unemployed and socially disadvantaged; to organisations seeking to combat it; to new sustainable products and services and to some extent a closure of local financial facilities. Social economy banking encompasses such well known names as the Grameen Bank of Bangladesh, Finansol in Latin America, Shore Bank in Chicago and Triodos Bank in Europe. However, it also includes many much smaller institutions, some not strictly credit institutions and therefore without banking status, which are seeking to provide credit in these fields. Some of these are regulated as banks by national laws.

Social economy banking raises a number of competition questions for the supervisory authorities. Many social economy credit institutions have developed because of an absence of the provision of credit services to particular markets, or at least an inadequacy of provision. The development of credit unions in Ireland and the United Kingdom, and the development of credit institutions specialising in environmental funding in Germany and Switzerland, meet market needs which are otherwise unsatisfied.

In the United States the various Community Reinvestment Acts have been developed to bring more transparency into banking operations to use not, for the purpose of credit risk assessment, but for the purpose of ensuring appropriate market coverage in what are perceived to be, but are not necessarily, high risk areas of lending to businesses and individuals in poor communities. Whilst there has been some examination of whether a Community Reinvestment Act should become a new European Union Directive, discussion has so far been fairly limited as to the merits and demerits of this approach. If a more laissez faire approach is to be taken to community reinvestment by banks in Europe, then should there be a more uniform approach to the development of the regulation and supervision of social economy credit institutions within the European Union?

One cap fits all?

The intention of the first Banking Directive of 12 December 1977 was that the scope of the measures relating to credit institutions would be as broad as possible, covering all institutions whose business is to receive repayable funds from the public whether in the form of deposits or in other forms such as the continuing issue of bonds and other comparable securities, and to grant credits for their own accounts. However, it was recognised that some exceptions must be provided in the case of certain credit institutions to which this Directive cannot apply. Article 2(2) of the Directive set out a list of credit institutions of member States to which the Directive did not apply. In Ireland this included credit unions and in the United Kingdom it also included credit unions, although there was no separate law for credit unions in the United Kingdom at the date the Directive was enacted.

The Council, acting on a proposal from the Commission, is entitled to decided on amendments to the list in Article 2(2). Subsequent Banking Directives have established minimum capital adequacy and other supervisory thresholds for regulated credit institutions which are linked to the Basel Committee on banking supervision.

At the time when the Directives were first crafted 20 years ago, it was envisaged that it would lead to increased competition between credit institutions. Whilst competition between regulated institutions has undoubtedly increased, it is much more arguable whether the range of services and their reach in terms of population has increased or decreased. In some communities within the

European Union, not only is there an absence of competition, there is an absence of a product or service. The European Central Bank rightly has concern about the restrictiveness of certain labour markets within the European Union and is pressing for their deregulation. A similar argument could be made in respect of credit supply, whose purpose is to tackle, quite often, that same problem.

Safeguards for exempt credit institutions

The consultative paper on a new capital adequacy framework makes the point that 'The financial world has developed and evolved significantly during the past ten years, to the point where a bank's capital ratio, calculated using the current Accord, may not always be a good indicator for its financial condition'. The collapse of Barings Bank was a high profile illustration of this. The regulation of credit unions in Ireland and the United Kingdom demonstrates that it is possible to create credit institutions which do not, in their early development, meet the capital adequacy ratios of regulated credit institutions under the Banking Directives. This does not mean that they are not prudent and solvent credit institutions which lack supervision. Over time, a system of supervision has been developed for them. Why, however, should the establishment of these institutions be restricted to the United Kingdom and Ireland? Would they not equally meet the needs of consumers in other member States of the European Union? Similarly are there exempt institutions in other member States which should be permitted in the UK?

Some credit institutions, such as credit unions, are based on the assumption there is proximity between the investor and the borrower, as well as restrictions on lending, which together with internal assessment procedures and market discipline, involving restrictions to certain markets in which they specialise, ensure the safety and soundness of those institutions in conjunction with their supervisors. Such credit institutions are sophisticated within their own niche area of operations in which they have specialised.

The minimum regulatory capital requirements have on the whole served the European Union constructively in promoting safety and soundness in the financial system. Article 4(2)(a) of the second Banking Directive of 15 December 1989 grants the option for supervisory authorities of member States to grant authorisation to particular categories of credit institution, initial capital of which will not be less than one million ecu. If a competitive credit market is to continue, then social economy credit institutions, in particular, whose purpose is to invest for the general good, deserve particular support for development. The minimum requirement should apply to them, provided that they restrict their activity whilst growing their sophistication in their particular niche.

The Basel Committee in its proposal for the new capital framework, bases it on three main pillars. The importance of the retention of the minimum regulatory capital requirements. The second pillar is the importance of a Supervisory Review of an institution's capital adequacy and internal assessment process and the third pillar is the need for greater market discipline. The Basel Committee takes the approach that some banks may be more sophisticated than others. There is an inference in the paper that this sophistication is likely to be based on computerised systems and other techniques which enhance knowledge of the bank about its operations. The sophistication can take other forms too.

The Grameen Bank, for example, has developed a very sophisticated technique of lending relatively small amounts to poor people in what has become known as 'microcredit'. Each borrower, before receipt of a loan, becomes involved in a small group of four or five persons, (in the case of Grameen Bank predominantly women), who themselves assess the person who should receive the loan first in addition to the Supervisory Officer of the bank. This type of sophistication, which arises from specialisation and the use of credit risk techniques which are not generally used in the same manner by non-social economy banks, can lead to a low risk credit institution. On the other hand, the use of that same technique by a more sophisticated non-social economy bank may not be successful since it is not specialised in that field. The Committee is examining the capital treatment of a number of important credit risk mitigation techniques and it is hoped that it should examine the techniques of the microfinance banks too, in order to give comfort to regulatory authorities that the social economy banks can be sound even though the traditional risk rating of this type of loan portfolio would be considered unsound.

The Committee suggest that external credit assessment institutions might evaluate the banks and this might be taken into account as the basis for regulatory capital requirements. Social economy finance institutions have, under the umbrella of INAISE, been engaged in sharing experience and, more recently with the assistance of the European Union, benchmarking of best experience. Supervisory authorities might gain comfort from the external assessment of social economy finance institutions. Such external valuation would give comfort to advisory authorities in new member States of the European Union in which communities are seeking to respond to credit deprivation by the establishment of their own financial institutions.

The Committee's paper enhancing bank transparency discusses how a bank that is perceived as safe and well managed in the marketplace is likely to obtain more favourable terms and conditions in its relations with investors, creditors, depositors and other counter-parties than a bank that is perceived as more risky. This is one of the core elements of social economy banks whose transparency often involves the provision of information on all loans which they make and whose investors are more patient investors tied to the financial institution through support for the social purpose in which they are engaged. Nonetheless, supervisory authorities would need to mitigate this patient investor quality as the financial institution grows in size and perhaps become somewhat more remote.

Corporate risk and micro lending

The Committee recognises that a shortcoming of the current Accord has been that inadequate recognition is given to the differing credit quality of claims on corporates. The Committee proposes preferential risk only for the very highest quality credits. Proposals such as this are of little comfort to micro lenders to corporates since they essentially leave such loans classified as high risk. If credit mitigation techniques of the social economy micro lender are working, then its track record will demonstrate that a lower risk rating may well be appropriate. If the risk assessment techniques of social economy finance institutions are to make a significant difference, then it will be important to provide better information on the internal ratings of risk by social economy banks. The Committee appears to have an open mind and recognise that different banks and different systems may have equal validity and their problem is how can supervisory authorities understand the deviation from the standardised supervisory approach. The Committee welcomes a meaningful dialogue with the industry on these issues, which leaves open the opportunity for social economy banks to engage in this dialogue.

Importantly, the Committee seeks to evaluate the extent of risk reduction by guarantees, a technique that is used strongly by the anthroposophical social economy banks as well as some micro lenders. The Committee is concerned about the relationship between the default probabilities of the original borrower and the guarantor. The question for social economy banks is to how to evaluate what is often a personal guarantee in a manner which supervisory authorities can take into account.

So far as the second field is concerned, the supervisory review of capital adequacy, often the biggest hurdle for social economy banks, is the understanding by the supervisory authority of the nature of the bank's activities. This is not to say that other banks are not engaged in the same type of lending. What it usually means is that in other banks there is an absence of transparency and specialisation which would permit the bank itself to identify that type of lending as a particular subset of its overall activities. For example, the NatWest Bank plc only identified its lending to the charity sector, for the first time in its history, in 1999. For some social economy banks, this is a key area of their lending and data is regularly available. For the bank supervisors, this presents a problem because of their lack of experience with non-social economy banks' activity in these fields. Understanding by the regulators would be critical for the application of principles of bank supervision.

The Committee indicates that it will continue its efforts to enhance a supervisory review process. This gives an opportunity for social economy banks to share their experience with the Committee so as to enable it to make sounder judgements about the quality of social economy banks. The existing transparency of social economy banking is a key feature of its market discipline for its investors and borrowers and supervisory authorities. As social economy banks grow, they will inevitably compete with non-social economy banks who may themselves seek to develop market niches in competition with those developed by the social economy banks. If social economy banks are to remain true to their purposes, they should not let this competitive threat obscure their principle of transparency.

The growth of social economy banking since the first Banking Directive in exempt and regulated credit institutions has demonstrated the many shortcomings in the regulatory regimes for these institutions. Social economy finance institutions have demonstrated that there is a competitive market for their products and services, and by engaging in those markets where many non-social economy banks have retreated or reduced their service, create a competitive banking environment.

Regulatory authorities

The scale of operations of social economy banks, whilst still very small, has found itself on the agenda of national governments in the European Union as they seek to provide different ways of tackling social exclusion and sustainability. If the Committee can recognise that the existing capital adequacy framework is a 'blunt instrument' which requires elaboration, perhaps they can also recognise that to sustain competition in banking that provides services to all sections of the community, the regulation of social economy banking by both exempt and regulated credit institutions merits a more sophisticated treatment too.

A European regulation for social responsibility of banks? Learning the lessons from the US Community Reinvestment Act[1]

Jan Evers
(IFF, Institut für Finanzdienstleistungen, Hamburg, Germany)

This article aims to discuss if and in what form regulation may prove efficient in implementing social responsibility[2] into the banking business. It uses the US-American regulatory framework, in particular the Community Reinvestment Act,[3] as a benchmark to develop ideas for an efficient European regulation.

A. Introduction

Banking has to be sound and safe for its customers as well as for the stability of the currency and economy. The development of European banking within the globalisation of financial services creates tendencies which may undermine stable economies. Both the effects of banking products and services, as well as the absence of banking in certain areas, quarters and regions as well as among certain groups and citizens should be taken into consideration not only by the public or the bank authorities but also by the banks themselves.

A new approach in bank policy is required due mainly to two contradictory developments in financial services, wherein an increasing need for financial services is contrasted with an increasing discrimination towards less profitable sectors of the economy.

There is an increasing need of access to financial services for people of all classes and with different expectations because adequate access to financial services has become:

*   *indispensable* for many parts of economic and social life that were formerly available without access to bank services (i.e. retirement, payments, investment)
*   *a basic need* for new forms of financed consumption, housing, job creation, small business and charitable work.
*   *more necessary* because the welfare state is gradually reducing its scope in favour of more private responsibility of citizens, which impacts on the use of financial services.

The increasing need is contrasted with increasing pressure on banks and financial institutions to select clients, regions and areas more precisely according to cost-benefit criteria in a process of advanced competition which is driven through:

- globalisation of financial services,
- deregulation of financial markets,
- privatisation of formerly public banks,
- informational technologies that render the identification of cost elements easier and further non-personal service provision,
- standardisation of retail banking and a trend to cost efficiency through bigger units.

Banks have always been viewed as semi-public institutions. The idea of social and public responsibility of banking is far from new. There is a multitude of forms, structures, ownership schemes as well as products and relationships through which banks and financial institutions have tried to comply with such expectations.[4]

But in spite of this variety these aspects have remained partial and peripheral to banking itself which tends to diminish its effect at a time of major banking developments.[5] It is legitimate to question how such effects can be ameliorated by somehow adding a collective element to each individual transaction, transforming the market into a more complex exchange mechanism into which individual transactions and individual marketing efforts are embedded into policy requirements (act as an agent of public interest, as economic theory would put it).

Community Reinvestment – A specific instrument against insufficient supply

The US regulatory environment for the majority of credit institutions including banks and thrifts makes these institutions' business activity particularly transparent in as much as they must disclose specific and detailed information about the geographical and economic profile of their customers vis-à-vis where they undertake business activity. Behind this regulation one may perceive a presumption that credit institutions should conduct their core business in a socially responsible way with particular regard to geographical impact. The law itself is very broad:

Community Reinvestment Act 1977 12 USC 2901
SECTION 804 – Financial Institutions; Evaluation
(a) In general. In connection with its examination of a financial institution, the appropriate Federal financial supervisory agency shall -
1. assess the institution's record of meeting the credit needs of its entire community, including low and moderate-income neighbourhoods, consistent with the safe and sound operation of such institution; and
2. take such record into account in its evaluation of an application for a deposit facility by such institution.

However, any such social responsibility is only *facilitated* through the law and the regulations prescribed under it. The regulations do not actually force institutions to be socially responsible, rather encourage them just by asking the respective questions. And the question of social responsibility is circumscribed by the principle of anti-discrimination, rather than any wider starting point such as, as some have argued, that credit institutions fulfil a *quasi*-public function.

The basic idea of CRA is that credit is an 'investment' which enables any community to use capital for the development of housing conditions, job creation, improved conditions for individual consumption and the raising of children in a supportive environment. It is seen that with more and adapted credit social costs for the public – otherwise needed for upgrading the public conditions in the community – can be saved and that the instrument credit is more focused and sustainable than subsidies spent by public authorities. As banks are the most important creditors in society the public has to keep on eye their credit behaviour especially towards communities, regions, classes and groups of people with difficulties with the pace capitalist markets require. It is Adam Smith revised: *Each individual should take into account in its personal decision in the market that its individual situation also depends on the situation of the whole which again is characterized by the situation of its weakest part.*

The US regulatory environment makes sense of the market economy paradox that investors en masse, such as credit institutions or equally pension funds, may jeopardise factors such as regional economic prosperity or job security for the very people who contribute to them and live or work in those areas. It does this by giving consumers the information that illustrates this rather abstract relationship enabling them to see the connection. While it is a common assumption that the United States is among the most free market orientated economies, especially when compared to Europe, the qualification that private enterprise there is concomitantly expected to fill gaps that would otherwise be left by smaller government is perhaps less immediately obvious. In fact, the US legislation with which this study is concerned stems from the philosophy that there is some sort of contract of reciprocal rights and obligations between private, shareholder owned credit institutions and the US taxpayer. In exchange for the latter guaranteeing the deposits of the former, these institutions have an obligation to extend credit and financial services in general to their entire communities in a non-discriminatory way, including those areas populated by low and moderate-income households and minorities.

Viewed from the EU banking regulatory environment, the US situation raises questions about the purpose of banking and financial service regulation beyond the questions of deposit protection, safe and sound operation and maintaining the integrity of payments systems. But again, this is not some broad social responsibility, based on a requirement that institutions undertake activity which cannot properly be described as business. Rather, it assumes that there are areas of profitable business activity which would otherwise be left unprovided for because of discrimination and prejudice. However, the question of anti-discrimination is especially problematic in this area because of the etymology of the word credit, *credere* in Latin meaning to trust. And trust is not always something which is easy to build when there are a variety of reasons mitigating against a positive credit authorisation. Some of these may be linked to income and repayments ratios or screening for financial responsibility (*legitimate*) and others linked with other factors such as mere area of residence (*illegitimate*). However, it may occur that illegitimate reasons can be concealed behind legitimate ones, consciously or sub-consciously, and this is an area fraught with difficulties – hence the element of subtle positive discrimination within the framework of the legislation to achieve results.

Since 1992 the commercially sensitive information which the institutions must disclose has been entirely in the public domain, and from that point all financial service consumers, including federal and state government, have potentially been able to base their choice or preferment of institutions and products on *more* infor-mation. In any event, rather than simply *having* money in a bank, consumers (and regulators) are given information relating to what their money is *used* for.

In fact there have been three perceptible steps to CRA regulation

(i)   1977-1992   CRA disclosure to the bank authorities only
(ii)   1992-   CRA disclosure to the public
(iii) 1997-   results rather than process CRA regulation

It is important to note that the CRA came in the wake of the highly draconian Home Mortgage Disclosure Act[6] which will have focused the minds of US bankers in a very severe manner. And, it is submitted that following this juncture the need for and implementation of highly detailed regulation has diminished. Instead bankers increasingly have a *socially beneficial bottom line* to aim for rather than a prescribed way to get there. The effect of post-1992 public disclosure cannot be underestimated.

Although the legislation is concerned with the general concept of an adequate provision of financial services, it is the extension of credit which is its focus, including within its scope the activities of both wholesale and retail banks although many credit–giving and financial services institutions are left outside the regulation.

As will become apparent, the CRA has been heavily criticised from all sides but it is important to distinguish between the desired goals of the regulation, the principles behind the regulation and the regulation itself. As a result of criticism, the bank regulatory agencies adopted the new Community Reinvestment Act regulations in May 1995 and established a transition period for institutions to develop compliance procedures. Since July 1997 the new regulation is in fully in place. A brief description follows:

(a) Technical Requirements
·   Public notice posted in the bank lobby

· Public file which includes

> CRA performance evaluation
> Branch and service information
> Map of Assessment Area
> HMDA data (if applicable)
> Loan data information (Large banks)
> Description of efforts to improve performance (if rated less than satisfactory)
> Written comments from the public

(b) CRA Performance Evaluation Criteria

Performance tests	Performance standards
Large bank: Lending test	· Number and amount of loans in assessment area
	· Geographic distribution of loans
	· Distribution of loans based on borrower characteristics
	· Community development loans
	· Innovative or flexible lending practices
Investment test	· Dollar amount of qualified investments
	· Innovativeness and complexity of qualified investments
	· Responsiveness to credit and community development needs
	· Degree to which investments are not made by private investors
	· Benefits to assessment area
Service test	· Distribution of branches and record of opening and closing branches
	· Availability and effectiveness of alternative systems for delivering bank services to low- and moderate-income people and geographies
	· Range of services provided
	· Extent of community development services provided
	· Innovativeness and responsiveness of community development services
Small bank: Lending test	· Loan to deposit ratio
	· Percentage of loans in the bank's assessment area
	· Record of lending to borrowers of different incomes and businesses and farms of different sizes
	· Geographic distribution of loans
	· Action taken in response to CRA complaints
Wholesale or limited purpose bank: Community development test	· Number and amount of community development loans, qualified investments, or community development services
	· Use of innovative or complex investments, community development loans or services and extent that they are not routinely provided by private investors
Strategic plan	· Responsiveness to credit and community development needs
	· Achievement of strategic plan goals

It is important to note that even after that reform the major impact of the CRA is not through transparency effects on positive customer behaviour (that they use banks with good CRA performance) but through negative pressure: community groups openly complain if they feel or see evidence in the public data of being underserved of a specific bank. This is noticed by regulators who give the bank trouble with its next requests as permission for a merger. In the effect, the bank reacts itself on community group complaints and works out 'contracts' for exploring financial need with adapted products. As it can be imagined banks feel quite often 'bribed' in that process and keep on maintaining pressure against the

Act.[7] At the same time individual bankers openly admit that they accept the responsibility of banks for some social problems: 'My personal view is – it has to be done and who if not we (the banks) are in a better position to do it... everyone in the management today sees what a difference CRA activity makes in the communities. The task is overwhelming – we have to do it.'[8]

B. Conclusions for European regulation

The CRA regulation also responds to the problems analysed for the European market. It is a good starting point for a new approach in bank regulation where banking is no longer evaluated only by safety and soundness towards its own customers or the stability of the currency, but monitored on its impact on a community, a city borough or a region.

Twenty years' experience of the CRA could suggest that such concerns are much more developed in the United States. Indeed the opposite is true. In many Member States of the EU, the balanced economic and social development of regions has a constitutional foundation. In Germany for example, the regions are bound to support each other by constitutional law. This principle is equally present in the European Treaties where the structural fund as well as different contributions are designed to compensate for structural inequalities throughout the EU. The true difference between the US system of affirmative action and the European system of redistribution lies in their respective private and public status. CRA is not an answer to the question of how to cope with inequalities in modern society as such. In this respect observers of the American social situation would have reason enough to think that Europeans have little to learn from the Americans. The question is whether the private sector contribution to anti-discrimination could be significantly more developed in Europe than it is until now.

In this respect the US example is indeed interesting. Just because equal distribution of economic and social opportunities is a generally accepted public good in Europe provided by States and the European Commission through subsidies and home State action, private efforts to support such policies are less developed than they could be. As it is generally assumed that public efforts will no longer suffice to counteract rising tendencies towards regional and social discrimination, Europeans have good reason to take a closer look at the US system of Community Reinvestment for elements which could be incorporated into an emerging European system of more private responsibility for the public good in general.

Two aspects have to be kept separate: *Firstly*, mistakes that have been made in the US do not have to be copied in Europe and *secondly*, differences in the banking environment in both continents necessitate a tailored approach for the EU.

- The starting point of the CRA in the US, that is to develop community reinvestment performance only as between banks and their supervisory institutions has shown little effect (but may have given the banks sufficient time to comprehend the philosophy of the CRA and integrate its requirements into their reporting system). Reporting about social effects of banking must be public in order to be successful.

- Administrative rules defining precisely how social effects should be measured and demonstrated may lead to an inappropriate bureaucratic burden for banks and divert their attention from the purpose of the required action to its administrative requirements. Such bureaucratic rules may equally produce unnecessary hostility to the regulation itself. A regulation should therefore focus on the purpose of the new 1996/97 CRA approach leaving as much discretion as possible for its fulfilment to the banks itself and enabling them to put up their own agenda as a yardstick for their respective social responsible behaviour.

- Negative sanctions for non compliance are certainly an important starting point for making banks respond to community reinvestment ideas. But banks should have the opportunity to develop more positive incentives through the use of social banking procedures in marketing, product design and public relation.

- Mere quantitative approaches such as the social distribution of products among customers have two important disadvantages: *Firstly*, the bureaucratic part of disclosure is maximised and *secondly*, data suggesting success may disguise inappropriate or bad products which diminish instead of improving economic opportunities in the long run.

- In addition, the US-American culture of pressure groups and heavy lobbying have developed an atmosphere that bankers just hand over social purpose money to communities and their pressure groups to keep them quiet.[9] At the same time, the CRA asks banks only to do profitable business which produces another force to outsource social lending portfolios to hide losses or deliver more sponsoring than social banking. As a result, attempts to integrate social banking methodologies into mainstream banking have weakened.

- An important European contribution to the CRA could be the combination of minimum standards for the social acceptability of bank products (usury interest rate ceilings, control of costs in repayment default, rights to adaptation in difficult social situations etc.) with a general monitoring of access.

- The European market would equally have to consider the existing state owned banks, coop banks and specialised financial institutions with social purposes and give them preferential treatment if they can show that they emphasise community reinvestment more than the legislation requires.

C. Recommendations

On the background of the above analysis of the strength and weaknesses of the American CRA and of the European regulatory regime, the following points try to focus some crucial elements for an efficient European regulation.

Develop a legal basis for non-discrimination on social grounds

(1)   In spite of the emphasis the European Treaty puts on equal rights and access, it is to acknowledge that there is no robust principle of anti-discrimination, either on ethnic, geographical or social grounds informing the provision of financial services in any of the large EU countries Germany, France and the UK.[10] The Second Banking Directive refers vaguely to the general good and the European Court has decided that this can cover the interests of consumers, the protection of workers, the social order and related matters. However, this is not a universal responsibility using similar criteria applied evenly throughout the European Union as a requirement under which all banks must operate. Rather each banking authority may establish what it considers to be in the general good and apply that within the boundaries of European law. This contrasts starkly with the USA position. With the globalisation of banking services creating European if not global banks it is submitted that in order to progress the principles of non-discrimination and universal equality of access to financial services it is likely that a legal basis must be developed both in administrative and private legal relations at a European level. The Banking Directives might be an appropriate scheme for such legal basis.

(2)   In France and Germany, at the State level, there is a principle of equal treatment whereas for private entities there is no equivalent. With a privatisation of public tasks it is assumed that the US anti-discrimination approach must gain grounds, particularly in areas as central as financial services. In the UK one can see the development of minimum standards of social responsibility among some of the utility companies in relation to the provision of basic services such as gas, electricity and telephone. In the latter case, British Telecom will soon be introducing a low cost service which permits incoming calls only and outgoing calls to emergency services only.

(3)   Whether the goal of non-discrimination on social grounds ought to be achieved through legal non-discriminatory principles in the EU, as it has been in the USA, is queried considering the strength of social equality heritage of continental European countries and principles of existing non-discrimination in EU law. One lesson from the US CRA development could be that it makes less sense to focus on ethnic discrimination than on social discrimination. However, if the legal approach is not to be one of non-discriminatory principles, the question of how to enforce principles to *act in the general good* becomes a matter of administrative law.

(4)   EU structural funds, in the same way as German federal arrangements, demonstrate a commitment to regional balance with regard to economic prosperity and consequently social equality. The concept of this type of non-discrimination is thus already well-understood within the EU. The legal place for anti-discrimination regulation remains to be identified.

Flexible regulation allowing priority to private initiatives

(5) Whereas a robust commitment to achieving social goals through banking and its regulation is desired, any legislative instrument would, it is submitted, have to be of a preliminary nature, be very flexible and ultimately reflexive to market adaptation to principles of social responsibility.

(6) There is another lesson to be drawn when looking on the US CRA: not the procedure demanded by the regulators, but the effects of banks examining their social impact, and developing new strategies and products, has been demonstrated as being successful. The force of regulators, fixed procedures and documentation requirements make the CRA inefficient and something of a last resort measure in its USA form. It is believed that in order to get credit institutions' attention to the subject of social responsibility, measures of that magnitude ought not to be required. However, it is important to ensure that at a national and at a European level appropriate regulatory bodies are given the responsibility of ensuring that there is an adequacy and effectiveness of financial services for low income consumers and for social purposes.

(7) It is desirable to achieve certain minimum standards in the provision of financial services such as equal access for all. There should not be cost penalties for low-income consumers. But beyond such minimum standards in, for example the areas of basic banking services, mortgage loans and small business finance, market forces should be allowed to direct activity. It has also to be questioned whether European Union funds be used to support low interest loans instead of market rate loans because this delivers wrong incentives and as a consequence fails to help the target group.

(8) Whilst it may be appropriate to annex any legal measures on social responsibility to the Social Chapter where much of the social dimension of EU law is found, a *Recommendation* on the social responsibility of credit institutions setting out a European Code of Practice and a set of goals for Governments to aim towards may be more appropriate. Together with the Recommendation a review committee could be established to follow the implementation by Governments and private credit institutions of such proposals.

(9) If credit institutions are to have minimum standards of social responsibility then they should be motivated to show commitment for equal access to financial services. One possibility could be a *self regulated Code of Practice* defining a basic banking service and covering responsibility for access, for quality and cost of financial services. A step in that direction was made by the European Savings Bank Association when it issued its statement of social principles in 1996. There should also be structures for review of the implementation of such statements to see how progress is being made.

Social Transparency to compete for the good

(10) Transparency of these issues is highly desirable to allow the proper functioning of market mechanisms and it is imperative that information about the activities of credit institutions in respect of their social responsibilities should be in the public domain.

(11) Transparency in three areas seem to be necessary: *distribution, social effects and best practice of financial services*. A Code of Social Responsibility in Banking practice might be drawn up which sets out what such responsibilities might be and how they should be reported. It might include the proposal in the UK report that information on a geographic basis should be provided as part of an initiative to combat inadequacies of financial services, coupled with data from reports by banks to the committees which review breaches of Codes of Practice.

(12) In order to measure social effects quantitative and qualitative sociological studies could be undertaken on behalf of credit institutions and their associations, particularly to ascertain what were the effects of certain products on low income consumers.[11] Best practice studies could be placed with relevant international bodies.

(13) It may be desirable to include incentives towards best practice, to publicise the most successful initiatives and to allow institutions themselves to evaluate what they undertake in this regard as much as possible. Some external and independent assessment may also be required to consolidate a robust framework. Subsidies are certainly to be considered in all areas where contamination of the credit institution business decision making process is avoided. In the example of commercial micro loans it is obvious that even best practice is not commercially sustainable and therefore subsidies are essential. However, the technique of subsidy should foster market creativity and striving for efficiency on the one hand while concentrating on that part of the business where the social responsibility leads to over average costs – in the case of the previous example, because of the high support involved.

(14) In addition, the EU Banking Directives need to remain sufficiently flexible to permit new social financial institutions to develop within appropriate prudential criteria. Further examination of this area is overdue.

(15) At a consumer level there is also room for considering what tax incentives might encourage bank customers to save and invest for social purposes and thereby provide specific funds for such purposes. Making transparent what money is used for by particular institutions can only encourage consumers to make informed decisions.

ENDNOTES

1   The backbone of this article is a European study by Benoît Granger, Malcolm Lynch, Leo Haidar, Udo Reifner and Jan Evers finished in 1997 and published in Evers/Reifner: *The Social Responsibility of Credit Institutions in the EU*, 1998 ISBN 3-7890-5567

2   Social responsibility of banks is defined as ensuring access to financial services. This does NOT mean that every one gets every banking product but that access is decided on individual features and not limited by customers statistical bankability (e.g. entrepreneurs with three and or more children are less credit worthy) or regional location.

3   Please note that in the US are a range of acts with the objective ensuring access to financial services for example the Home Mortgage Disclosure Act (HMDA) of 1975. See: Evers/ Reifner, p. 402-410

4   For example: state banks, saving banks, co-operative banks, mutuals, non-banks as intermediaries. A detailed analysis for Germany, the UK and France in the country reports of Evers/ Reifner 1998

5   For an evaluation of reasons see Evers/ Reifner, p. 69-70

6   This was implemented 1975 to fight racial 'red-lining' (encircling map areas in red as areas in which no more investment would be made) by asking all financial institutions that undertake mortgage business to add to their mortgage business intelligence further statistical information about the racial and income backgrounds of their borrowers. The figures that were made public through this legislation showed that levels of credit given to minorities and low-income consumers was disproportionately low. See: Schieber, P.H.: 'Community Reinvestment Act Update', in: *The Banking Law Journal*, Jan.-Febr. 1993, p. 65

7   As a contemporary example see *Wall Street Journal*, 'Gramm's Glass-Steagall Beef', 6.01.1999, page A22

8   In an interview with the Northern Trust Company Chicago 1995, full documentation in Evers/ Reifner et. Cit. P. 418f.

9   In the quoted *Wall Street Journal* article it is described that to get the acceptance of the regulators for recent mergers, Travelers and Citibank announced a CRA commitment of $115 billion (double Citibank's US deposit base) and NationsBank and BankAmerica created a 10 year package worth $350 billion

10   This was analysed in the above quoted country reports (in Evers/ Reifner 1998)

11   Europe has hundreds of state subsidized research institutions for city development, housing, labour market etc.. Nearly none of them emphasises the research on new banking products that are especially designed to meet the needs of low income communities. As the banks equally do not invest into such developments, there is also a lack of ideas and of necessary consulting to make the general aspirations of CRA viable and practical. Much of discrimination is also a lack of imagination that other tools could do better. Probably the best European research the area of access to finance is done by the Private Finance Research Centre (PFRC) in Bristol – some of it financed by the British Bankers Association. More of such research would make it clearer for the state and the banks how with adopted products tax money and write offs could be saved.

Conclusion:
This is only the beginning

Ed Mayo
(New Economics Foundation)

Concerns about inequality and poverty are now everybody's business. An era of opportunity has also been an era of inequality. As banker to the world's governments, Michel Camdessus warned in his closing remarks as head of the IMF in 2000, this could not continue. 'Poverty' he said 'is the ultimate systemic threat facing humanity… The widening gaps between rich and poor within nations; and the gulf between the most affluent and most impoverished nations, are morally outrageous, economically wasteful and potentially socially explosive…poverty will undermine the fabric of our societies through confrontation, violence and civil disorder…'

Yet Camdessus himself had little to offer about how to tackle poverty, beyond freeing up capital and promoting open markets. But despite huge advances in doing just that around the world, the gap between rich and poor has increased, both between nations, more than doubling between 1960 and 1997, but also within nations. Countries that have turned away from global markets have fared no better, caught in what Klaus Schwab, Director of the World Economic Forum, calls the 'globalisation trap'. The idea that turning your back on the economy is best for human development has been discredited. But the alternative, of designing economic institutions and systems that promote wellbeing, has barely begun.

The promotion of free movement of capital, new technologies and the deregulation of financial services has seen product and market innovation and a significant increase in competition. Whereas previous phases of globalisation were led by trade and corporate activity, the defining characteristic of world economic development over the last decade has been that of finance capitalism. With the integration of all three through new communication technologies, a new set of economic drivers are emerging, of hyper-competition, deflation and new corporate models, as traditional functions are dispersed from the core into value based webs. It can be argued indeed that we have been living in an era of soft globalisation. A new phase of fabulous opportunity for those at the top and brutal denial for those at the bottom awaits.

The European model of social development stands as a counterweight to such forces of inequality. And yet the model itself is in question. The traditions of social partnership are being unravelled by the forces of globalisation and economic change, unpicking the historic settlement between labour and capital and eroding the power of the state in relation to markets and enterprise. There is space to recreate the same model at a higher level, the level of the European Union, given the political will, but at the same time, there are good reasons to think afresh. Ironically, in the field of social banking covered by this book, there are good models and lessons to be learned from Anglo-Saxon countries in terms of innovative roles for the state as well as best practice in continental Europe in terms of state action to secure citizens' rights in the market.

Within Europe, a major trend identified by a number of the contributors in this book is the threat of financial withdrawal. Technological change, disintermediation and securitization, the growth of capital markets, coupled with the EU's attempt to create a common framework for financial services, the transition to a common currency and the shift from pay-as-you-go to funded social security systems mean that the European financial services sector is now entering the most far-reaching process of transformation of the post-war period.

Within a more integrated financial system, the bottom line search for maximum return on capital has a direct effect on every financial service, from current accounts and savings through to enterprise credit. The raising of the threshold, in terms of financial returns sought means shifting away from all such services that attract only a modest return. This phenomenon of financial withdrawal has been most marked in the Anglo-Saxon economies, where the model of financial capitalism has been strongest and where finance has been redistributed most rapidly from traditional sectors to growth areas such as the internet and biotechnology sectors. So, whereas the European industrial revolution was financed largely by patient capital at low rates of interest, today's political economy of globalised financial markets looks for five times the equivalent annual return.

Over the next five years, as financial services adapt to the new market emerging in Europe, the phenomenon of financial withdrawal is likely to bite deeply between and within regions. And yet financial services in the modern era have become a central component of economic citizenship. They are also critical to the economic health of neighbourhoods, cities and regions. The rise of financial withdrawal is therefore starting to show up in evidence of personal exclusion and social and geographical disinvestment and discrimination.

The experience of such 'redlining' in the USA, where this process, symbolised by bank branch closures, started earlier, in the 1970s, is that the local effect can be a vicious cycle of disinvestment and disadvantage. The perception that an area is becoming a no-go area for financial investment can all too quickly become a reality. This means a higher business failure rate, fewer start-ups and less employ-ment. The withdrawal of financial services represents a new form of systemic risk, which regulators will need to understand. Services such as credit and money transmission are the lifeblood of economies at any level. Banks indeed are granted the profitable privilege of credit creation by the award of a banking licence. The process of financial withdrawal therefore raises new questions for democratic debate. Is credit creation and opening up access to other financial services is just privilege of banking, or should it be a responsibility? And if it is a responsibility, how then should it be organised and paid for ? What are the roles of the state, the private sector and civil society?

The field of social banking addresses some of these questions. But it should be seen as offering not one response but many. It has therefore been specialist groups, in particular pioneers in the co-operative sector, that have pioneered social banking in Europe. These are structured as non-profit financial intermediaries or as for-profit investment societies or banks. Often, they will involve direct part-nerships with mainstream banks. But as is also made clear by authors in this book, a small number of mainstream banks are also engaging directly in social banking. It is in this area that social banking has the greatest untapped potential, given the scale of resources available.

How will social banking now develop ? These are three possible scenarios.

The first is that social banking starts as innovation at the margins of the economy and attracts support from the growing number of concerned consumers and investors. Growth is voluntary and likely to be tilted towards models, such as ethical investment trusts, in which financial return is highest. The state has little role to play in this, except possibly moral exhortation in favour. If social banking proves as competitive as other forms of investment, then it will become a signif-icant financial sector.

The second is that social banking will in fact be driven out from the market, either for competitive reasons, because ethics does not pay or pay as well, or for regulatory reasons, if social banking falls outside of approved models of banking and risk assessment. The role of the state in this case is one of enforcement against the diversity of social banking models.

The third scenario is that the public sector plays a pro-active role in creating the conditions in which social banking can succeed, by adapting existing activi-ties, from welfare reform to business support, to improve the chances of otherwise marginal enterprises and create incentives to bring the profile of risk or return in social banking closer to market norms

In reality, social banking in Europe is diverse enough for all three scenarios to happen. If environmental lending, such as in renewable energies, proves itself a market success, then in a competitive market it will succeed. There are already cases in a number of European countries of a regulatory crack-down on unorthodox specialist social banking institutions, and new Basel Convention ratios for risk assessment make it harder to pursue small business lending because of the perceived risk involved. If micro-credit only proves itself in an industrialised country setting with an element of subsidy, perhaps in the form of an income bridge from welfare payments into enterprise, then it will only develop at scale with creative support from the public sector, and when its record is proven it will attract large-scale private finance.

The state itself does not have a good record of directly doing social banking, which is better done with the proper investment disciplines and horizons of an independent initiative, although it can be an important partner. In this, there are a range of models for creative and effective public policy in support of social banking, ranging from special tax and regulatory dispensations for credit unions in Ireland and Cigales in France, public subsidy for enterprise development among disadvantaged groups in Belgium and the development of targeted loan guarantees in the UK. However, the most effective state action is likely to be a reorientation of existing spending, such as welfare payments, and existing initiatives, such as the semi-public sector infrastructures of post offices and caisses municipales.

The review of regulatory action in the US by authors in this book also confirms the benefits of an approach of creating an affirmative obligation in favour of social banking. The Community Reinvestment Act in the USA, they conclude, 'has played an important role in expanding access to credit to help rebuild housing, create jobs and restore the economic health of communities across the United States.' Under the Act, US retail banks have committed over $1 trillion to low income neighbourhoods and discovered that such lending can be profitable. The Act achieves this through two key actions: public disclosure of banks' record in serving poorer communities and regulatory sanctions for poor performance. In Europe, there are practical options for how to do the same, perhaps starting with an initiative of the European Commission to complete an annual Community Reinvestment Rating of financial service providers in the EU.

Promoting better information on the social impact of banking is a first step towards better social banking. Banks and their key stakeholders can then make productive use of the information. Wider and deeper information and disclosure is in any case the way that the world is going to be. This is particularly so in the financial services sector, where clear and trusted information is needed to underpin the development of capital markets. The emergence of models for social and environmental reporting over the last decade could shift from being a framework for corporate best practice to become a market norm, part of the licence to operate. Indeed, new market-based standards are emerging around issues as diverse as child labour, forest stewardship and staff training. These set benchmarks against which corporate performance is scrutinised by media, government and civil society. Social banking, perhaps with the development of a European voluntary code of conduct among banks, could be next.

This new partnership approach can be seen as one element of a paradigm change in the way that poverty is tackled. The post-war European settlement was that poverty and exclusion was the boundary between public and private sector. It was where governments, not markets, stepped in. The new social banking approach does not do away with government. Rather it finds ways for government to support enterprise and the efforts of people themselves to win access to livelihoods and opportunities in the market. From pensions to insurance, from enterprise credit to basic banking, financial services is being elevated to a prominent new social role in twenty first century industrialised countries. Any prudent bank wishing to invest in its own future will wish to investigate social banking. Any prudent citizen or politician, looking for alternatives to insecurity and inequality, will welcome those that do.

About the writers

Francesco Bicciato is the director of Fondazione Choros and former Research Centre Manager of the 'Banca Popolare Etica'. He also was senior research fellow of the Fondazione Eni Enrico Mattei (FEEM) where he still is scientific coordinator of the research programme on 'Non-profit, Environment and Ethical Finance'. Within this context he is carrying out several studies about the new orientations of Third Sector development in Europe and in LDCs. He has a Ph.D. of the Department of Geography, University of Padua, where he is also assistant professor on 'Environment and social economy in Europe and LDCs. He has acted as a researcher and advisor for various institutions, such as Italian and foreign NGOs, Universities, Municipalities and the European Union. He was co-operator in Latin America within a programme of International Co-operation managed by MLAL (an Italian NGO) and financed by the Italian Ministry of Foreign Affairs. He is a member of the National Council of the Permanent Forum of the Third Sector.

Pat Conaty is the Managing Partner of Common Futures – a community finance development consultancy in Birmingham. He has either founded or led the development of many social investment ventures in Great Britain including the UK Social Investment Forum, Aston Reinvestment Trust, and the Rebuilding Society Network. He is currently working on the development of the London Rebuilding Society – a community reinvestment trust and social venture capital provider

Rosalind Copisarow was from 1979 to 1994 a banker at Citicorp, Midland Montagu and JP Morgan. Her work covered project finance, corporate finance, private banking and capital markets development in the UK, North and South America and Eastern Europe, on behalf of governments, financial institutions and major corporations. Her final position with JP Morgan was as Vice President responsible for developing their Polish operations from inception. In 1994, she established a nationwide microfinance institution in Poland, Fundusz Mikro, under the auspices of the Polish-American Enterprise Fund. After five years from start up, Fundusz Mikro has made 30,000 loans, disbursed US$45 million, opened branches in 33 cities and currently employs 94 people. Through its group-lending methodology, over 80% of clients have become members of mutually supporting community networks and between them have created an estimated 7,000 new jobs. The loan repayment rate on loans has consistently exceeded 98% and, since March 1999, the company has become fully self-financing. Rosalind also serves on the Policy Advisory Group of CGAP (the Consultative Group for Assistance to the Poorest), a multi-donor organisation coordinated within the World Bank. Previously she founded the Microfinance Centre for Central and Eastern Europe and most recently established Street (UK) to serve the poor and financially excluded micro-entrepreneurs of the UK.

Paul H. Dembinski is Professor at the University of Fribourg (Switzerland) and Executive Secretary of the Finance Observatory (Observatoire de la Finance), Geneva, an independent foundation under Swiss law. The goal of the Observatory is to encourage new thinking debate and proposals to back up the financial sector's contributions to the common good. By its formal and informal activities it aims at meeting the challenge facing today's world due to the development of financial activities. The Observatory provides material for thought and establishes links between groups and centres spread across different countries. Finance & Bien Commun/Common Good, is the quarterly review of the Observatoire de la Finance.

Jan Evers, born 1968, holds an MA in European Business Administration and has worked for IFF since 1994, now heading the Social Investment and Corporate Finance department. At the moment he is conducting research in quality of bank advice and finance packages for small enterprises, reasons for start-up failure and in implementing the concept of micro-lending into Europe. (NB: for a note on IFF see 'Udo Reifner')

Laura Foschi studied economics in Bologna and has a European Masters in Environmental Management from EAEME, the European Association for Environment Management Education. Since 1998 she is a Junior Reasearcher with the Research Centre of Banca Popolare Etica where she works on ethical finance, development of social enterprises, environmental and social rating, the implementation of the Environmental Managment System, microcredit programmes in LDCs and other environmental projects of Banca Etica. She also is co-ordinator of Research and Training Programmes at the Fondazione Choros.

After almost 5 years working for a Japanese trading multinational, developing business in the Former Soviet Union, **James Giuseppi** felt that his efforts would be better employed promoting corporate social responsibility rather than earning a profit for a company which displayed little concern for such issues. In September 1998, James was contracted by NPI Global Care to conduct a survey of the European Banking Sector. Soon after joining, NPI announced demutualisation and was later bought by AMP. James was subsequently requested to join the team full-time when it transferred to Henderson Investors, another recent acquisition of AMP. A new Henderson Socially Responsible Investment team is one of the largest SRI organisations in Europe, with four fund managers and six in-house researchers, and over £650 million of SRI funds under management.

Paul Gosling is author of *Changing Money* and *Government in the Digital Age*, both published by Bowerdean. He is also a freelance journalist specialising in new technology and finance.

Thierry Groussin is in charge of executive training within the 'Confédération Nationale du Crédit Mutuel' in France.

Ronald Grzywinski is Chairman of the Board and Chief Executive Officer of Shorebank Corporation, a regulated $900 million commercial bank holding company that implements community development strategies. The company currently operates in Chicago, Illinois, as well as in Ohio, Michigan, and Washington State. The company also provides management and operating consulting assistance to development banking institutions world-wide. Mr. Grzywinski is a trustee of several non-profit development organisations, and was formerly president of Hyde Park Bank and Trust Company in Chicago and of the First National Bank of Lockport, Illinois. He has a B.S. in English Literature from Loyola University.

Christophe Guene has been working since 1995 at INAISE, where he is responsible for research and project development. As an economist he had specialised in environment and development issues, which led him to work as a research assistant at the University of Louvain (IRES / UCL). Since then his core attention has gone on the various forms of domesticated monies and finance, as well as on economic entropy in a larger sense. INAISE – the International Association of Investors in the Social Economy – is an international network of environmental and social finance organisations that have emerged these last 15 to 20 years. They serve mainly those sectors and groups of people that the mainstream banks are no longer willing or able to finance and that the social welfare systems are unable to reach.

Peter Hughes manages public policy issues for the NatWest Group. He concentrates on public policy issues such as financial exclusion, community development and ethical issues. He also helps manage and prioritise the range of issues which can affect or are influenced by the actions of the Group. He also spent 12 months with the Charities Aid Foundation helping launch an innovative loan fund for charitable organisations and is a trustee of a theatre in education charity. NatWest Group is a primarily UK and Irish based financial services group, which provides a broad spectrum of financial services to its customers. NatWest Group is the leading provider of banking services to British businesses and an innovative bank for over six million personal customers.

Dan Immergluck is senior vice president of the Woodstock Institute, a 26 year-old organisation based in Chicago, Illinois, which conducts applied research and policy analysis, both in Chicago and around the USA, in financial services and economic development. Dan has researched, and written extensively on, financial services trends, access to commercial and residential credit, U.S. Community Reinvestment Act policy, development finance, and various other community and economic development topics. In addition to authoring more than a dozen Woodstock Institute publications, he has published research and commentary articles in a wide range of journals and magazines, including *Urban Studies*, *Economic Development Quarterly*, *Inc. Magazine*, and others. Dan holds a Master of Public Policy from the University of Michigan and a PhD in Urban Planning and Policy from the University of Illinois at Chicago.

Koert Jansen (1969) is Policy Advisor at Triodos Bank. Triodos Bank was founded in 1980 in the Netherlands and is a fully-licensed independent bank, owned by private shareholders. Triodos Bank has offices in Belgium, the Netherlands and the United Kingdom and employs about 100 people. The green investment funds of Triodos Bank (for wind energy and organic farming respectively) acted as models for the Dutch green investment scheme. Triodos Bank was involved in the design and preparation of the scheme.

Marcel Jeucken is an economist working at the Economic Research Department of the Rabobank Group. **Bart Jan Krouwel** is head of the Sustainable Development Department of the Rabobank Group.

Paul A Jones is a senior lecturer in the School of Law and Applied Social Studies at Liverpool John Moores University where he specialises in organisational management, community development and community enterprise. His research publications include the national report, 'Towards Sustainable Credit Union Development' (1999), published by ABCUL in collaboration with the Co-operative Bank plc. and the English Community Enterprise Partnership, and 'Sustainable Credit Unions. Guidance Notes for Local Authorities' (1999) published by the Local Government Association. He is also a member of the national supervisory committee of the Association of British Credit Unions Ltd (ABCUL). ABCUL is the leading credit union trade association representing 84% of all credit union membership in the UK.

Masaru Kataoka – Representative of Press Alternative Co. Ltd: After retiring from Mitsubishi Trust Bank, in an attempt to solve society's problems through business, he established 'Press Alternative Co. Ltd.' In 1986. It comprises 'The Third World Shop' which tries to narrow the north-south gap through fair trade and 'The Citizen's Bank' started in 1989, which cooperates with the Japanese credit unions. He supports small businesses locally and internationally as a citizens' business leader.

Elaine Kempson is currently the director of the Personal Finance Research Centre (pfrc) at Bristol University. Previously she was programme director for family finances research at the Policy Studies Institute and, in 1998, transferred the research programme to the newly formed centre. She and her colleagues, have undertaken a wide range of empirical research studies on all aspects of financial services – including banking, savings, insurance, mortgages and credit. Much of this work has been concerned with individuals who are on the margins of financial services (full details can be found on the pfrc website www.ggy.bris.ac.uk/pfrc.htm). Elaine was also a member of the recent UK Government Treasury Policy Action Team on access to financial services.

Malcolm Lynch – After qualifying as a solicitor in 1983, Malcolm worked as a corporate lawyer in the City of London. He then became the first Economic Development Solicitor for Kirklees Metropolitan Council, gaining detailed understanding of the way in which local authorities work. He worked as the in-house solicitor to ICOM, the UK National Federation of Worker Co-operatives, before founding the practice in 1989. Malcolm works primarily on company, commercial, finance and banking matters for charities, housing associations and commercial companies generally. Malcolm Lynch Solicitors are a leading charity law firm and advisers to companies seeking to make a positive contribution towards tomorrow's world. They are a leading adviser to organisations seeking to access social investment.

Ed Mayo joined the New Economics Foundation in 1992 as Director. He studied Philosophy at Cambridge. On graduation he became a management consultant in financial services at Andersen Consulting. In 1990 he became Head of Campaigns at World Development Movement and in 1992, Acting Director. His work involves promoting all aspects of ethical and sustainable economic activity. He is currently a board member of UK Social Investment Forum and the Local Investment Fund, Chair of the Jubilee 2000 Coalition and has been a member of the Social Exclusion Unit's Treasury Policy Action Team 3 on business and finance. He was in Davos with the World Economic Forum 2000 talking about corporate accountability to business leaders. Ed has written numerous books including a book on Social Auditing as a fellow of the City University Business School in London. He has also written extensively on all aspects of economics.

The **New Economics Foundation** (NEF) is an independent think tank promoting innovative and practical approaches to build a just and sustainable economy which delivers quality of life and respects environmental limits. To this end it acts both to promote accountability and participation in business and civil organisations and develop tools for autonomy through community economic initiatives.

Andy (A.W.) Mullineux is Professor of Money and Banking in the Department of Economics at the University of Birmingham. He has published numerous books and journal articles on a range of topics including: Divisia monetary aggregates; financial sector restructuring in Central and Eastern Europe and South East Asia; and business cycles and financial crises and their prevention through bank regulation and supervision.

Helmut Muthers and **Heidi Muthers-Haas** are owners of the 1994 founded Institute for Strategic Opportunity-Management in Banks and the 1998 founded

Network for Innovative Bank Development. Both are practitioners who themselves have been in the bank business for 25 and 17 years, respectively. Today they accompany as opportunity-manager the processes of change and new thinking in banks, savings banks and especially co-operative banks in order to activate their future potential through new, inimitable business fields and a different form of customer care.

Maria Nowak holds a degree from the 'Institut des Etudes Politiques' (Institute of Political Studies) in Paris and from the London School of Economics, and she has made her career in development. Director of Policies and Studies at the 'Caisse Française de Développement' (French Development Bank), then seconded to the World Bank in Washington, she currently divides her time between setting up micro-credit programmes in central Europe and ADIE ('Association pour le Droit à l'Initiative Economique'), which she founded and of which she is voluntary president. Maria Nowak is a member of the CGAP Policy Advisory Group (the World Bank initiative to fight poverty, based on micro-credit). She is the author of *Banquière de l'Espoir* (Albin Michel 1994) and has received the 'Prix des Droits de l'Homme' (Human Rights Prize) awarded by the readers of the Fribourg newspaper *Croix et Liberté* for her activities in promoting community credit in France. She is also a 'Chevalier de l'Ordre du Mérite' (1994) (Knight of the Order of Merit) and 'Chevalier de la Légion d'Honneur' (1998) (Knight of the Legion of Honour).

Patrick Ochs is a researcher-cum-teacher in France and North America. With his Doctorate in Management Science and his skills in directing research, his work in the field of management science focuses principally on intangible investment and its impact on competitiveness and company value. The author of several works and scientific articles, he has also, for more than 20 years, worked as a consultant for national and international companies.

Christophe Perritaz, an economist, works as an assistant at the department of international strategy and competition at the University of Fribourg (Switzerland) and is responsible for the Finance and Technology programme for the 'Observatoire de la Finance', a Geneva-based foundation which studies the workings of the financial system in terms of its contribution to the common good.

Lynn Pikholz joined Shorebank as a Corporate Analyst after completing her Masters in City Planning at MIT where she specialised in international development and poverty alleviation with a focus on enterprise development and low-income housing. Shorebank Corporation, the first community development bank in the USA, is committed to restoring opportunities for residents living in underinvested areas. At Shorebank Advisory Services, Shorebank's consulting company, Ms. Pikholz works with domestic and international clients (financial institutions, multilateral donor agencies and NGOs) primarily in the area of microfinance and small business / enterprise development. Prior to coming to

Shorebank, Lynn Pikholz worked as an economist at a commercial bank in South Africa, and later as a senior policy analyst at a leading non-government organisation in South Africa. Her post graduate degrees include: Masters in City Planning from MIT, Honors in Economics from the University of the Witwatersrand, South Africa and Business Science Marketing Honors from University of Cape Town, South Africa.

Pilar Ramirez is a Bolivian citizen professionally working in her country, was trained as a Clinical Psychologist in the United States and she also has a Master in Public Administration degree from the John F. Kennedy School of Government at Harvard University. Upon returning to Bolivia she founded FIE in 1985, a non-profit organisation, as the first microcredit organisation offering this service to the then called 'urban informal sector' of the city of La Paz. The success of FIE and other similar programs have placed microfinance activity in Bolivia at the top of this industry in the world today. FIE is the creator and a major shareholder of FIE Private Financial Fund, a fully regulated microfinance institution, and Ms Ramirez is the President of the Board. Ms Ramirez is divorced and a mother of two adolescent sons.

Udo Reifner, born 1948, is director of IFF and Professor of law at the Hamburg University of Economics and Politics. He has published widely in the areas of legal theory and sociology of law, banking law, banking and new products as well as on consumer protection in financial services. The current focus of his research is social banking and access to financial services. The **Institute for Financial Services (IFF)** is a private, independent and not-for profit research institution, founded in 1986 and working internationally in all areas of banking and finance but particularly with regard to the customer-orientation of products and services, overindebtedness, construction finance, social investment and corporate finance. The broad aim of the Institute is to help create innovative and transparent financial services adapted to both individual and societal requirements, now and in the future. IFF employs 17 members of staff (9 permanent, 7 part-time/freelancers and 5 students). For more information, see the internet pages in English and German on www.iff-hamburg.de

Bettina Schmoll is an adviser in the public relations department of the Ökobank. Ökobank is a universal and direct bank with a policy guided by ethical and ecological criteria. The bank was launched in 1988 and is now the largest alternative bank in Germany.

Leo Schuster, born 1937 in Fürth/Bavaria, studied economics and worked during many years at the University St. Gallen as private lecturer, professor and director of the Banking Institute. Since 1990 he is professor of business administration, in particular in the fields of financing and bank administration, at the economics department of the Catholic University Eichstätt. He is the editor of 'The Societal Responsibility of Banks' (Die gesellschaftliche Verantwortung der

Banken), published by Erich Schmidt Verlag, 1997.

Josef Stampfer, born 1946, has been working in the co-operative sector for 30 years. Since 1981 he is director of the Raiffeisenbank Kötschach-Mauthen, which was founded in 1894. Between 1981 and 1983 ten former independent Raiffeisenbanks amalgamated to the Raiffeisenbank Kötschach-Mauthen serving the region Oberes Gail- und Lesachtal, a relatively unspoilt valley bordering Italy. The aim of the bank – of which its customers through membership are also its owners – is to take responsibility and offer services for the development of the region and the community.

The paper from the **U.S. Department of the Treasury** was a collective contribution. **Michael Barr** is Deputy Assistant Secretary for Community Development Policy; **Dr. Lynda Y. de la Viña** is Deputy Assistant Secretary for Economic Policy; **Valerie Personick** is a Senior Economist in the Office of Economic Policy; **Melissa A. Schroder** is a Program Analyst in the Office of Community Development Policy. The authors of this paper are employees of the U.S. Department of the Treasury, however, the views expressed in this paper are those of the authors and do not necessarily represent the views of the U.S. Department of the Treasury.

David Vallat is an economist and researcher at the Walras Centre (University of Lyon 2 / CNRS-ISH / France) and is part of the working group on 'Finance, Exclusion and Activity'. The purpose of this working group is to study financial and monetary practices, the financial determining factors in exclusion, the fight against exclusion through the decentralisation of finance, the relation to employment and the statistical construction of indicators. An important characteristic is that the studies are based on active collaborations with the organisations being studied. Its field of research focuses on both north and south. This work is carried out from theoretical and operational perspectives.

Jacques Zeegers is General Secretary of the Belgian Banker's Association (ABB). He is a Doctor of Law, with a degree and a Masters in Economic Sciences (Catholic University of Louvain) and fellow of ICHEC ('Institut Catholique des Hautes Etudes Commerciales'). He is also economic columnist for the daily newspaper *La Libre Belgique*.

The Grip of Death

A study of modern money, debt slavery and destructive economics

Michael Rowbotham

This lucid and original account of where our money comes from explains why most people and businesses are so heavily in debt. Rowbotham writes about subjects very close to home: mortgages, building societies and banks, food and farming, transport, worldwide poverty, and what's on the supermarket shelf.

He explains —

- why virtually all the money in the world economy has been created as a debt; why only 3% of UK money exists as 'legal tender'; and why in a world reliant upon money created as debt, we are kept perpetually short of money.

- how and why mortgages are responsible for almost two-thirds of the total money stock in the UK, and 80% in the US.

- why business debt is at its highest level ever.

- why debts mean that a small farm can be productively very efficient, but financially not 'viable'.

- why national debts can never be paid off.

- how debt fuels the 'need to grow', revolutionising national and global transport strategies, destroying local markets and producers and increasing waste, pollution and resource consumption.

- how 'Third World debt' is a mechanism used by the developed nations to inject ever-increasing amounts of money into their own economies, and why debtor nations can never repay the debts.

- why politicians can't fund public services.

- why 'debt-money' is undemocratic and a threat to human rights.

The author proposes a new mechanism for the supply of money, creating a supportive financial environment and a decreased reliance on debt.

Michael Rowbotham is a teacher and writer.

£15 pbk   352pp   1 897766 40 8

Essential reading for social and environmental reformers. It fills a major gap in accepted theory ... Rowbotham's work places him on a par with the social reforming economists E. F. Schumacher and Henry George.   The Ecologist

ALSO PUBLISHED BY JON CARPENTER

Goodbye America!
Globalisation, debt and the dollar empire
Michael Rowbotham

This provocative analysis of globalisation and the international debt crisis as aspects of Western economic imperialism explores the origins of the crisis, and its connection with unjust trade and its underlying monetary structure.

It argues the case for the complete annulment of Third World debt.

The author's conclusion is that the debts of the developing nations are completely invalid. The worldwide backlog of international debt is merely an expression of the failings of the current financial system.

At Bretton Woods in 1944, the United States insisted on a trade ideology that favoured their economic and political aspirations. Since then, the World Bank and IMF have carried this agenda forward. As they are drawn ever deeper into debt, Third World countries have been obliged to submit to the demands of free-market, deregulatory economic policies, forced to cut or abandon spending on education, health and welfare, end support for domestic industry, produce food for export instead of home consumption, and sell their businesses and factories to Western buyers.

With the unrepayable debts of the developing nations mostly denominated in US dollars, two-thirds of the planet now finds itself subject to American corporate, financial and economic imperialism whilst the US enjoys an unearned income from overseas poverty. This book argues that developing nations should be released from these debts as they lack both economic and moral validity. The options for full debt cancellation are discussed; developing nations would regain control over their economic policy, concentrate on domestic needs and achieve social progress. A more even balance of power would emerge at the international level together with more localised, resource-efficient commerce.

The book also considers reforms to trade accountancy, a new 'financial architecture' covering investment and lending, and a new development model for the emerging nations.

£11 pbk   224pp   1 897766 56 4

Private Planet
Corporate plunder and the fight back
David Cromwell

*P*rivate Planet takes a critical, new and revealing look at the destructive impact of economic globalisation on the global environment and communities everywhere. Citizens are losing power to undemocratic institutions and private corporations – by a process of stealth. This trend to economic globalisation is being sold to the public by politicians, the business community and the media as 'inevitable'. It isn't. David Cromwell examines how and why the forces of globalisation are opposing ecological sustainability, human rights and social justice – and draws on examples from around the world to show how we can reverse the process.

John Pilger, journalist:
The fightback against the inequalities of globalisation has begun in earnest. David Cromwell's book provides us with a powerful weapon of words that are both incisive and encouraging.

Dr Caroline Lucas MEP:
World trade rules have to be changed – it's that simple. David Cromwell has done us all a favour by revealing the sustainable alternatives and citizen resistance that rarely get reported in the media. Private Planet is compelling, warm-hearted and ultimately hopeful.

Andrew Rowell, author of *Green Backlash*:
Cool-headed, clear, compelling. Read this book if you want to be able to read between the lines of political and corporate rhetoric.

Barry Coates, Director of the World Development Movement:
The question is not whether globalisation is creating massive social and environmental damage – it is – but what we need to do in order to achieve a fairer and more sustainable future. *Private Planet* makes a provocative and important contribution to the development of alternatives.

£12.99 pbk   256pp   1 897766 62 9

TO ORDER any book published by Jon Carpenter, please phone 01689 870437 or 01608 811969 and pay by credit card, or send a cheque to Jon Carpenter Publishing, Alder House, Market Street, Charlbury OX7 3PH.
POSTAGE IS FREE IN THE UK.